Praise

Hilarious one moment, poignant the next, *Once Upon a Villa* is the journey of an American author and his young family through Europe as few have ever experienced it. I devoured this memoir, thrilling at the vicarious adventure, the often hysterical scenes filled with celebrities and even royalty. An author with ten lifetimes' worth of experiences, Kaplan has penned far more than a writer's story but an evocative and witty tour back in time to the French Riviera as most only dream of it. Clever and—best of all—true, *Once Upon a Villa* belongs at the top of every reader's list.

— *NY Times* bestselling author Tosca Lee

Reading *Once Upon a Villa* is as joyful as a great vacation . . . only less expensive.

— Peter Bart, *Deadline Magazine*, former Editor-in-Chief of *Variety*

With his sharp eye for detail and wicked sense of humor, Andrew Kaplan's memoir of a newly minted American novelist moving his young family to the south of France made me feel as if I were right there with him. The end result is a delightful page turning Franco/American discourse on creativity, culture and cuisine (and I'm not talking a can of spaghetti).

— Sandy Krinski, TV writer, *Spencer, Alice, ABC Playhouse, Three's Company*

I fell in love with Andrew Kaplan's *Once Upon A Villa* from the first page. It has to go in my top-ten list of the most entertaining and endearing books I've ever read! *Villa* is a wonderful insight into a writer's life of living abroad with his mostly supportive family, peopled with delightful characters and vivid descriptions of zany adventures. Kaplan's elegant prose made me feel like I was there with him. *Et mon dieu... that stove!*

— John Russell, author of *Riding with Ghosts, Angels, and the Spirits of the Dead*

Andrew Kaplan's *Once Upon a Villa* is a pure delight. Ruefully funny and entirely relatable, this memoir of a young family's experience living on the French Riviera will have every reader entertaining thoughts of getting away from it all. Highly recommended.

— Dennis Palumbo, psychotherapist and author of the *Daniel Rinaldi mysteries*

Storyteller Andrew Kaplan serves up a delicious "*mille feuille*" that features crisp, puffed up layers of French society separated by rich, funny impressions of life abroad as a father, husband, and writer.

— Robin Gregory, author of *The Improbable Wonders of Moojie Littleman*

The immensely talented novelist Andrew Kaplan has written a wonderfully entertaining memoir about the time that he and his family lived on the French Riviera. He paints an amazing portrait of this exceptional part of the world. For those of you who would love to travel to the French Riviera but don't want to fly, this is a great way to go. The most fun too!

— Larry Jacobson, TV writer, *Married with Children, The Tonight Show, The Late Show with David Letterman*

Andrew Kaplan's vivid writing and warm narration had me savoring experiences with him and his family on the French Riviera. I hankered to follow in the path of their adventures, and through Kaplan's words, I have.

— Ed Scharlach, TV writer/producer, *Quantum Leap, Scooby Doo*, author

If you ever wanted to live on the Cote d'Azur, here is your chance to do so vicariously. In this book a writer's family experience, the pleasures of France— the food, celebrities, kindness and difficulties. Imagine living in the same house that Roman Polanski rented and swimming in F. Scott Fitzgerald's beach!

— Valerie Harms, author of *Blood and Water*, book consultant

Once Upon a Villa

ANDREW KAPLAN

This book is a memoir of our lives during the time when we lived on the French Riviera. The names of certain persons have been modified to protect those individuals' identities and privacy.

Smugglers Lane Press, U.S.A.
First Smugglers Lane Press printing: March 2024
Copyright © Andrew Kaplan 2023

ISBN (eBook): 978-1-7368099-4-5
ISBN (Paperback): 978-1-7368099-5-2
ISBN (Jacketed Hardcover): 978-1-7368099-6-9

Cover by Jane Dixon-Smith

Title Production By The BookWhisperer

All rights reserved. No part of this book may be used or reproduced in any manner whatsoever without the written permission of the author, except in the case of brief quotations embedded in critical articles and reviews.

As always, for Anne

Preface

While there have been many books about Brits or Americans living in Paris or Provence or Tuscany or other romantic or exotic locales, little has been written about what it is like to be a young American family living in that extraordinary corner of the world – part international café society, part billionaires' playground, part provincial France – of the French Riviera. That was the genesis of this book.

This book is also a memoir, specifically of the years 1985 and 1986, when we lived on the Côte d'Azur.

Everything in this book actually happened, the sole exception being name changes to protect certain persons' identities and privacy. What does come through, I hope, is the incredible kindness and generosity that was shown to us by so many people, from the Italian border guards who were so careful to ensure that a child like Justin would not come to harm to friends who helped us countless times to Princess Caroline of Monaco to the presumably stand-offish French, some of whom, like Colette, not only helped us, but took us in and made us part of their family. What may also be of interest to readers planning to travel to France or Italy, is that nearly all of the locales, hotels, restaurants, cafés, etc. mentioned in this book are still there.

Preface

In writing a memoir, or anything for that matter, one of the things you have to decide is what to put in and what to leave out. I wish I could have put in more about the bicycle riders in Antibes, or my own investigations into what really happened to Nietzsche in Eze, or our explorations of the hill villages, or more of my conversations with Auguste, the barman at the Colombe d'Or in Saint-Paul de Vence about Picasso, Jean-Paul Sartre, Simone de Beauvoir, Yves Montand, James Baldwin, and other famous persons he'd known who hung out there, or so many other things, but the book would have been twice as long and perhaps not the better for it.

Also missing is what happened afterwards. I have left out what happened with those we knew on the Riviera, some now gone, some still very much a part of our lives, or what happened with us or some of our friends like Stuart and Glenda, which taught us yet again, if we still needed teaching, that while great wealth buys many things, peace of mind isn't one of them. But that's another story.

Andrew Kaplan
Rancho Mirage, California

PART 1

Cap d'Antibes

Chapter 1

Polanski's Villa

"You are not anything like Roman Polanski, are you?"

"Why do you ask?" I said. I wasn't sure whether it was because we were from Los Angeles, where Polanski, the famous film director, was still wanted on a sex charge or in general because we were Americans.

"It took two weeks to clean the villa. The drugs, the parties, the girls running naked, *oh là là*," the real estate agent said. We were driving on the coast road in Cap d'Antibes past tall cypresses and villas, their pastel-painted walls sun-faded and covered with ivy. On the seaward side were the bright-colored sails of windsurfers out on the bay. Coming around a curve, we saw an enormous yacht anchored off the point. It was the size of a small cruise ship, blinding white in the sun, complete with a helicopter on a landing pad on the stern.

"Whose boat is that?" Anne asked.

"The King of Arabia. He comes every year at this time. That way," the real estate agent, her name was Martine, pointed where she wanted me to go.

"The King of Arabia! Of course. We'll have him over for bagels," I heard Anne mutter from the back seat.

We turned down a street shaded by overhanging trees and bordered by expensive villas behind high stone walls. The leaves were dusty in the late afternoon sun; dust motes floated in shafts of light streaming through the branches. A street sign on a stone pillar read: *Chemin des Contrabandiers.* Smuggler's Lane, I translated to myself. Perfect.

I stopped the Renault in front of a massive wooden gate. A wall topped by a hedge at least ten feet high surrounded the property. From the street, it was impossible to see the villa or the grounds. Martine got out and unlocked the gate with a skeleton key big enough to be used on the door to a castle. The wooden gate was heavy and she had to lean into it to swing it open, revealing a long gravel driveway leading up to the house.

The property was like a park, with stone paths and plane trees in the midst of an extensive lawn. The villa itself was white with dark shutters, a red-tiled roof, and a stone-paved courtyard in front bordered with flowers. It was a good deal larger than we expected or needed. As soon as we got out of the car, Justin, our two-and-a-half-year-old, began running around the grounds.

"He can't get out, can he?" I said.

"It goes all around," Martine said, indicating the hedge. It looked as impenetrable as the hedges in Normandy that had almost stopped the American GIs after D-Day. If there were no breaks, Justin would be as safe as in a fortress.

"How far is the beach?" Anne asked.

"Only one block. Afterward, I'll show you," Martine said, leading us to the house.

"Why did she ask if you're like Polanski?" Anne said. I could see she was worried. Cap d'Antibes was for millionaires, not struggling writers trying to escape the rat race.

"I don't know. It's not a question I get asked a lot."

"Well, you're probably more normal than him – most of the time," she said, taking my arm and calling Justin.

"Taller too," I said.

Martine showed us around the villa. The living room was somewhere between imposing and comfortable, with overstuffed furniture, a big marble fireplace and arched windows looking out over the front grounds. The bedrooms had electric candlestick sconces and flowery yellow drapes on the windows. The bathrooms were white, with telephone spray faucets and tiny bathtubs, the kind you have to sit in with your knees up to your chest. The kitchen had an antique gas stove that looked bigger than our car. It sat there giving no hint of danger or that, as we were to learn, it was visible proof that the French were a nation of fatalists.

"What do you think?" Anne said. Justin was jumping up and down on one of the beds like a trampoline.

"We don't have much choice," I said. "We're running out of time." We only had three days left before we had to vacate the apartment in Villefranche.

For a month, we had been trying, without success, to find a villa to rent. When we had planned it back in California, finding a villa had seemed simple enough. We would be coming after the summer tourist season. We thought about trying to book a place before we went, but we were told that we would get better prices once we were there and we weren't sure where we might want to live. In any case, the French consulate in Los Angeles assured us, there was nothing to worry about. In the fall, there were always lots of empty villas to rent.

What we hadn't counted on was the then-French Socialist government passing a law that basically allowed renters to squat free after paying three months rent. As soon as the law passed, almost every French landlord promptly took his property off the market. As a result, the Riviera was filled with empty villas, their windows shuttered, no longer available. Up till now the only rental we had been able to find had been a stone *bastide* (country house) in Provence; a massive hulking structure in a remote region of the Luberon mountains, far from the nearest village and gloomy even in bright sunlight. One could only imagine what it would be like in the dark of winter, an icy *mistral* howling outside the shutters. "If we live here," Anne had said, her voice echoing in the dusty drawing room, "one of us will end up killing the other."

Sensing a sale on the Polanski villa, Martine delivered the clincher. "There's another floor below," she said, opening a hidden door. We went down a narrow staircase to the lower level which included a garage, three more bedrooms and baths and a furnace room. One bedroom was below ground level, with a table against a blank wall that formed the part of the house next to the driveway. It was perfect for an office. I would be able to work and Justin wouldn't even know I was there.

"When did Polanski leave?" I asked.

"Two weeks ago," Martine said. In Hollywood, Polanski had left behind a tabloid reputation even beyond the charge involving a teenage girl. There had been rumors of drugs, parties, and of course, while he himself had had nothing to do with it, the horrific murder of his beautiful pregnant wife, actress Sharon Tate and their friends by the notorious Charles Manson clan. The types of movies Polanski made only reinforced this image. Dark, edgy films, like *Rosemary's Baby* and *Chinatown*. The whole thing was a little creepy. For a long time in that villa, every time I opened a closet, I half-expected the naked body of a teenage girl to tumble out.

"What about the furnace?" I asked, feeling ridiculous. It was a gorgeous autumn day on the Côte d'Azur, the kind you put on postcards. The sun sparkled on the sea, temperature was in the high 80's. Winter seemed an impossibility.

Martine took me around back and showed me a metal trap door in a flat concrete slab. As I heaved the trap-door open, checking to make sure Justin was nowhere near, Martine came marching out of the garage with a stick at least twelve feet long that she held parallel to the ground, looking like she was planning to pole vault over the house. She told me to stick the pole down the opening. When I pulled it back up, there was a film of oil about six inches from the end.

"I can send the oil truck around in the morning," she said.

I went to talk to Anne. I could see she was worried.

"Can we afford it?"

"Until next summer when the higher rates kick in," I said. Afterwards, Martine showed us the Plage de la Garoupe, with its restaurant overlooking the small sandy beach that we later came to think of as Gatsby's beach because it was at a nearby villa that F. Scott Fitzgerald had written much of *The Great Gatsby*. We went back to Martine's office in Antibes, where she brought out a plate of olives and a bottle of wine to cement the deal, Provençal-style.

As we were about to sign, she said, "Monsieur, Polanski is a true genius, but *pas facile*. The landlord requests no wild parties, no naked girls, *bien*?"

"You'll have to talk to my wife," I said. "She's in charge of dealing with naked girls."

That evening, we celebrated over dinner at Maria and the Chef's in Villefranche. Maria and the Chef's wasn't the restaurant's real name, but that's what we called it. Monsieur le Chef made a wonderful fish soup, a toasted slice of *baguette* dabbed with *aioli* floating in the dark broth. Every restaurant on the Côte d'Azur serves *soupe de poisson*, but after I had tasted le Chef's, I never ordered anything else. Justin only wanted the *moules marinières* (mussels) and Anne liked what he did with the local *loup* (sea bass). Best of all, since Justin, like most two-and-a-half year old boys, would get restless and want to explore other tables, in order to let the other patrons dine in peace, the owner Maria would take him down the medieval cobblestones to the wharf to feed breadcrumbs to the schools of tiny fish attracted by the harbor lights shining on the water. She would ask me to mind the cash register while she was gone. Her willingness to do that, something we thought inconceivable in an American restaurant, was one of the reasons why we loved France and had wanted to come in the first place. Anne and I clinked "*Santé*" over a bottle of

Bordeaux.

"What do you think?" I said. "If I were a genius like Polanski, would Martine and the landlord let me have naked girls at the villa?"

Anne playfully punched my arm. "I'll give you naked girls," she said.

We'd done it, I thought. We were going to live in a villa by the sea on the French Riviera. Just a few months earlier, it had barely been a distant fantasy.

Good luck and bad luck often come wearing each other's clothing. You don't always know what you're getting. Because we never would have come to the French Riviera if I hadn't broken my foot.

It happened during a racquetball game with a business pal, Jerry. I tried to change direction to get at a shot he had slammed off the back corner, slipped, and as I fell I could hear the bone snap, like a twig breaking. Jerry helped me to the car and I drove home with just my left foot.

The next day, the doctor showed me on the X-Ray where the bone was broken and told me I had to have a cast. I told him that I couldn't drive or work with a cast and to just tape it up. I was a junior partner in a marketing agency specializing in technology accounts. My partner and I were already experiencing difficulties both in terms of cash flow and disagreements about the direction we wanted the company to go and if I couldn't drive and deal with clients, that might be the end of the partnership.

In truth, my heart wasn't in the agency. What I really wanted to do was write – I had published one novel, a spy thriller called *Hour of the Assassins*, had sold a second, *Scorpion*, and had played around with Hollywood – but with a wife, a toddler, and a house with a mortgage in Canoga Park, part of the endless suburban sprawl of the San Fernando Valley near Los Angeles – writing full time seemed an impossible dream.

"You won't be able to stand the pain," the doctor said.

"Sure I will. I'm a tough guy," I said.

Two days later, I was back, begging him to put the foot in a cast. A few weeks later, with me unable to drive and see clients because of insurance liabilities, my partner ended the partnership. He gave me a severance package and wished me luck. I spent the next month on the couch, trying to figure out what to do, watching daytime TV and complaining. Finally, Anne had had enough.

"I'm tired of listening to you complain," she said. "It's boring."

"I know it's boring. I can hear brain cells dying every time I open my mouth."

And then she asked the absolutely best question anyone had ever asked me: "If you could do anything in the world, if money was no object, what would you do?"

"You really want to know?"

"Yes, absolutely."

"For two bits I'd sell the house, the cars, the whole shebang, move us all to France and write my book." I had an idea for a new novel, triggered by photos I'd seen in National Geographic magazine about temple ruins in the Cambodian jungle. I thought it would make a wonderful setting for an action adventure thriller, but with a touch of resonance from the Vietnam War. I didn't have a title yet; we just called it the "Southeast Asia book."

"Fine. That's what we're doing. When do you want to leave?" Anne said.

I was stunned. I hadn't expected her to take me up on it. It was crazy. Still, not completely crazy. If we were ever going to do it, now was the time, while Justin was still a toddler and not yet in school. And of course, there was the 'Pago Pago Syndrome.'

The Pago Pago Syndrome was a theory of my brother Gil's. "Everyone," he explained, "has a fantasy place. For some it's a garret on the Left Bank in Paris, or a cabin by a lake, or a South Sea island, sipping coconut drinks, surrounded by brown-skinned maidens (*I could tell which one he wanted*). Some secret place where you think you'll be happy." For both Anne and me, France was our Pago Pago. We'd each spent time in France separately before we'd met and loved it. Later, we'd gone to Paris and the Loire Valley on our honeymoon. But whenever we day-dreamed aloud about living there, she'd say, "As long as we're fantasizing, why not go all the way? Why not a villa overlooking the sea on the French Riviera?"

"What about your job?" I asked. Anne was a school psychologist with the Los Angeles Unified School District.

"I can take a year's childcare leave and still have a job to come back to."

"Are you serious?"

"I want you to be happy," she said and at that moment, I fell in love with her all over again. "You're not happy now. I don't want you to use Justin and me as an excuse not to do what you want."

Three months later, our goodbyes said, at a party where friends and family wished us well and privately looked at each other in ways that indicated they thought we were nuts, our house sold – to a lucky Mexican-American who had hit the *trifecta* at Santa Anita racetrack for over $200,000 and whose wife had been eying the "For Sale" sign on our lawn for weeks – we, along with seventeen (seventeen!) pieces of luggage, including Justin's stroller and car seat, boarded a flight for London. We decided to start in London so that I could meet with my English literary agent, June Hall, and also because we thought it might be best to ease into Europe in a place where they speak English, of a sort.

We also brought letters of introduction from a movie producer named Nancy Darling, who with her ex-husband had co-produced the movie, *Beach Holiday Hawaii*, starring Annette Funicello and spent the proceeds on a yacht they sailed along the French Riviera where they "knew absolutely everyone," Perhaps one of the people she knew might be able to advise us once we arrived on the Riviera.

Of course, leaving California wasn't quite that simple. My phone conversation with my mother was emblematic. After I told her we were going to live in France, there was a long pause. Finally she said:

"You're taking my only grandchild off forever to a foreign country?" (You had to hand it to her. The woman was good. If there were an Olympics for Guilt, the other competitors would just hand her the gold medal and walk away.)

"It's not forever, Mom. Besides, you can come and stay anytime you want."

"I don't like Paris. They have those places where the men pee in the middle of the street. The smell is disgusting!"

"They got rid of those ages ago. Besides that's Paris. We'll be in the south."

"The Metro stinks. They never take a bath, the French."

"Mom, we really want you to come. Justin would miss his Grandma terribly."

"What language would he speak? French or English?"

"Both, hopefully."

"Wonderful!" she said. "I won't even be able to talk with my own grandson."

Dealing with our parents wasn't the only concern. During the months that we had been getting ready to leave, I had written a first chapter and a one-page outline of the Southeast Asia book and had sent it off to June. I didn't want her to try and sell it; indeed, she had cautioned me that the British book market was too small for publishers to take a chance on an incomplete manuscript by someone who wasn't a "brand name." You could only sell a completed manuscript in England, preferably one already sold to a major trade publisher in the States. I desperately wanted to get her feedback before we sold the house and took the fatal plunge. Did what I was working on have any kind of a chance of selling, or had I gone off the deep end completely? She hadn't responded, which didn't bode well. But we had already sold the house and said our goodbyes. It would've been too embarrassing to back out now. Boarding the flight to London, that was one of many things I tried not to think about.

The flight from Los Angeles to London began uneventfully. Justin was very good. Anne had cleverly bought ten small toys that she gave him at a rate of about one an hour. Just as he would start to get bored with one, she would hand him a new one. Our plan, if you could dignify our thinking by calling it that, was to stay in London for a few days, while I met with June. Afterwards, we would fly to Germany, where we would buy a used car, maybe a BMW, then drive on down to the south of France. On the advice of Anne's dentist, we had booked the Lonsdale, a moderately-priced (for London) hotel near the British Museum.

The trouble began as we approached London. The pilot came over the intercom and announced that he was landing at Gatwick because of wind shear conditions at Heathrow. Unfortunately, he hadn't cleared it properly with the British authorities, who would not allow anyone to deplane. This led to a standoff between the airline and British Immigration with the passengers in the middle. The Immigration authorities insisted that the pilot fly the plane to Heathrow; the pilot refused, citing airline safety regulations.

Each side assumed that increasing the discomfort of the passengers would force the other to crack. We sat trapped on the tarmac like hostages, hour after hour, the air conditioning off, the toilets overflowing, the passengers sweating and ready for mutiny and Justin getting more and more cranky by the minute (by this time Anne had run out of toys). Anne looked at me. It wasn't an auspicious beginning.

The cabin air became foul; passengers' eyes grew furtive. The situation was becoming desperate. Suddenly, we could hear a thumping from the back of the plane, passengers rhythmically pounding the seat in front of them. "Let us off! Let us off!" they chanted. The plane began to vibrate with the rhythm of the pounding. Everyone was restless. Passengers muttered sidewise under their breath to their neighbors. The scene was like something out of one of those old black and white prison movies. Any moment I expected someone to whisper that the "big break" was set for tonight. "I don't want to be here!" Justin wailed loudly. Anne tried to calm him. A sweating businessman stared daggers at Justin.

"He's only two and a half," I said apologetically.

"Forget it," the man growled. "He's only saying what we're all thinking." Finally, after nearly four hours, the crisis was resolved. Without a word of explanation, the plane turned around and took off again for the five-minute flight to Heathrow.

It was night when we finally got to the hotel, arriving in state in two taxis to carry all the luggage. Staggering into the room at long last, we found a large bouquet of flowers and a note from June Hall telling me to call as soon we got in. I rang her at once.

"Congratulations," June said. "We sold the book."

"What book?" I wasn't sure what she was talking about. Had she sold some additional rights to *Scorpion* or something?

"The Southeast Asia book. To Century Hutchinson - Random House. I'll tell you all about it tomorrow."

"I thought they didn't buy partial manuscripts."

"They don't." My mouth grew dry; I could literally hear my heart beating. Something was about to happen.

"So this is unusual?" I asked, hardly breathing.

"Very," she said.

I took a deep breath. I couldn't wait till tomorrow. I had to know now.

"How much?"

"Um, it's quite good, *eckshully*" she said in that English way that seems to imply that someone of a better class is doing you a favor. "12,500 pounds."

I did a quick mental calculation. At the then-current exchange rates, that was almost $28,000! I hung up the phone in a daze and looked at Anne. Maybe, just maybe, we weren't so crazy after all.

I spent the next few days meeting with June and my editor. There was good news all around. In England, *Scorpion* was going into its third printing and it had hit the best-seller lists in the U.K., Canada and Australia. One curious note, my editor told me, was that my books were reportedly the most stolen of any author's in Britain. No one seemed to know what to make of it. My editor acted as if it was some kind of distinction.

They also told me that while they had a number of best-selling women writers, they were short of what they called "Boys' books." Apparently, the head of Century-etc., someone referred to within the company only as "God," had indicated that he saw me as potentially one of their top three thriller writers. Actually, the way they put it, in a tone even more sepulchral and intimidating, was: "God is interested in you." Since Thriller Writers One and Two were Frederick Forsythe and Len Deighton, at that time, two of the top-selling writers in the world, this was heady stuff.

But as they talked, I began to get queasy. Having "God" interested in you can be a dangerous thing. I felt a sudden pang of understanding for Moses and his reluctance to get involved at the burning bush. All this time I had been alone with an idea and that's all it was – an idea, with maybe twenty pages written. It wasn't a book, not by a long shot. I had no idea whether I could finish it or even how to go about it. In a way, I told Anne back at the hotel, I was just playing. I figured we had enough money to last for a year, maybe a year and a half if we were very careful, and if it didn't work out, we could just come home and I could get a real job. But these people were serious; we were signing contracts. They actually expected me to write the thing!

The next day, we went down to the American Express office to check flight schedules to Germany (how we did things in those pre-Internet days). We couldn't decide whether to fly to Munich, where the BMW factory was, to get a car or to go directly to Paris or possibly, Nice.

"How about calling someone?" Anne said.

"Who?"

She got out the list.

"Nancy Darling said the first people to call were Max and Sally Byrne. She said they know *everyone*."

We went outside and I dialed the international call from a public street phone, Anne beside me with Justin in the stroller.

A man, I assumed it was Max, answered the phone. I told him

who I was and mentioned Nancy Darling. It was hard to hear because there was something noisy going on at his end and a double-decker London bus was rumbling by only a few feet away.

"We're stomping grapes. Everyone's plastered," Max said. "Are you coming over?"

"We're in London actually," I said, throwing in the *'actually'* to sound more British, so he would believe me about being in London. I asked him what he thought about buying a car in Germany.

"Forget Germany. You're better off buying a French car here. That way, if something goes wrong, the Frogs will at know how to fix it and they won't charge an arm and a leg extra the way they would on a German car."

"How hard is it to get a used car there?"

"There are lots of cars. I'll help you buy one. Got a place to stay?"

I told him we hadn't, that we weren't sure what we were doing yet.

"Look, there's a wonderful little hotel in Roquebrune, not far from us. Overlooks the Mediterranean, nice patio. I'll book you a room. Sure you can't make the party today? Plenty of wine," he said.

I told him we'd be down tomorrow and got the information on the hotel.

"Well?" Anne asked, when I hung up.

"We're invited to a party. They're stomping grapes," I said.

"So we're going to Nice?"

"Unless you're dying to go to Germany. Do you have a preference in airlines?"

"British Airways. Maybe they won't keep their own airline sitting on the tarmac," Anne said, pushing Justin in his stroller ahead of us and we marched back into the American Express office. As the clerk, a young man whose teeth were unmistakable evidence that the British National Health Service didn't adequately cover dental visits, booked the morning flight to Nice for us, Anne said, "I just had the weirdest thought."

"What?"

"What on earth would one wear to a grape stomping?"

"A dress," the clerk said, handing us our airline tickets.

"How do you know?" Anne asked.

"I saw it on an *I Love Lucy* rerun," he said, flashing those awful British teeth at us. "She stomps grapes in a dress." He was right. I remembered the episode. Anne stared first at him and then at me as if she had fallen amidst a tribe of lunatics.

"I'm being punished," she said. "For something I did in a previous life. Maybe two previous lives."

That night back in our hotel room, Justin playing on the floor, Anne suddenly turned and demanded, "That clerk in the American Express office, the one with the teeth. What was he trying to say? Lucy Ricardo is supposed to be a role model for women?"

It was the kind of question husbands learn to dodge if at all possible. "Maybe it's some kind of existential metaphor. Life as an absurdity like an *I Love Lucy* episode," I offered lamely, hoping she wouldn't ask me what I meant.

Anne glanced at the TV, where two incredibly boring Oxford professors were discussing the mating habits of birds. Not even showing pictures of the birds, mind you, just talking about it! We were learning that not everything on British telly was Masterpiece Theater. Justin crashed two toy mini-trucks into each other, making sounds of a noisy head-on collision.

"You know," Anne said thoughtfully, "that clerk might be onto something."

The next day at Nice airport, we began our life in France. It was, as Margot would say later, like Dorothy landing in Oz. Suddenly everything was in technicolor.

Chapter 2

Gatsby's Beach

The hotel *propriétaire* took one look at our rented station wagon packed with luggage, a large pile of suitcases tied on top of the roof and gave me the famous French finger, a gesture that consists of wagging one's index finger in the offending party's face back and forth like an admonishing metronome. We were to become very familiar with this particular form of communication, which in France indicates that you have transgressed some invisible, but very real social taboo, anything from committing murder to something really serious, like bad table manners.

I had parked the station wagon as best I could in front of the hotel. However, the space reserved for check-in was designed for a kiddie car at best and the back end of the station wagon stuck well out into the *Basse Corniche* at an angle, blocking traffic behind me. *Monsieur le Propriétaire*, however, was unmoved.

"Impossible, Monsieur," he said. "*Les bagages* are too many."

We had been through this before in London, where we had ended by stacking the luggage like bricks, literally building a wall of suitcases in order to get them all into the room at the Lonsdale. After London, I figured I could handle this and asked to see the room anyway. He responded with that eloquent Gallic shrug which suggests that indulgence is the best policy when dealing with idiots and foreigners. As promised, the room was charming, with floral wallpaper and a wonderful view of the Mediterranean. It was also the size of a broom closet. I went back down to the station wagon to tell Anne.

"He's right," I said. "It's impossible."

"I'm not moving," she said. "I'm hot and exhausted and I've got a two-year-old who's already thrown up once, so you take care of it because I'm not moving."

Trapped behind the station wagon stretched a line of cars, shimmering in the sun. Some were honking, cursing, or gesturing obscenely, others had given up and had opened their newspapers and started to read. The driver in the car behind me had popped into a café and ordered a *pastis*. People came out of shops and restaurants to watch. We were becoming an event.

"I'm open to suggestions," I said. It was hot and I was perspiring.

"Tell him we'll take two rooms. One for us, one for the luggage," Anne said.

I told him. We went inside to the tiny lobby, where the *propriétaire's* wife, a buxom woman with curly hair, stared at her husband from behind the front desk.

"He wants two rooms?" she asked him in French.

"One for *les bagages*."

"*Ils sont excentriques, les américains*," she said.

"For the second room, do you require a room with a view, Monsieur?" he asked.

"Is it more?"

"*Naturellement*."

"No, *merci*."

"*D'accord*," he said with great seriousness. "*Les bagages* do not require a view."

Later, after we had checked in and cleaned up, we drove back down the *Basse Corniche* to Villefranche. By chance, we found *La*

Frégate, a restaurant on the *quai* beside the harbor and had a late lunch. Next to us, a woman with two small poodles sat with a friend. Justin squatted and played with the dogs.

"First thing we need is a place to stay. We can't keep going across the corridor to change clothes," Anne said.

"And a car. The station wagon's too big," I said. It was the only rental vehicle big enough for all our luggage. It was also taxed by the French as a super-luxury vehicle, which made it insanely expensive.

"Where should we look for a place?" I said. It wasn't a simple question. The French Riviera, called the *Côte d'Azur* (the Azure Coast) by the French, stretches roughly 75 miles, from St. Tropez on the west to the Italian border on the east (or at least the portion of the Riviera we came to know, although some will argue it extends all the way west to Marseilles).

Going along the coast from west to east, the largest cities are St. Tropez, Fréjus, Cannes (site of the film festival), Nice (the second largest city in France), Monte Carlo (in the principality of Monaco), and Menton (next to the Italian border). The terrain is mountainous, with medieval villages and resort towns built on hillsides that come down nearly to the sea. The mountain range, the *Alpes Maritimes*, acts as a barrier to cold weather and good television reception. Three main roads run parallel to the coast. The *Basse Corniche* (Lower Coast Road), nearly at sea level, is lined with palm trees, beaches and villages and is the one you usually see in movies set on the Riviera. The *Moyenne Corniche* (Middle Coast Road) runs along the mountains about midway up the heights (in the James Bond movie, *Goldfinger*, when Tilly Masterson takes a shot at Goldfinger, she and Bond are on the *Moyenne Corniche*); the *Haute* or *Grande Corniche* (High or Big Coast Road) winds along the top of the coastal range. The *A8 Autoroute* is further inland.

"What about here?" Anne said, meaning Villefranche.

I looked at the picturesque harbor and beyond to the blue Mediterranean, white sails of boats in the distance, the medieval fortress and cobbled streets. If you've ever seen a movie called *Dirty*

Rotten Scoundrels and seen the scene where Michael Caine shoves Steve Martin into the water, you've seen Villefranche.

"Why not?" I said.

The first two real estate agents we tried were not encouraging. Neither had any villas for rent. They blamed the lack of available properties on French President Mitterand and the Socialists.

"They are all *communistes*," a young woman agent assured us. She was pert and young in a white blouse and blue skirt that she wore like a uniform. "Since everyone cannot be rich, they prefer in the name of equality that everyone be poor. It is because they are lazy and do not wish to work."

"It's true, Monsieur," an older woman doing a word puzzle added. "There is nothing. Perhaps in a month or two."

"There is one possibility," the young woman said, checking her notes. "An apartment in Breil."

"Is that near here?"

"*Oh là là*. It is far, on the *Grande Corniche*."

"Could we see it?" Anne asked.

"Impossible, Madame," the young woman said.

"Why?"

"I have an appointment," she said, taking her handbag and getting up to leave.

"Is it so important?" I asked as we walked her out.

"*Oui*, Monsieur. I must get my nails done," she said, waving her fingers as she walked away.

"Good thing she's not a communist or she'd never show up for work," I heard Anne mutter under her breath.

The third real estate agent we tried showed us a two-bedroom apartment in a modern block apartment building in Villefranche. It was furnished in 60's modernist style, with a geometric red couch and a space age lamp with a long arching metallic arm in the living room, with aluminum shutters that could be lowered over the panoramic glass door to the balcony. The balcony ran, Riviera style, along the length of the apartment and overlooked the harbor and a stretch of Mediterranean coast. The apartment was available for thirty days.

"It isn't exactly the Pierre Deux kind of place we had in mind," Anne said.

"It'll give us thirty days to find something – and it's a lot cheaper than the hotel."

"At least we won't have to go across the hall to visit our clothes," she said.

The next day we moved in and the day after that, Max and Sally invited us to our first Riviera dinner at their house in Cap Martin. Sally walked us around their neighborhood. It had a rural feel, with lemon trees, overhanging vines, dusty hedges and fields that the locals had turned into mini-vineyards.

Sally looked more French than Midwestern American, which was where she was from, fashionably thin, with long curly blonde hair and fine hands. She pointed out a garden where Winston Churchill used to sit and paint landscapes. She and Max lived in a small villa next to Churchill's. The living room was like a library, the walls covered with shelves overflowing with books, and a large garden in back.

There were a dozen people chatting and drinking wine and more out in the garden. We added the bottle of wine we had brought to the collection on an outside table and sampled some of the quiches and cheeses Sally had put out.

"We didn't realize you had a two-year-old," Sally said.

"Two-and-a-half. He's very particular about that," I said. Justin was playing outside in the garden with a toy truck Anne had brought to keep him busy.

"You can't bring him to parties. No children, I'm afraid," Emma, a bleached blonde Englishwoman with an accent that wandered somewhere between the BBC and Manchester, said. According to Sally, Emma was married to Chuck, a millionaire who owned a computer company headquartered in Monte Carlo.

"Do you have children?" Anne asked.

"Two boys," Emma said.

"Where are they?"

"With the *au pair*, of course," she said, moving away.

"Don't mind her," Sally whispered. "She used to be Chuck's old *au pair*, until he dumped his second wife and married her after the wife caught them together in the tub."

"How'd he meet his second wife?"

"Come to think of it, she was an *au pair* too," Sally said.

"Wonder who's watching the kids tonight?" Anne said.

"Hey bud, you like vodka?" said a voice in an unmistakable Midwestern twang.

"Sounds good," I said to a sandy-haired man in a white shirt and golf pants.

"Bobby G. is the souvenir king of the Riviera. He produces the tourist souvenirs for places all over the Côte d'Azur," Sally said.

"Yeah, and it's thirsty work," Bobby G. said, pouring me a glass of vodka large enough for a Russian battalion.

"Where's Max?" I asked.

"Somewhere," Sally said, vaguely indicating the garden.

"What does Max do?" Anne asked Sally.

"As little as possible," Carl said. He had ridden up on a BMW motorcycle. Sally had told us he was the personal pilot of the Count di Portanova, an Italian nobleman by way of Houston and Texas oil money, who kept a private Lear jet on call twenty-four hours a day. According to Sally, Carl had quit the Air Force and came to Europe after his wife, a spiritualist, had divorced him on the channeled advice of a dead American Indian who had fought with Geronimo.

"Max does some business with Chuck," Sally said.

"Bullshit," Bobby G. whispered to me. "He's in the CIA. He'd kill you as soon as look at you."

"Max? Really?"

"You kidding? All those years in Germany – on both sides of the Curtain. Why do you think he's so buddy-buddy with the Prince?"

"Prince Rainier?"

He nodded and headed for the bar. Just then, Max came over.

"Vodka," he said, glancing at my drink. "You must've met Bobby G." He motioned for me to follow him out back.

Max was a well-muscled man with a cropped military-style haircut. His face beamed good humor as he walked me around the garden, pointing out his vegetables and his small vineyard. He apologized for getting us too small a room at the hotel and promised he'd go shopping with me for a car the next day.

"Your wife is very attractive. You ever cheat?" he said.

"No," I said.

"That's it. Hold on to your convictions." He studied me. "You've been in the military. Where?"

"The States. Also the Middle East."

"I thought so. We're going to have a lot to talk about, you and I," he said.

The party was still going strong when we left that night. Justin had fallen asleep on a chair and we carried him to the station wagon.

"What did Max want?" Anne asked as we drove back on the *Basse Corniche* to the Villefranche apartment. The road curved as it followed the hills in the darkness, the lights along the coast reflected on the water.

"He wanted to know whether I cheated."

"What did you tell him?"

"No."

"Are we ready for this?" she asked.

"You can handle anything," I said.

"What about you?"

"I've got you."

The next day, Max and I went to a car dealer where I bought a used blue Renault 5 sedan. It was small, perfect for the narrow streets and tiny parking spaces on the Côte d'Azur, but with a decent-sized trunk and a back seat big enough to handle Justin's car seat. Max said it would prove reliable and that turned out to be true. We returned the station wagon back to the rental agency at Nice airport and began searching for a villa.

We first explored the coastal towns and medieval villages between Monaco and Nice, but found nothing. Many businesses were closing for the annual winter *fermeture annuelle* and though the weather stayed warm and sunny, life was beginning to slow.

We enjoyed the flower market in the old town in Nice, sitting under an umbrella, eating a *pain bagnat*, a kind of *salade Niçoise* sandwich, made with tuna, tomatoes, and onions in a round *baguette* that is the Riviera's equivalent of a hot dog, and a cold beer, watching the shoppers at the colorful flower stalls. But there was little available in Nice, except for a few expensive apartments in the middle of the city.

Finding little, we explored the villages in the hills away from the coast, towns like Biot and Vallauris, known for their pottery industry set up by Picasso, Grasse, where they distill flowers to make French perfume, Vence and its neighbor, St. Paul de Vence, with its Disney-like medieval charm overrun with tourists, all the way up to La Turbie on the *Grande Corniche*, with its massive marble monument to Caesar Augustus built by Roman soldiers after they added this part of Gaul to his empire. Everywhere we went it was the same; there was nothing available.

We went further inland, exploring Provence all the way up to Aix, with its narrow streets, Cezanne mountains, and college town feel, the pretty French co-eds and their T-shirted boyfriends smoking *Gauloises* in the Café des Deux Garcons on the Cours Mirabeau, possibly the most beautiful street in Europe with its plane trees and eighteenth-century buildings.

We explored villages in the Luberon mountains and back along the rest of the French Mediterranean coast, nearly all the way to the Camargue. There were places of unbelievable beauty, like the Esteral coast between Cannes and St. Raphael, a breathtaking landscape of red rock cliffs, green trees and white villas overlooking the blue Mediterranean.

"This is the most beautiful place I've ever seen," I told Anne as we drove along the winding coast. Below us were cliffs and olive trees with silver leaves growing out of the crevices in the red rock and below that was the sea.

"It's a long way from everyone we've met. We'd be isolated."

"We'd meet people," I said. But here too, there were no villas available.

"What are we going to do?" Anne said. Our rental on the apartment in Villefranche was almost up and the concierge had told us that someone else was waiting to move in. We were spending all our time and money traveling and villa-hunting and I still hadn't started on the book.

"Maybe France wasn't such a great idea. Maybe we should try the Italian Riviera, or Spain. They say Portugal is cheap," I said.

"I like France."

"We're running out of options. Besides the French are difficult. And they do weird things, like make cars shaped like clams," I said as I passed a Citroen that looked exactly like an elongated metal clam.

"We'll find something," she said.

The next day we found the Polanski villa in Cap d'Antibes. It took us three trips with the Renault to move in. In the days that followed, Anne set about making the villa livable, while I started work on the Southeast Asia book.

I had begun the book with the disappearance of a CIA agent in Bangkok, the chapter Century-Hutchinson had bought. Now I brought my protagonist, a CIA agent named Sawyer, onto the stage. His assignment was to find out what happened to the first agent and complete the mission, which involved warlords in the jungles of the Golden Triangle, morphine base (from which heroin is made) and the Vietnamese army in Cambodia.

The writing was interesting and we began a routine. At one o'clock, we would have lunch. We tried various restaurants in Antibes. One day, we had lunch at the restaurant overlooking the sandy beach a block from our villa. The beach was deserted this time of year. From the restaurant, you could see along the beach and across the bay to Nice. On one side of the beach was a heavily-wooded promontory that was fenced in and patrolled by guards with automatic rifles and police dogs.

"What's the name of this beach?" I asked the waiter.

"La Plage de la Garoupe, monsieur."

I asked him what a *"garoupe"* was and he just shrugged. "They call it 'the American Beach,'" he said. When I asked him why, he said he didn't know. In a moment, *la propriétaire*, a plump Frenchwoman with permed blonde hair appeared.

"There is a problem, Monsieur?"

Why do they call it 'the American Beach?'"

"My mother said there was a famous American writer here long ago. The one who shot lions."

"Hemingway?"

"*Oui, c'est lui.* There were other rich Americans. They had a big white villa, 'La Villa Amerique,' but it is gone."

In college I had read about the wealthy Murphys and their 'Villa America,' which became a kind of writers' retreat for the Lost Generation. It was said that Hemingway had written a portion of *A Farewell to Arms* there. Scott and Zelda Fitzgerald had rented a villa nearby where he had written much of *The Great Gatsby* and *Tender is the Night*.

"What's the place with all the guards?" Anne asked.

The *propriétaire* looked around nervously as if fearing to be overheard.

"That is the Heineken estate, Madame," she whispered.

"The beer company?"

"The son was kidnapped in Holland. They are very strict. You live in the Villa Closerie on the Chemin des Contrabandiers? Where Monsieur Polanski stayed?"

"You knew Monsieur Polanski?"

"He came here for the *bouillabaisse*. Ours is the only true *bouill-*

abaisse on the Côte d'Azur. You must try it." This statement was something we were to hear at every restaurant on the Riviera. It was an article of faith of every local chef that all other *restaurateurs* were imposters and that he or she alone possessed the only authentic recipe for *bouillabaisse*. On no other subject were the locals so passionate. One might argue about the politics of Le Pen, or debate the fine points of upcoming bicycle races, but fistfights could result over whose *bouillabaisse* was the most authentic. As Monsieur le Chef at Maria and the Chef's put it, laying his finger alongside his nose, "*La vraie bouillabaisse*, that is *serieuse*, no?"

That evening, we took a walk on the Plage de la Garoupe beach and along the path around the Heineken estate with its barbed wire fence and back to the beach. The sun was low, the sea towards Nice a liquid gold. Anne pushed Justin in his stroller and the only the sound was of waves lapping on the sand.

"What good is money if you have to live like that?" Anne said, talking about the Heinekens. At the end of a jetty was a lone white navigation light shining in the advancing darkness. A bizarre idea occurred to me.

"Could that be the green light in Gatsby?"

"It's white," she said.

"Yeah, but suppose Fitzgerald actually wrote it here, like the *propriétaire* said. He must've come down here for walks. He would have seen it. Maybe that's what gave him the idea." At that moment, the white light did look distant and almost, but not quite attainable in the darkness, like the light on Daisy's dock that Gatsby had watched in the night.

"I guess it's possible," she said. "Do you think he came here with Zelda?"

"I think she was having an affair with some French guy, as in *Tender is the Night*, which he also set here in Cap d'Antibes."

"Maybe they came here together," she said, tucking Justin in. It began to get cold. We looked at the lonely navigation light and the pale line of surf and the lights of Nice in the distance.

"I don't think so. The green light is all about yearning, not fulfillment. He must have been alone."

"Glad you came?" she asked, taking my arm.

"God yes," I said, but Gatsby's Beach, which was how we thought of it ever after, made us feel lonelier and less safe and that was even before we met the 'Other Americans' and came to realize that Roman Polanski wasn't the only one on the Riviera running from the law.

Chapter 3

Caviar and Calvados

We came to Nice because of the Algerians. The problem was laundry. There was a tiny washing machine, not much bigger than a child's sand bucket, in the villa, no dryer, and we were running out of clothes. We had tried the local laundry in Antibes, but it was too expensive. When we came to pick up our laundry, every article of clothing, each individual sock and piece of underwear, was neatly wrapped in tissue paper and tied with a ribbon. It turned the simple act of picking up the laundry into Christmas, but it also cost the equivalent of nearly half a month's rent.

Then there was the matter of Justin. To deal with the dry cleaner required two free hands and complete attention, not something we were able to do with a two-year-old around, not to mention that it took at least an hour, if you were lucky, to find a parking space. So it took two adults, Anne and myself, to pick up the laundry. While Anne dealt with the dry cleaning, so as not to waste the luck of finding a parking space, I took Justin with me to a *cave* across the street to buy some wine.

The *marchand de vin* was a small man with a leather apron and a red nose that suited his trade. I asked him in my half-way decent French when the Beaujolais Nouveau might be coming in. He glared at me as though I had come to rob him and shook the forbidding French finger in my face.

"*Impossible*, monsieur. This is an honest *commerce*."

Somehow I had insulted him, although I wasn't sure what I had said that had set him off. I explained that I was an American, as if that excused all social breaches.

"Ah monsieur is an *étranger*. By French law, the Beaujolais Nouveau may be released no earlier than midnight of the third Thursday in November. Not one second before. To do so would be *criminel*," he explained. He told me he would have it the day after that and asked would Monsieur care to reserve several bottles?

Monsieur would and then bought a Bordeaux he recommended. "Although," he said as he wrapped the bottle, "strictly speaking, Beaujolais Nouveau should be more correctly termed 'Beaujolais Primeur,' since the law requires that a wine released between the time of its harvest and a date in early Spring is *primeur*, whereas the designation *nouveau* is reserved for a wine released before the following year's harvest." He sighed at the general ignorance of the wine-drinking public and humanity in general, then motioned me close and asked whether Monsieur drank more than just wine. I leaned forward, wondering if he was about to offer me a hot bottle of Beaujolais.

"We specialize in cognac and Calvados, Monsieur," he whispered. Instantly, I was seized with an irresistible desire for Calvados. I was a huge fan of the Inspector Maigret novels of George Simenon, a writer that all other writers hate for the twin crimes of being both incredibly prolific (over 500 novels) and consistently good. In Simenon's *romans policiers*, somehow it is always a cold rainy day in Paris and whenever a case reaches a critical point, Inspector Maigret always stops in a bar and has a Calvados. All these years I had been reading about Calvados, a kind of brandy made from apples, but had never tasted it. With an instinct bordering on the occult, the *marc-*

hand de vin had divined that the instant he mentioned Calvados I would have to have it.

I asked him what was a good brand of Calvados.

"*Mon Dieu*," he sighed, an artist forced to deal with the philistine masses. "There is no *marque* of Calvados, Monsieur. Every farmer in Normandy makes his own. One must know the farm for the good Calvados. *Par exemple*," he said, handing me a bottle with a plain label without a picture or brand name, just the hand-lettered name of a farm.

"Is this good?" I asked.

"Monsieur will be back," he said.

"What are we celebrating?" Anne asked that night at the villa.

"Calvados," I said, clinking glasses. It tasted warm and smooth with just a hint of apples. I had another taste and felt as wise as Inspector Maigret.

"What are we going to do about the laundry? It's cheaper to buy clothes here than to dry clean them."

"We need advice. Who can we ask? Martine?"

"Wrong person."

"Why?"

"She wears a Chanel blouse and skirt," Anne said knowingly. "She would never admit she deals with anything as mundane as laundry."

"So who?"

Which brought us to Colette, who, according to the film producer, Nancy Darling, more-or-less ran the Nice harbor. Colette had an apartment in St. Laurent du Var, not far from a huge apartment complex on the coast just west of Nice that looked like a futuristic pyramid designed by Stephen Spielberg. Colette's reaction was typically French. She invited us over to discuss the matter over lunch, which we ate on her small tree-shaded balcony overlooking the street.

It was, as promised, a simple Riviera-style lunch. For *hors d'oeuvres*, grilled sardines, tiny calamari with *aioli*, artichoke hearts, two kinds of *pâté*, one a duck *pâté de compagne* she had made herself, the second a pork *pâté de campagne*, and for the *entrée*, a *coq au vin* accompanied by fresh asparagus in butter, and a lamb *couscous*.

Colette was a short Frenchwoman with blond hair who had spent much of her life in Morocco and was something of a stickler about her *couscous*, which by our lights deserved at least one, maybe two Guide Michelin stars. Anne wondered why she had been in Morocco and she told us about her father, who had been a colonel in the *Maquis* during the war. Captured by the Gestapo and sentenced to be executed, he had made a famous escape. After the war, he had been an important person, but was forced into an administrative position in Marrakech by political enemies, so Colette spent time in her youth there. She had married a French businessman with interests in Morocco, but after they got divorced, she moved back to France.

By the time we mopped up the last bits of lamb gravy and couscous with pieces of *baguette* and Colette brought out a tray with half a dozen different kinds of cheeses, she and Anne had become fast friends. In truth, we found it easy to make friends in France, mainly because we had two great assets. The first was that Anne was a very attractive woman who, as a school psychologist, had a way about her that was immediately seized upon by people for free therapy. Whereas I considered myself lucky if I could get someone to tell me the time of day, within minutes of meeting, strangers would confide to Anne their most intimate problems, things they wouldn't tell their best friend or doctor or priest. This extraordinary effect she had on people happened so often that I took it as a matter of course. When I asked Anne what was her secret, how she got people to so completely reveal themselves in a couple of minutes, she said she just asked them. My explanation was that great artists have abilities that may be secret even to themselves.

The second was that the French – and as we were to learn, the Italians – contrary to popular belief, enjoy children and having a handsome, well-behaved two-year-old who knew how to charm people, like Justin, was as close as you could get to a slam dunk. We knew Justin had worked his charms on Colette because before lunch was over, she had volunteered to baby-sit for us for free any time we needed.

She and Anne discussed practical matters, like laundry and what to do with Justin in the morning so Anne could get her shopping done. Colette had to leave to get back to work, but she invited us back for Sunday dinner with her cousin and his wife, who were visiting from Champagne along with her daughter and son-in-law, down from Paris.

This, of course, was a major coup and Anne and I understood it as such. The French have a reputation for coldness and snobbery in part because they prefer to meet publicly, in cafes and restaurants, where there is no requirement to reveal anything personal other than one's opinion, which any Frenchman feels qualified to offer on any subject whatsoever. However, invitations to share a meal *en famille* are rare and to receive such an invitation is to be accepted virtually as a member of the family. Our tummies were full and we were feeling happy and confident, a feeling that lasted only till the explosion.

The next day, I was working on the book in the lower bedroom that I had converted into an office. My CIA agent protagonist, Sawyer, was being sent on a mission down the same rabbit hole where a previous agent, Parker, had disappeared. Sawyer searched the backstreets and *klongs* of Bangkok, trying to get a lead on anyone who might have seen Parker. The writing was interesting, but it was still work. It hadn't reached that point, that if you are lucky it sometimes does, when the world you are creating becomes as real as your so-called "real world." At that point the story starts to write itself and you find yourself living in two parallel and equally interesting universes at the same time.

In the story, Sawyer was meeting with an old Thai general who held no official position in the Thai government, but who seemed to have enormous influence. Sawyer had discovered that two Thai police agents had been tailing Parker the night he disappeared. One of the Thai police agents had been killed, the general was telling Sawyer, when a loud explosion rocked the villa.

I raced up the stairs to find Justin staring wide-eyed at his Mom. Anne was sitting on the floor of the kitchen. I looked around, trying to understand what had happened. Except for Anne on the floor and soup splattered all over the stove, walls and floor, everything seemed intact. Anne just sat there, white-faced. I asked her if she was OK and she nodded.

I helped her to her feet and when I asked what had happened, she pointed at the stove, never taking her eyes off it as though if she did, it might attack her again. When she had tried to light the stove, there had been a gas explosion. I got Anne and Justin outside the villa and opened the doors and windows to clear the gas. I checked the gas lines and pipes with soapy water, but there was no sign of a leak. It wasn't the pilot light, because the stove didn't have one. You lit it by putting a wooden match directly to the gas through an opening. There must have been an accumulation of gas down there and when Anne had tried to light it, KABOOM!

After we cleaned up the kitchen, I called the appliance repair number Martine had left for the *cuisinière a gaz*. A certain Monsieur Ledur told me he would be there *demain* (tomorrow). This left us somewhat uncertain, as we were already learning that time in southern France is as elastic as anything Einstein could have ever conceived. *Demain* might mean *tomorrow*, which it technically did, or it could mean sometime this week, or even month.

Three days later, Monsieur Ledur still hadn't come, but I had discovered that you could light the stove by dropping a lighted match into the blow hole exactly one second after turning on the gas. Often, there would be a *bang* when the gas caught, but after that, everything would be fine. Lighting that stove was a little like playing Russian Roulette. On any given attempt, the odds were in your favor, but you knew that sooner or later your luck would run out. Anne, of course, recognized the stove for the dangerous creature it was and although she would cook on it, she refused to ever light it again.

A week later, Monsieur Ledur showed up at the villa gate unannounced. Anne came and grabbed me from my office. I asked

Monsieur Ledur if he would like to see the stove and he asked me for a hundred francs. After I gave him the hundred francs, he marched into the kitchen, took one glance at the stove, made a face as if to say, "What can you expect?" and turned to leave.

"What is it?" I asked in French.

He touched the side of his nose. "I know this one. She is old and *capricieuse*."

"What should we do?"

"*Ah Monsieur*," he said, holding up a warning finger, "*fâites attention*," and left.

Thereafter, anytime we needed to light the oven or gas burners, we would clear the house. We would open all the windows, Anne and Justin would stand a safe distance from the villa and I would put on gloves and *fâites attention* (be careful) as I tossed the match into burner opening and dived for the kitchen door. This bizarre behavior came to seem quite normal to us. So much so, that we actually discussed putting a mattress by the kitchen door to help cushion my dive when I hit the floor. Other than that, the stove worked perfectly and we cooked on it every day.

Colette had recommended a laundry and dry cleaner in Nice. But when Anne went to Nice to take in the laundry, she came back swearing she would never do it again. She was afraid of the Algerians.

The position of Algerians in France was somewhat similar to that of the Chinese in the U.S. in the early part of the twentieth century. Like the Chinese, Arab Algerians (as opposed to French *pieds noirs* who returned to France when Algeria won its independence in the early 1960's) were often in the laundry business. Anne, however, thought they might be gangsters. "I'm not going back there by myself," she announced. I asked how she knew they were gangsters.

"You'll see. You'll have to because you're coming with me when I pick up the laundry."

A few days later, after driving around the narrow streets near the harbor area of Nice for more than an hour and not finding a parking space, I gave up and parked like a Frenchman, with the Renault wedged into a tiny gap between a minivan and a Citroen truck that looked like it had been hammered out of tin, such that the back of the Renault stuck perpendicularly out into the narrow street. We walked to the laundry and when we went in, I could see what Anne had meant.

Two tough-looking young Arab men in sunglasses were smoking and talking in Arabic on separate telephones. Arabic music was blasting from the radio and beyond the laundry soap and chemical smell, I caught a whiff of something else, incense, or maybe hashish. At another counter, a sullen, muscular young man in an undershirt was using a vicious-looking stiletto to cut string to tie laundry boxes. One of the men took off his sunglasses and sized Anne up. Barely looking at us, the Arab behind the counter took the laundry and handed us a slip, then said something in Arabic to the one with the knife. I asked him in French if he knew Colette.

"*Ah oui, la capitaine du port*. Everyone knows her." He asked how old Justin was. I told him he was two and a half.

"I have a brother the same age!" he said, bringing out a picture of himself with a toddler in front of a car. He rummaged around behind the counter and came up with a toy top that he gave to Justin. He and his brothers insisted we join them in a glass of wine and brought out a dish of sugared almonds. "*Attendez*," he said and wrote something on the slip he had given Anne. "Fifty percent off *pour nos amis*." The one with the stiletto brought us our finished cleaning wrapped in paper tied with string. It turned out they were three brothers. The one with the stiletto was a serious bicycle racer, who was training for the Tour de France. The one behind the counter was studying electronics at the university.

As we drove back to the villa, I asked Anne if she thought it would be too dangerous to go herself next time into such a den of vicious killers.

"Shut up and drive," she said, neither of us aware that we were about to meet real criminals.

In the morning, Martine called. There was another American

family living in Cap d'Antibes, a couple with a young daughter a little older than Justin. Would we be interested in meeting them? Anne thought it was a good idea. It would be nice knowing other people and Justin really didn't have anyone to play with. Also, as winter approached we were feeling more isolated. Each day we would discover that another business had closed for the *fermeture annuelle*. There was never an advance warning. You would go to a shop or restaurant that you had been to just previous day and find it boarded up with a little handwritten sign stating they would be closed until the following year.

Life on the Cote d'Azur is seasonal: in winter, empty and a little remote, almost rural; in summer, packed wall-to-wall with people on holiday. The insanity reaches its peak during the month of August, when virtually the entire nation of France heads south for the annual *vacances*. This is a mass migration of the population unlike anything Americans have ever experienced. Cars and campers create traffic jams that can extend for a hundred miles and more on the *autoroutes*. Masses of families and teenagers swamp the streets, souvenir shops and restaurants in every village on the Cote d'Azur. The stony beaches become wall-to-wall carpets of greased bodies in string bikini bottoms.

Unpleasant as it sounds, those poor French citizens who have to stay behind in Paris or Lyons because of their jobs actually become aggrieved and irritable at missing this annual ritual of French life. American tourists who visit Paris during August, when the weather is hot and sticky and utterly unlike Paris at any other time and who complain about French rudeness and indifference, should remember that although Parisians never need an excuse to act self-absorbed and superior, in August they start out already angry and deprived because they know that in the great scheme of things, they are not supposed to be there. Existentially, they are supposed to be getting sunburned and overpaying for everything on the Cote d'Azur along with everyone else.

But when the annual summer migration is over, the Cote d'Azur empties and many businesses, having made more than enough money in the three-month season, close for the rest of the year. For *les commerçants* on the Riviera, taking nine months off each year was the good life, but it left us feeling increasingly isolated.

Anne also thought it would be nice to have another woman, an American, with whom she could talk and go shopping with. So phone calls were made and that afternoon we met Greg and Janie and their four-year-old daughter, Sloane, at their villa. They lived on a quiet street not far from the famous and *très* upscale Hôtel du Cap.

The idea that Sloane and Justin might play together was dispensed with within the first minute. The gap between a two-and-a-half year old boy and a four-year-old girl is enormous and she simply refused to have anything to do with him. Janie was a pretty, brown-haired twenty-something second wife, the kind you run into at an art show or a charity affair. Greg was a former financial manager for a number of Hollywood celebrities. He said he had retired young and moved to the Cote d'Azur to enjoy life and write a novel.

He had acquired many of his wealthy clients through his first big catch, a well-known psychologist who billed herself as "Sex Therapist to the Stars" and who had written a best-selling book on women and sex. As it happened, Anne and I had met her once, when she was seated at our table at a PEN Awards dinner. All I could remember of her conversation was that it consisted of a lot of name-dropping, of the "As I was saying to my good friend, the Pope," variety. When Anne suggested that we found "the famous Sex Therapist" a bit full of herself, Greg commented he had dropped her because she was "too high-maintenance." The midnight calls, the crying on his shoulder, all got to be too much, especially when they couldn't get her extra tickets to the Grammy Awards, a night, which Greg and Janie announced solemnly, was the high moment of their lives. Anne asked them why they had come to the Riviera.

"To meet royalty and nobility," Janie said. "Think of it. Millionaire princes, exiled kings, the royal family in Monaco. You know, the British royals come down here on vacation. Prince Charles, even," she whispered breathlessly, her eyes shining. I could see what she meant. The social-climbing possibilities were enormous.

"In America, all you've got are Hollywood stars, most of whom are lower class people who just got lucky and then act superior. But in Europe, you've got the real thing. Kings, counts, all kinds of lords. Real old money. It makes you think," Greg said. He brought out a football and wanted to know if Justin and I wanted to toss it around. When we got outside, he asked me if I wanted any cocaine. When I shook my head, he offered me a joint. I told him to put it away. He then explained his philosophy, what he called, "the secret of life."

"There are two kinds of people in the world," he said solemnly. "Those who get high and those who wish they could."

"That's it? The whole human race?" I asked. "That's the secret of life, what I traveled 10,000 miles for?"

"That's it," he said, motioning for Justin and me to go deep. He tossed a long perfect spiral pass with the ease of someone who had been a jock in high school that I surprised myself by catching. I gave the ball to Justin and told him to throw it to me. Justin threw a wobbly three or four foot pass. As I caught it and turned to throw back to Greg, I caught him staring at us in a way I didn't understand. It made me uneasy until I recognized it was envy, the envy of a jock father who had only a pretty little daughter with no interest in sports instead of a son to throw a ball around with. I found myself feeling more uncomfortable by the minute.

Back at the villa, Anne asked what I thought of Greg. I didn't answer.

"That bad, eh?" she said.

"He might not be the biggest jerk in the world. I haven't met everyone."

"The kids didn't get along either. It's the age gap."

"Yeah, Justin's two-and-a-half going on three and she's four going on thirty."

We decided that spending time with them wasn't a great idea and we would try to limit it. Janie, however, was irrepressible. During one phone call, Anne had an "Aha!" moment when Janie confided how she had helped Greg through a "horrible divorce" from his first wife, Barbara. As Janie described this Barbara, Anne realized that by an unbelievable coincidence she had once worked on a graduate research project at UCLA with this same Barbara, Greg's first wife. Anne decided to write to Barbara and find out what we could about Greg and Janie.

Later that week, Anne signed Justin up for a *crèche*, a French pre-school, the *École de Cap* in Cap d'Antibes. This would give her a couple of free hours every morning during which she could run errands and maybe even have the luxury of being able to sit over a cup of coffee at a sidewalk café and read the *International Herald Tribune*. With Justin taken care of, the only thing she had to worry about were French drivers who, she claimed, seemed to regard the act of getting behind the wheel of a car as an opportunity for national suicide.

On Sunday, we went to Colette's for our initiation into the important French ritual of the Sunday lunch. As promised, Colette's cousin, Georges, and his wife, Annette, were down for the weekend. Georges was a well-dressed businessman in his sixties, who owned a large stocking factory in Troyes, a medieval city in the Champagne country.

Colette's daughter, Freddie, and her husband, Jean-Claude, were down from Paris. Freddie, for Fréderique after her grandfather, the *Maquis* hero, was a beauty, with short dark hair that she wore *gamine* style and a wonderful smile. She was a commodities trader on the Paris Bourse and immediately wanted to spend all her time with Justin. She and Jean-Claude were trying to have a baby and she wanted the practice of being with a toddler. Her husband, Jean-Claude, who looked like Louis Jourdan in *Gigi*, only younger and handsomer, smiled indulgently. Jean-Claude was the mayor of Compiègne and the deputy in the National Assembly for the *départment* of Picardy. I seemed to remember that Compiègne had been a place of importance during World War One. Indeed, Jean-Claude reminded me, the armistice ending the war had been signed in a railway car in Compiègne. When the Nazis defeated France in 1940, Hitler had insisted on signing the cease-fire in Compiègne in the same railway car.

It was, as Colette insisted, a simple lunch, or as she called it, a *"déjeuner très simple"*: caviar from a shop in Cannes (one which we would get to know well), that only sold caviar, dozens of different varieties. There were three kinds of *foie gras*, one with truffles from Perigord, the region famed in France for the best truffles, a lobster *mousse*, *boeuf Bourguignon*, a salad with local vegetables, a dozen cheeses with two types of *baguettes*, and for dessert: Napoleons and *glace aux fraises*. Georges supplied the champagne for the caviar, revealing that he owned several medieval houses in Troyes, one of which he had turned from basement to roof into a multi-story temperature-controlled wine cellar to house his enormous champagne collection. When I told him that I planned to someday write a book about a murder that had occurred in the year 1146 in the village of Ramerupt near Troyes, he became extremely interested and we were soon deep in discussion about Troyes during the Middle Ages. He invited us to come to Troyes where we would, as he put it, "drink our way through the best champagne collection in the world in his own *maison de vin.*"

Lunch went on for hours, blending into dinner. This would become a ritual for us on Sundays. Our eventual record for Sunday lunch was twelve hours, with a lunch that began at a country inn with Max, Sally and friends and eventually migrated to Max and Sally's villa for dessert. But that day, sitting with Georges, Jean-Claude, Anne, whose French wasn't as fluent as mine, speaking a *mélange* of French and English with Colette, Annette and Freddie, Justin laughing at cartoons on TV, Freddie and Jean-Claude looking impossibly attractive and sophisticated, Anne and I caught each other's eye and at that moment, I believe we shared the same thought, that the French were so incredibly good at what they they care about, which is living. Next to them, we felt like ragged immigrants, self-consciously working at food and conversation that seemed to come so naturally to them.

I asked Jean-Claude for advice about our visa situation. Before we had left the States, we had gone to the French embassy in Beverly Hills to get our residents' visas, our *cartes de séjour de résident temporaire*, which we needed to stay in France. They told us it would take a minimum of eight weeks to get a visa, which was warp speed as far as they were concerned. There are times when it seems as if the French invented bureaucracy; indeed, French bureaucracy is so maddeningly slow and difficult one suspects they take a secret delight in it. Since we were set to leave the U.S. in less than a month, especially with our house in escrow, they suggested we go as tourists, which would allow us to stay for three months without visas and afterwards, we could take care of it in France. However, I had gone from one government office to another in Nice and everywhere I had been told the same thing: we could not get a *carte de séjour* in France.

"That is correct," Jean-Claude said. "One can only get a resident's visa from a French embassy in another country."

"So let me get this straight," I asked. "If one is a resident in France, one cannot apply for a French resident's visa. Only if one is not a resident in France and one is outside the country can one get a French visa. But you can't get the actual *carte de séjour* outside France. For that one has to be in France."

"*Exactement*," Jean-Claude said and laughed when I told him I didn't even know what I had just said. However, one thing was paradoxically clear. If we wanted to stay in France, we would have to leave the country. I asked him what we should do.

"What everyone else does, go to England or Italy. Some place with a French consulate. Like Milan or Florence."

At the word "Florence," Anne looked up.

Alarm bells rang in my head. "What's in Florence?" I asked.

"Gucci's," she said.

We left Colette's full of food and talking about trips to Troyes and Florence. Because we were intimidated about reciprocating with a dinner invitation which would involve cooking for the demanding French palate, we invited Colette to share Thanksgiving with us at *chez Polanski*. Anne figured that the novel cultural experience and a decent turkey dinner would make it acceptable and if Colette ended up disappointed, the failure would be blamed on American cuisine in general, instead of our less-than-*cordon-bleu* cooking skills. However, when we got home, Janie called. They had discovered another American couple, Hal and Darlene, "hiding out" as she put it, in Cap d'Antibes. She wanted us all to get together for Thanksgiving, except, she warned us, Hal and Darlene were "a little unusual." Coming from Janie, that was like saying World War Two was 'a little violent.'

Anne tried to beg off, but Janie came back with how we were the only American families in Cap d'Antibes, hitting Anne with the unfair tactic of patriotism. It'll be fun, she insisted. When Anne mentioned Colette, Janie insisted we bring her along. The more the merrier. Anne looked at me in despair; there didn't seem to be a graceful way of getting out of it.

Thanksgiving was starting to shape up as a disaster. Anne called Colette to see if she could get her to back out. Anne tried to paint the other Americans as vaguely sinister boors, which – the more she described them – sounded more and more on the mark, but Colette's curiosity was aroused and she insisted she wanted to come. "We're stuck," Anne said, hanging up. The phone rang again. It was Janie. She was thrilled to learn Colette was coming. She also asked Anne whether one was supposed to use wine or milk to make the gravy. It seems she had never actually cooked a Thanksgiving turkey before.

"Florence," Anne said, after getting off the phone, "is starting to look very good."

Chapter 4

Spaghetti Land

The weather had begun to change. The Riviera of travel-poster sun and blue seas turned cold and rainy. A chill wind stripped yellowing leaves from the trees on the Chemin des Contrebandiers. The leaves lay brown and sodden on the driveway and the grounds of the villa and at night we kept the windows shuttered against the rain. The beach was deserted and no one sat outside at the cafés in Antibes.

Now when we walked by the beach, we wore our raincoats and kept Justin bundled in his stroller. The wind blew across the white-topped waves, sending a cold spray over the path and when we walked along the fence around the Heineken estate, we would see the guards standing around a fire in a trashcan, warming their hands and smoking cigarettes, their automatic weapons slung across their backs. We went by often enough that they got to recognize us and would wave when they saw us.

Sometimes when I was stuck in the book, I would walk alone along the rain-empty streets and down to the beach. I would stop at the restaurant by the beach for a glass of red wine, the windows steamed so you couldn't see the sea and think about how the beach had belonged to the Murphys, after whom Fitzgerald had modeled Dick and Nicole Diver in *Tender is the Night*. Back then it had been a Gatsby summer of endless parties, one blending into the next, with Zelda and her aviator and F. Scott Fitzgerald, who had a crush on Sara Murphy, and Hemingway, working on *A Farewell To Arms* still with his first wife, Hadley, Picasso and his mistress, and Archibald Macleish, only now it was late autumn and like that long-ago summer, the parties had ended.

And not just the parties, but their world too. Even the writing had changed. Literature didn't seem to matter any more. Real writing, novels, the thing I loved, the thing that Hemingway and the Fitzgeralds and the Murphys had argued about and loved and lived for, was a tiny segment of the Entertainment industry. Novels had become genre pieces, Stephen King-type horror thrillers, spy thrillers like mine, private eye procedurals, women's paperback romances with bare-chested Fabio's on the cover; something people did to keep themselves busy on a plane, or at the beach. You'd better stop thinking like that or you'll never get this book done, I told myself.

In the book, I was working on an action sequence. An unknown assassin was about to try to kill my CIA agent Sawyer in the courtyard of Wat Po, the Temple of the Reclining Buddha, in Bangkok. It was good action stuff in an exotic setting, but I was anxious to get past the plot-driven aspect of the thriller and into the characters and what the book was really about. At the core of the novel was a love story between Sawyer and a mysterious Eurasian beauty, Suong, who hadn't yet made her appearance (already a problem – I was well into Part One) and I needed to decide when and how to bring her onstage. For me, Sawyer represented us Americans and how we had bumbled into Asia, devastating it all the while convinced we were doing good, while Suong in some way embodied Asia itself, violated but not innocent.

I sat in the restaurant bar, listening to the waiter and the chef discuss what they needed to order from the market and whether there was a chance of getting a decent *loup* in tomorrow's fish catch. In the book, I felt as if I was working around the edges of something hidden in a fog, chipping away at the spy stuff while what was important was right in front of me, only I couldn't see it.

I was also feeling guilty about sending Justin to the *crèche* at the Ecole du Cap, throwing him into an environment where he was the only kid who didn't speak French. It had to be hard for him, but Anne thought that since he was only there from 9:00 AM till 11:30 AM four days a week, it would be all right. A lot of French expressions, like *c'est tout, voilà, non merci, allons,* and *oui Madame,* in a perfect French accent, were starting to creep into his language, but if we tried to encourage him to speak French outside school, he refused. When I mentioned the *crèche* to him, he looked at me with mistrust as if as if he wasn't sure what other nasty tricks I had up my sleeve to pull on him. I wondered if the whole thing hadn't been a terrible mistake. Still, those hours in the morning when I was working and Justin was in the *crèche* were necessary for Anne and if we stayed in France, he would need to learn French anyway. At least I tried to rationalize it that way, though I still felt guilty.

Meanwhile, as Thanksgiving approached, there were lots of calls between Anne and Janie. Trying to find American-style food, things that you would pick up in the supermarket back home without a second thought, was turning into a full-time undertaking for both of them. A major coup was finding a can of cranberry sauce in a store in *Carrefour,* the big shopping center in St. Laurent de Var. Another time, Anne was thrilled beyond belief when she discovered a can of pumpkin pie filling gathering dust in a small *épicerie* in Cannes.

On Thanksgiving Day, Colette arrived at our villa after work, driving up in an old yellow Morris Mini. She had brought a bottle of her cousin Georges' champagne, assuming as any French person would, that champagne is perfect for all occasions.

Anne added a half-dozen bottles of Beaujolais Nouveau — that I had picked up just that morning from the *cave* in Antibes, the *marchand de vin* handing the bottles to me with greater solemnity than when I had been handed my college diploma — and a pumpkin pie she had baked in our oven that only took two desperate dives onto the mattress we placed by the kitchen door to light.

We piled into the Renault and went over to Greg and Janie's villa, where there was a woman named Marianne, a friend of Janie's from Colorado, who kept asking us why we had come to the Riviera. When Anne told her about our fantasy about the Riviera and my wanting to write a book, she responded "Yes, of course," but wanted to know why had we *really* come?

We sat around waiting for the other American couple, Hal and Darlene, to arrive. In France, there is a whole protocol about when to arrive for dinner, as had been carefully explained to us by Sally. First of all, it is considered *gauche* to arrive on time. If you are meeting someone at a café or restaurant, one should always be five to fifteen minutes late. This allows time for the other person to get through traffic and above all, so that one never shows any degree of anxiety about the other person showing up. This is particularly critical if the meeting is *une affaire de coeur*, Sally cautioned. To arrive early, or at the appointed time, was a bit *impertinent*. On the other hand, to be more than twenty minutes late to a café *rendez-vous*, is to show a lack of interest. A man or woman kept waiting more than twenty minutes would certainly be allowed to, at the very least, begin a flirtation with someone at another table.

For dinner at someone's home, however, according to Colette, to be correct one should be from thirty to forty-five minutes late. This allows the hostess sufficient time to prepare and for her to appear perfectly calm and in control, not a hair out of place, when the doorbell rings.

On the other hand, she cautioned, to be more than forty-five minutes late was an insult to the food, which might then become overcooked; in France, a crime barely second to murder in its seriousness. As it was, after more than two hours, Hal and Darlene still hadn't arrived. All the while, Marianne kept pumping Anne trying to find out what was our *real* purpose for coming to the Riviera and Janie fluttered around, worrying about the turkey. "The turkey's going to burn if we don't start," Janie announced mournfully, so we all sat down. We had nearly finished eating when Hal and Darlene finally showed.

Hal was a balding bearded man in his early forties; Darlene was an aging long-haired flower child left over from the Sixties. Without a word of apology, they sat down and began to stuff food into their mouths like refugees at a UN camp. Between bites, Hal told us he had come to France to write a novel about his experiences in a commune during his hippie days. Greg chimed in that he was working on a book, too. I began to feel less like a writer and more like I was part of a demographic trend.

Hal explained that he had met Darlene at the commune, but they were no longer hippies. They had bought a place in Connecticut and turned it into a Bed and Breakfast, which they said they had sold "for an obscene amount of money" to a hotel chain. The day after the money was in the bank, they had boarded a plane for Paris. Anne asked them what they had done in Paris, probably thinking about museums, sidewalk cafes and walks along the Seine.

"We went to the Mercedes dealer. Told him to give us the most expensive car he had. Paid cash and as soon as we signed the papers, we drove down here," Hal said. I asked him how he liked Cap d'Antibes.

"It's all right now that I've found a video store. All they have around here is one movie house showing stupid French movies," he said. Meanwhile, Darlene confessed to Anne that every once in a while, she worried about the kids.

"You have children?" Anne asked.

"A boy 15 and a girl 18," she said. Anne asked where they were now.

"I don't know about Kim, my daughter. Last I heard, she was in New York. But I think that's better, don't you? Girls need to be independent. She'll be all right. We arranged for a line of credit for her," Darlene confided. As for her son, he was still in high school in Boston.

"Where does he live?"

"He's got his own place," she said.

"Don't worry about him. I gave him a Mercedes and a platinum Visa card with a $50,000 limit. It'll cover him and his girlfriend, especially now that she's pregnant," Hal added. "Nope, the only real problem was our other Mercedes. It was still on lease."

"What did you do?" I asked.

"We didn't have time to get anybody to take over the lease, so we left it."

"What do you mean?"

"Just left it parked on a street in Boston. Then we took a taxi to Logan airport to come here," Hal shrugged. Justin was playing by himself in a corner, making car crash sounds with a toy truck we had brought. Sloane, the four year old, was watching a video of Warren Beatty and Faye Dunaway in bed in *Bonnie and Clyde*.

"Except he crashed the Mercedes," Darlene added. "He's OK though, just a broken leg."

"My God, what did you do?" Anne asked.

"Bought him another Mercedes," Hal said, still eating. I glanced at Colette, thinking of her beat-up old car and tried to imagine what she was thinking. Meanwhile, Greg kept trying to talk me into moving to Aspen. I told him I liked France, in fact we had just gotten here. Besides, while I liked skiing, it wasn't what I wanted to build my life around, not knowing that we were soon to meet the son of a famous novelist who had done just that. "What's so special about Aspen?" I asked.

"It's just cool. Besides, on any given day, you can walk down the street and see really cool people, like John Denver," he explained solemnly. "Eating, shopping, just like anybody else. Only it's John Denver, man!"

"Rocky Mountain High?"

"Exactly!" he winked. He wanted to open a women's boutique in Aspen. "All these unbelievably hot women trying stuff on. Imagine fitting them. Can you dig it?"

"But why have you *really* come to France? What's the real reason?" Janie's friend, Marianne, asked Anne again, who looked at me as though she were sinking for the third time. Meanwhile, Greg, Hal and Darlene had gone off into the other room. The scent of marijuana began to overpower the smell of roast turkey.

That night, on the drive back to our villa, I asked Colette what she thought about Thanksgiving. She thought the other Americans were *"très intéressants*. One doesn't get to meet *ces types-ci* very often," she added.

"What do you mean?"

"*Alors*, they talk many things, but no matter what they say, they are always talking about money," she observed.

"Colette, you're a philosopher," Anne said.

"*Ah oui*," she smiled. "Money is always good, but there are the truly important things in life, such as," she leaned forward on the car seat, "food, wine, and *surtout*, the chance for us all to gossip a little, *non?*"

After we got Colette safely off in her little Morris Mini, Anne and I tried to figure out how we were going to deal with our fellow Americans in Cap d'Antibes in the future.

It wasn't just the drugs, although we didn't want Justin around any of that, or that they were almost caricatures of "ugly Americans." We had a bad feeling about them, something we didn't trust. As always, the French have a word for it. When something is shady or suspicious, they say it is *louche* (derived from the verb *loucher*, to squint). From our point of view, Greg, Hal, Janie, their friend Marianne, were all definitely *louche*. On the other hand, Cap d'Antibes was a small place. We were bound to run into them. "And what was that business about why are we really here?" Anne wondered.

"Maybe they think we're running from something."

"Maybe *they* are. I can't wait to hear from Greg's first wife Barbara and find out what's really going on. I kind of feel sorry for Janie though," Anne said.

"That's because she's pretty. She and Greg probably have pictures of themselves turning disgusting and ugly in the attic."

"How can we avoid them? I run into Janie and Darlene when I'm shopping."

It looked like we were going to be stuck with them, until the next day, when Janie called, Anne had a brainstorm. She told Janie she couldn't talk because we were leaving for Florence to get our visas and do some Christmas shopping. "That'll hold them for a while," she said when she hung up.

I nodded and went back to trying to close up part of the house. The fuel oil bills for heating were killing us. Something else we hadn't foreseen. The problem was that our villa, like most of the houses on the Cote d'Azur, was built with little or no insulation on the theory that they were usually only used during the summer. As a result, the heat escaped through a thousand invisible cracks in the walls and roof. It was costing me a fortune to heat the air over Cap d'Antibes. By closing off part of the house and leaving those rooms unheated, we might be able to save a little. Suddenly, the phone rang again and I heard Anne say, "I wish we could, but we're leaving today" and then "I'm not sure we'll still be here."

She looked at me and didn't have to say another word. It was time to get out of Dodge. While I got the suitcases, Anne called our ultimate information source, Sally, who recommended the Hotel Lucchesi in Florence. It was in the middle of town, near both the Santa Croce and the Piazza della Signoria and if you made a point of it, Sally said, you could get a room with a view of the Arno River.

Anne called the Lucchesi, found out we could get both a hotel babysitter and a view. Twenty minutes later, we were packed and on our way to pick Justin up from the *crèche*. Soon, with Justin safely in the car seat, we were on our way to Italy.

We drove through Nice and Monaco. Just beyond Menton, driving along the harbor road, we crossed the border into the Italian town of Ventimiglia. Justin wanted to know where we were going. Since *spaghetti Bolognese* was his favorite food, we told him we were visiting the country where they made spaghetti. You can have all the spaghetti you want, I told him.

"That's funny, Daddy. We're going to Spaghetti-land," he said. Some people call it 'Italy' I told him, but after that, amongst ourselves, we called it 'Spaghetti-land.' That was Justin's second favorite part of Florence, the pasta. But what he really liked in Italy were the tunnels. As we drove the *autostrada* along the hilly Ligurian Coast, we began to go through tunnels in the mountains. Justin had never been in a tunnel before. He found the sudden change from day to night, the cars with their lights on in the daytime, the cave-like feel and the roaring echoes of the cars fascinating. Each time we entered another tunnel, he would sing out "Tunnel!" When we came out, the sun would be shining on the windshield and he would say, "More tunnels, Daddy." Further on past Genoa, the *autostrada* took us through the Apuane Alps, where there were longer tunnels. Some of them seemed miles long. Italy, we all agreed, was hands-down the best country for tunnels. Justin couldn't have been happier.

We stopped for lunch and gas at an *autostrada* stop near Rapallo. Around us, Italian families were talking and eating, washing their pasta down with liter-sized carafes of red wine. People smiled and talked with their mouths full. It was like being in a boarding house. After lunch, we drove through brown and green Tuscan hills dotted with fields and whitewashed villages. We crossed an iron bridge over the Arno in Pisa and headed inland to Florence. By the time we got into town and found the hotel and checked in, it was almost dark.

The hotel concierge suggested an *osteria* up the street near the Piazza della Signoria for dinner. Justin had the *penne Bolognese*, Anne and I had the "drunken spaghetti" (*spaghetti dell ubriacone* cooked in red wine) and a bottle of *chianti*. After dinner, we went to Harry's Bar for drinks. Anne and I toasted having escaped our Cap d'Antibes American colony. When we came out, it was raining. We ran through the rain holding hands, Justin splashing through the puddles, back to the hotel, where we arrived wet and tired and as happy as we had ever been in our lives.

Chapter 5

Florence in the Rain

The attitude at the French consulate in Florence disappointed us. We had braced ourselves for a long bureaucratic siege, with endless rounds of paperwork, '*Impossible, monsieurs*, and, of course, the famous French finger wagging in our face. *Au contraire*, they couldn't have been nicer. They said it would take a couple of days to process the paperwork for our *cartes de séjour* and suggested that in the meantime, we enjoy ourselves in Florence. In a couple of days, when everything was ready, they'd call the hotel and we could stop by to pick up our documents. They even recommended a few restaurants, above all, the *Enoteca Pinchiorri*.

"Is it as good as French food?" I teased. Most Frenchmen would rather be torn limb from limb and have you set fire to what was left than to even consider the suggestion that food might be acceptable for human consumption anywhere outside France. The French consul looked around uneasily and beckoned me close to make sure he wasn't overheard.

"Better," he whispered, rolling his eyes at his own heresy. Speaking of which, we soon found ourselves in the Piazza della

Signoria, at the spot, marked by a dark marble circle in the pavement, where Savonarola had been burned at the stake.

"They pick interesting things to commemorate," Anne remarked, as we took snapshots in front of the fake statue of Michaelangelo's David, by Neptune's Fountain outside the Palazzo della Signoria. The day was cool and drizzly and Anne had Justin bundled in a jacket and a blue wool cap. The piazza was closed to traffic and we let him run freely. He splashed through the puddles until he found something even more fun: chasing the pigeons on the cobblestones in front of the statues in the Loggia. He was having so much fun, a small group of tourists began taking snapshots of him instead of the statues of Perseus and David. It seemed a shame to take him away, but Anne was a woman on a mission. We hailed a taxi, Anne said the magic word, "*Armani,*" and in a few minutes he dropped us off at the corner of the Via Turnabuoni. As we walked down the street, Anne's eyes grew wide.

"My God," she said. I could hear the awe in her voice. "They're all here. Gucci's, Bulgari, Prada – oh look!" Dragging Justin and me along. "Ferragamo!" The day passed in a Christmas shopping binge from one store to the next, from Ferragamo to Armani's, where she bought Justin a sweater, to Pucci's on the Via della Vigna Nuova to Bottega Veneta across the piazza from the Hotel Excelsior, then back to the "Holy of Holies," Gucci's on the Via Turnabuoni. When we collapsed back at the hotel that evening, wet and exhausted, Anne's eyes had the glazed satisfied look of a lioness after a successful kill.

"Christmas shopping done?" I asked hopefully. My feet were hurting so much from all the walking on cobblestoned streets, I could barely move. As for our finances, they'd definitely taken a hit.

"Almost," she said and I instantly panicked at the glimmer in her eye that there might be more. I turned on the TV. There were only three channels. On the first, some people on a panel were screaming at each other in Italian. They looked like they were about to kill each other, except that one man in a paisley tie kept smiling. He looked vaguely demented, but the fact that he was smiling and that none of the people shaking their fists and obviously threatening mayhem was actually doing anything, gave us the impression that whatever was happening was fairly normal. There was a spaghetti Western on the second channel and on the third, some young Italian women were running around topless in a department store. I thought all the jiggling might give Justin an earlier education than necessary and we settled on the Western. Little did I know, as Anne would say, that *'Cocorico Boy'* was coming.

After Justin was asleep, Anne and I stepped out on the balcony. It was cold and wet and we cuddled wrapped in a blanket as we looked out over the lights along the Arno River. The Oltrarno district, on the other side of the river, was dark and except for several neon signs, you could almost imagine yourself in another century.

"It's magic, isn't it?" Anne sighed and cuddled close. The Ponte Vecchio was lit by misty strands of electric lights reflected in the river.

"Yes," I said.

After that, we played tourist. The real David at the Accademia, the Duomo, the Pitti Palace. We did more shopping. We bought silver trinkets under the wet awnings of jewelry stands on the Ponte Vecchio. At the Uffizi, we rubbernecked with a crowd of tourists in front of Botticelli's *Birth of Venus*. The rain had driven everyone indoors; the museum smelled of wet clothes.

"Do you think she's beautiful?" Anne said.

"Sure," I said, thinking, a beautiful naked babe with long flowing hair popping out of a clamshell; no wonder she still drew a crowd.

"She wouldn't make it in L.A.," Anne said. "She doesn't have that anorexic Hollywood look they all have."

When we got back to the hotel, we learned the French Consulate had called. They wanted to know if they should send the papers to the hotel. It was as if we had somehow crossed into a kind of reverse-Twilight Zone. All the horror stories about French bureaucracy, supposedly the most obnoxious in Western Europe, were proving false. We wondered if maybe something sinister was happening.

Maybe, Anne suggested, they were going to send us to Germany instead.

That night, we hired a hotel babysitter, so we could go to *Enoteca Pinchiorri* for dinner. This was a tradition we had started on a trip up the California coast to Carmel when Justin was only six months old. We stayed at Quail Lodge, which had a five-star restaurant overlooking the golf course. The clerk at the front desk suggested a babysitter, a woman employee who had been there for years and who had a child of her own. She was German, they told us. Was that all right? We didn't think anything of it until she showed up in her hotel uniform about twenty minutes before our dinner reservation. Anne showed her Justin's formula, his little Teddy Bear and portable crib mobile and told her how he sometimes had trouble getting to sleep and what to do if there was a problem.

"There *vill* be no problems," the woman said in a thick German accent.

"But just in case..."

"There *vill* be no problems," she said. I believed her.

As Anne and I walked to the restaurant, I whispered, "See. That's what we've needed all along. A Nazi." Anne worried all through dinner, but when we came back to the room, Justin was peacefully asleep and as the baby-sitter said, there had been "no problems." Of course, that was when Justin was an infant and we worried all the time.

Now, years later, we were old hands at using hotel babysitters. Here in Florence, the babysitter supplied by the Hotel Lucchesi was very reassuring and she and Justin were playing with toys on the bed when we left.

It was still cold and raining when we got out of the cab and went up the elevator at *Enoteca Pinchiorri*. The dining room was luxurious and intimate, classical music was playing and the waiters outnumbered us three-to-one. The menu listed only two items: an eight-course *prix fixe* menu and something called the "Surprise Menu." No wines were listed and ominously, neither were the prices. I asked about the wine and the waiter told me that the appropriate wine for each course would be supplied, somehow implying that to use the same wine for two different courses was a sacrilege only a philistine would contemplate. Anne asked about the "Surprise Menu" and was told, "It's a *sorprendere... como se dice*, 'surprise,' *Signora*."

We picked the *prix fixe*. They brought us tiny antipasto cakes and a white Gavi de Gavi wine that was unbelievable, followed by *ignudi*, ricotta-cheese dumplings mixed, our waiter told us, with a lobster and a rooster's coxcomb fricassee – "Is he kidding?" Anne said – that was even better than the first dish, plus a different wine that made the Gavi de Gavi taste like mouthwash.

By the time we started the third course, a black octopus-ink pasta with truffles and yet another incredible wine, we knew we were in the presence of greatness. After the fourth course and another wine, Anne leaned over and whispered, "This is the best meal of my life." Her eyes were swimming and I realized that not only was she right, but that we both were becoming seriously tipsy. After the pasta came a Mediterranean sea bass *à la Florentine*. The wine continued to flow. An hour later, as the meal was ending over *expresso* and a final *digestivo* drink, we asked the waiter to bring over the chef so we could express our gratitude. In a moment, both the chef and the maitre d' were at our table. I tried to tell them how wonderful it had been, one of the great experiences of our lives, but since the room was spinning around me, I couldn't have been all that coherent.

"*Grazie, Signore,*" the maitre d' said.

"*Prego*, I mean it. Truly, *verdad*," I said, mixing Italian and Spanish. I motioned him closer. "Is it true you're getting a third Michelin star?" repeating a rumor the concierge at the hotel had told us.

"We don't want."

"Why not?"

"I tell you, *Signore*. We would have to raise prices. Maybe we lose the people who have been our customers all these years. We will be famous not just in *Firenze*, but all Italy. Then all is business – and where is the pleasure?"

"It was perfect," I said.

He bowed.

"It was our pleasure, *Signore*."

Anne and I staggered out of the restaurant feeling better than we had in our whole lives. We were also drunk. The taxi they had called was waiting for us in the rain.

"After that, we can't just go back to the hotel. It would be too – what's the word?" Anne said, snuggling close in the back of the taxi.

"Anticlimactic?"

"That too."

The concierge at the Lucchesi had told us that 'Jackie O's' on the Oltrarno side of the river was the hottest nightclub in town. I told the driver.

"That was incredible," Anne said as we drove off.

"That maitre d' is a great man," I said with drunken solemnity. "In America they'd turn it into a franchise. McPinchiorri, complete with a giant arch made out of gold-painted pasta. They'd make billions and the food would taste like crap."

"Thank you so much for that image, *Monsieur*," Anne said, as the taxi pulled up in front of Jackie O's. Inside the club, it was so dark the maitre d' used a flashlight to show us to our table. The room was filled with shadowy figures lit with smoky blue neon lighting. We ordered scotch and watched the dancing. Men in suits were dancing with other men and women in sexy gowns were dancing with other women.

"Are we in the right place?" I whispered to Anne.

"We're not the only ones." She pointed out a young couple getting up to dance. They looked like models: both were anorexic, blond, and good-looking in skin-tight black leather. The woman smoked a long purple-colored cigarette with a gold filter-tip. The man wore pearls around his neck. Anne stopped the waiter as he was going by.

"That man is wearing pearls," she said.

"What else with basic black, *Signora*?" the waiter shrugged.

"At the restaurant I thought 'Wow, we're sophisticated,' but we aren't, are we?" Anne whispered.

"Not even close," I said, pulling her onto the dance floor. "Europe has depths of decadence we can't even imagine."

The room swirled around us in a haze of blue smoke and loud music. The anorexic couple turned out to be Italian movie actors from Rome. I told them we were living in Polanski's villa and they shouted above the noise that they'd love to work with him. "We like to work naked," the woman assured me.

"I'm sure he'll appreciate that," I said.

Somehow, we wound up at five in the morning at the bar in the Excelsior Hotel. The blond couple had disappeared and a young Englishman was telling us that even though he was traveling around the world with a rich 65-year-old woman that did not make him a gigolo. It was source material; he was a writer.

"Jeez, another one," I muttered. I looked over at Anne and could see she was starting to tilt sideways like the Leaning Tower of Pisa. We went outside and walked back to our hotel. It was dark and misty and we were giggling trying to keep each other upright as we staggered on the cobblestones. We woke the babysitter up and paid her and fell into bed.

We hadn't slept more than twenty minutes, when I was awakened by Justin bouncing on my chest and singing, "Daddy, Daddy, Daddy, Daddy..." He was wide-awake and ready for fun. I, on the other hand, had what had to be the worst hangover of my life.

"Don't bounce on Daddy," I said. "Daddy's hung over and would like to die as quietly as possible."

"Daddy, Daddy, Daddy, Daddy... Time to get up, Daddy," Justin sang.

There was a knock at the door. It sounded like a bass drum from Hell. A housemaid came in and opened the curtains to bright morning light streaming into the room. My eyeballs felt poached. I heard Anne groan.

"This is the land of the Mafia. If you don't shut the curtains, I'm seriously going to hire someone to kill you. I'd kill you myself, but I have to wait for my head to stop exploding," Anne said, her eyes tightly shut.

"The maid did it," I said.

"They'll have to bump her off too."

"What's the matter with Mommy?" Justin said.

Anne pulled the pillow over her face. "Justin, Sweetie," she said, her voice muffled by the pillow, "play with Daddy. Mommy needs to go into the bathroom and never come out."

We were checking out that morning and the condition we were in may be judged by the fact that because Justin would not let us go back to sleep, we started getting dressed and packed at 6:30 AM and by noon, we still weren't ready. Somewhere in the middle of all this, a bellman brought us a thick sheaf of papers from the French consulate. I called to thank them and to ask them which of the papers was our *carte de séjour*.

"Ah no, *monsieur*," and I could imagine him wagging the famous French finger, "*le Consulat* does not provide the *carte de séjour*."

"I thought that's what we were doing," I said, wincing. Talking, or doing anything at this point, was incredibly painful.

"*Non, monsieur*. This is only the *demande*, the application, for the *carte de séjour*."

"So how," I asked, "does one get one's *carte de séjour*?"

"Ah, that is another matter, *monsieur*. For that you must go to the *préfecture locale*."

"Where is the *préfecture*?"

"I do not know, monsieur. But in any case, it does not matter."

"Why not?"

"Because you cannot go to the *préfecture*."

"Ah. And why is that?"

"Because you are not a French resident. For that you need the *carte de séjour*."

"So in order to get a *carte de séjour*, one must already have a *carte de séjour*?"

"*Pas du tout*," he said, annoyed. "That is not *raisonnable*."

I had made a *faux pas*. In France, to be considered illogical is a crime second only to not appreciating good food. When French mothers want to chastise their children, they use the famous French finger and tell them they are not *raisonnable*.

"*Mille pardons*," I said. "I am new at this. What should I do?"

"Perhaps *Monsieur* should inquire at the nearest *gendarmerie*," he said and hung up, the sound of the phone slamming making the top of my head feel like it was coming off. Justin was playing using his toy trucks like jet fighters shooting down enemy planes. Anne emerged from the bathroom, the color of her face matching the green velvet curtains.

"What did they say?" she asked.

"I have to go to the police station."

"What will they do?"

"The way my head feels, with any luck, the *guillotine*."

It took two porters, shaking their heads, to load us, the luggage and all the packages from shopping into the Renault. I drove toward La Spezia and up the Ligurian coast toward Genoa; it felt more like driving a boat than a car and I was getting sea-sick.

"You look terrible," Anne said.

"I look better than I feel," I said.

"More tunnels, Daddy," Justin ordered.

"I don't think we're cut out for the high life," I said, as the *autostrada* crested a hill revealing a dazzling view of the coast just as the sun broke through the clouds, beams of yellow light sparkling on the sea. It was beautiful and breathtaking and all I wanted to do was throw up.

"Mommy, I'm hungry," Justin called out. Anne checked the map.

"You know, I've never been to Portofino."

"Anything to stop driving," I said.

We drove down the winding road to the restaurant at the tip of the harbor in Portofino. The pastel-colored houses along the water front glowed in the afternoon sun. Anne ordered spaghetti Bolognese for Justin and herself.

"*per Signore?*" the waiter asked.

"Don't mind me, I'm dying. Hang-ov-er. *Como se dice* 'hangover' in Italian?" I said.

"*Signore?*"

"Too much *vino. Molto molto vino.*"

"*Ah, la malessere!*"

"*Si*, that. What've you got for *la grande malessere?*"

"*Grappa, Signore.*"

"What's that?" Anne asked.

"He's suggesting a hair of the dog."

"The sooner the better," she said.

The waiter brought us *grappas* and amazingly, in a few minutes we were feeling almost human. As we ate, we looked out over the yachts and fishing boats in the harbor, the setting sun turning the windows of the houses perched on the hills to gold. As we were finishing up, a burly American in an open shirt, a large St. Christopher on a heavy gold chain dangling on his hairy chest, and a thin blonde woman sat at the table next to us.

"Angelo and his goddamn Mercedes," the American said in an accent straight out of New Jersey. "Shoulda told him to get one of his *goombahs* to do it. He wants ta know made, I'll show him made."

"Smart. Real smart," the woman said.

"Whaddya talkin'?"

"There are people..." she glanced around.

Anne and I looked at each other. They could have come straight from central casting for *The Godfather*.

"Who gives a shit?" he said. When the waiter came, he ordered martinis. That was a mistake. We'd already learned that in Europe, except for Paris, there are very few places where you can get a decent martini – and not many in Paris either.

He lit a big cigar and leaned over to offer me one.

"Hey *paisan*,' you like cigars?"

"*Non, merci,*" I said, pretending I was French. This was just too good to miss.

"It's Cuban... Ha-va-na. In the States you can't get these, unless you know the right people," he said.

"*Non, merci. Je n'aime pas fumer.*"

"Whatever," he shrugged. "Where's the waiter? Goddamn country. Half the time they're on strike and the other half, they're on goddamn holiday. Can't even get a decent pizza. They invented it, for Chrissakes. Back home you can get a better slice on any street corner in Jersey City. We oughta go back."

"So whaddya want, Dominic?" the woman said.

"I wanna go home, is what I want. Where's that waiter?"

I motioned to Anne and paid the check. The waiter was just bringing them their food as we left.

"*Bon appétit, Monsieur, Madame,*" I said. He smiled and nodded.

"Goddamn Frogs," I heard him mumble as we walked away.

Back in the car, Anne and I exploded in laughter. Hearing us laugh, Justin joined in too.

"God, that was like something out of a movie. Why did you pretend to be French?" she asked.

"I figured if he'd be more open if he thought we didn't speak English."

"So what do you think? Is he really hiding out?"

"You mean like Michael in *The Godfather*? Could be."

"Al Pacino is cuter. Did you see that gold chain?"

"You could've strangled an elephant with that chain."

"Wow! A real mobster on the lam. Wait till I write my grandmother," Anne smiled, then paused. "I wonder who else we know here who's hiding out?"

We were about to find out.

Chapter 6

Cocorico Boy

Christmas was coming, but the French didn't care. Going into Antibes, we might see the occasional shop window on Avenue Thiers decorated with colored lights and a crudely-chalked *Père Noël* and a few of the *boulangeries* were starting to show their *buches de Noëls* in the windows, but there were no decorations or flags on the streets and shops as there usually were for a holiday or event the French considered important, like winning a soccer match. The weather stayed cool, the cafes were quiet, and there was a feeling of something missing.

In California, our Christmases had always begun with a Thanksgiving visit to Anne's family in Orinda, a wooded bedroom community over the hill from Berkeley. On the Friday after Thanksgiving, we would pile into the car and head across the Bay Bridge to San Francisco for a round of marathon shopping starting with the late and much-lamented I. Magnin's, Nieman's, Gumps' and after Justin came along, FAO Schwartz and their wonderful giant stuffed elephant. The stores would sparkle with Christmas decorations and the streets around Union Square were filled with vendors, shoppers, and anti-something or –everything protestors. Lunch was always

Chinatown, climbing up the narrow kitchen stairs at Sam Wu's on California Street for the deluxe raw fish salad, then more shopping and as the sun set over the bay and the city lights came on, drinks at the Top of the Mark. By the time we would get back to L.A., the malls would be decorated and full of people and in Beverly Hills, electric Santas and sleighs would be strung from streetlamps across Wilshire Boulevard.

But although France was a Catholic country, the French weren't interested. Colette said that Americans went overboard on these things. Too *commerciale*, she said, and besides, no one believed in such things anymore. Max however, had another explanation.

"In order to understand the French, you have to understand the Japanese," he said over dinner at the Petit Trianon, a bistro in St. Jean Cap Ferrat whose *mousseline de rascasse* (hogfish mousse) he had been raving about.

"That's ridiculous. They're nothing alike," Anne said.

"Exactly. Take whatever the Japanese do and reverse it 180 degrees. Cars, for example."

"What about 'em?" Gaby said, her fork pointed at him like a dart in a British pub. She and Bobby G. were shopping around for a new car.

"When the Japanese want to build a car, they study all the comparable models from the U.S., Germany, Italy, wherever. They take the best of each, improve it 10%, cut the price 10%, and sell a zillion of them. When the French want to build a car, the first thing they do is say, 'We must not consider anything anyone else does, especially *les américains*. Otherwise, it wouldn't be French!' So everything they do is like inventing the wheel for the first time. That's how you get cars that look like flying saucers and ride like boats."

What about clothes?" Anne put in. "They know how to make clothes."

"Baloney," Max said. "It only looks like clothes. The French models are all a size zero. Real women can't wear that stuff. If you want clothes, go to Italy."

"The French *are* funny," Anne said, getting into it. "Like why do they make you bag your own groceries at the *supermarché*?"

"And in such pathetic little plastic bags. Takes forever," Gaby smiled. We were all expats ganging up on the French. This was fun.

"Yeah. Why not hire a bagger, like in the States?"

"Because it is *déclassé* to do for people what they can do for themselves. What next? Hire *employés* to wipe people's *derrières* in public?" Colette snapped.

"What about the way they make you wander around a parking structure for hours looking for a *caisse* to pay your parking *ticket*? And then you've got to climb two, three floors to get back to your car... How about that?" Bobby G. said.

"It's the *Socialistes*. Gives employment to fools," Colette said.

"And when you go shopping... Talk about French *service*..." Max put in.

"'French service' is an oxymoron," Anne said.

"No kidding," Max said. "The other day I went to the *quincaillerie* in Menton to get a bunch of tools and stuff for the house. Must've bought three, four thousand francs worth. Weighed a ton. And of course you have to carry it all, because Heaven forbid there should be a basket or a cart! I'm standing there forty minutes waiting to pay while the only clerk in the store discusses with some old man about buying a screw! I'm not kidding, one screw! In America, you can't buy a single screw. They sell 'em in plastic bags of like, a hundred for a buck! And I'm staggering under all this merchandise. Finally, I said, '*Monsieur!*' and offered to buy the goddamn screw! Of course, you know what happened?"

"The French finger!" Anne exclaimed.

"He wags the finger in my face! All that for a lousy screw," Max said.

"No such thing," Bobby G. drawled and everyone laughed.

"The Frogs are weird," Max said. "Look at all the kissing they do."

"*Ja*, you've got to kiss everyone twenty-seven times. Even if you just see them five minutes ago. Takes an hour just to walk into a room!" harrumphed Yasper, a Dutch boat builder. He and his wife, Betje, usually lived on whatever yacht they were working on.

"*C'est normal*," Colette shrugged. "Don't Americans shake hands?" She pantomimed a humorless Midwesterner's grim handshake.

"Yeah, but we don't air-kiss someone six or seven times just to say hello, not to mention the hand-kissing," I put in, not wanting to be left out.

"I like the *baisemain*," the hand-kiss, Anne said. "It's romantic."

"Not very hygienic. You don't want to know where that hand's been."

"*Voilà les américains*! You all have the phobia *bactériologique*," Colette said.

"And after you kiss everyone when you come in, you have to do it all over again when you leave. In Holland, we'd be home in bed already," Yasper said.

"In France, the bed is saved for more important things," Colette said.

"So what's with all the kissing? Even people you don't like?" Anne asked.

"The *faire la bise*? *Bise* is what a kiss on the cheek is called. There are rules," Sally explained. "With people you don't like, you only kiss them twice, once on each cheek."

"Is that bad?" I asked.

"A slap in the face," Colette affirmed.

"So there's a whole system to this?"

"With people you know, but perhaps not very well, you want to *bise* them three times. Kissing four times actually shows affection. But it's not just the number, it's how you do it. How close you get, whether you actually graze the cheek, and so on. One must be *spirituel*," Sally said.

"Spiritual?" Anne asked.

"No, *spirituel*. It's an attitude."

"Like what?"

"One must have an air. Like when you *bise* a woman you can't stand three times and say, 'How chic of you to wear that color, *chérie*. Anyone else would look fat.' That is *spiritual!*"

"I'm still confused about the technique," I said. "You don't actually kiss the cheek?"

"Only with family or close friends," Sally said, wagging the famous French finger.

"Or lovers, of course," Colette added.

"So we've been doing it all wrong," I said.

Sally nodded. "We were wondering if you didn't like us."

Anne stood up and went over and kissed Sally's cheeks four times and everyone applauded.

"*Bravo!*" Colette said. "Perhaps, *après tout*, you begin to understand how to do things *à la française.*"

The next evening, our education on things *à la française* made a quantum leap when we discovered *Cocorico Boy*, a TV show impossible to imagine anywhere but in France. For one thing, there was the time. The show was on every night for exactly twenty minutes. Every show began with the same video of four pretty chorus girls dancing and singing the show's theme song, *Faites le Cocodingo!* Since it was always the same video, in Max's view, *les girls* had been doing the *Cocodingo* for twenty years and were all grandmothers by now.

After the chorus girls, came a few minutes of political satire, with muppet-like puppets representing well-known politicians hanging out in a bar. A distinctly recognizable Jacques Chirac was a fuzzy alcoholic frog, Mitterand was a plump chicken who was always clucking about things that had nothing to do with anything else, Le Pen was a mentally-deficient rabbit, and so on, with guest appearances by various other characters, including a Peter Sellers-like Inspector Clousseau. The jokes were forgettable, but the scene always ended in a slapstick brawl with all the puppets beating up on Le Pen.

Then came the part everyone waited for, a skit based on a hot new movie or TV show. In the middle of the silly jokes and regardless of what was happening, whether on the bridge of the star ship Enterprise, or in a Clint Eastwood Western saloon, or a confrontation between James Bond and an evil mastermind, out would come a sexy stripper who would peel all the way down to her G-string, kiss the leading comic and leave, at which point the comic would leer at the camera and say something like "I love *le business*," or "*C'est bon le cinq à sept*" ("It's good, the five to seven;" i.e., 5 – 7 PM is considered prime time for cocktails and extramarital affairs in France). This silliness was followed by another chorus from the *Cocodingo* girls (same video, why waste money?) and it was done. It had been the Number One show in France for years. Max and I often thought it would do well in America.

Meanwhile, Anne was getting frustrated with the French attitude towards Christmas. We had done our Christmas shopping in Florence, but we still needed toys for Justin. And there were no Christmas tree lots. It was impossible to find a tree.

"Maybe we should go into the forest and chop one down like people used to," I said.

"Great! I can see you chopping your foot off by mistake," Anne said, giving me the kind of look wives reserve for husbands and other congenital idiots.

By now, we had settled back into the villa routine. Justin spent mornings at the *crèche*, Anne spent her days looking for a parking space in Antibes and Nice, and I was back working on the book when I wasn't dealing with the French bureaucracy about our *cartes de séjour*. I had gone to the local *gendarmerie* in Antibes. It was a fortress-like stone building in a narrow side street. The inside smelled of disinfectant. The police *commissaire*, looking stern behind an old-fashioned French mustache, did not bother to look at the papers I handed him.

"You are the *locataire américain* at *la Villa Closerie* on the *Chemin des Contrabandiers* with your wife and the little boy," he said, surprising me at how much he already knew about us. "So what are you doing here? What is your *métier?*"

"I'm writing a book," I said.

"*Pourquoi?* America does not produce writers," he said dismissively.

"*Pardon, Monsieur.* I thought French education was better than that."

"*Pooh!* Name some great American writers."

"Melville, Hawthorne, Poe, Crane, Mark Twain *bien sur*, Jack London, Dreiser, Hemingway, Fitzgerald, Irwin Shaw, Updike, Bellow, Baldwin, James Jones, Heller, O'Neill, Henry Miller, William Faulkner," I said, heading south, "Tennessee Williams, Styron, Capote, Carson McCullers, Harper Lee, Pinky Lee, Peggy Lee, Robert E. Lee," I said, thinking, Jeez, the list of really good ones wasn't that long.

"*Rien*," he said, glancing at the other police *officier*, who was grinning widely. "Who is your Voltaire? Your Malraux? Your Zola? Your Balzac? Your Victor Hugo?!"

"Faulkner is our Hugo; Hemingway our Balzac," I said. This was getting interesting, a kind of literary parlor game.

"*Eh bien.* Who is your Gide? Your Anatole France?"

"For Gide, Dreiser or Updike. For Anatole France, Tom Wolfe, the second one with the white suit."

"I don't know him. Who is your Sartre? Your Camus?"

"We don't have one," I admitted.

"*Eh voilà!* There is no American literature, only *le Playboy magazine.*"

"You wouldn't say that if you had read *Gatsby*, or *The Bear*, or *Catch-22*."

"There are American writers," he intoned, "but no American literature."

"We've won six or seven Nobel prizes."

"The Swedes are idiots," he shrugged.

"It's true, Monsieur," the other *officier* nodded. "They come here for *les vacances*. They make the *vicieux* drunks."

"My father knew one of them," the *commissaire* said. "The Hemingway."

"Your father knew Hemingway? Truly?"

The *commissaire* responded with a Gallic shrug.

"What did your father say about him?" I asked.

"He said his French was *exécrable*," he laughed, handing me back my papers.

"*Monsieur le Commissaire*, do I get my *carte de séjour*?"

"*Pas ici*. For this, you must go to the *Ministère de l'Intérieur* in Nice. Still, come again. We must continue our conversation."

Driving back to the villa, I thought that was what I loved about France; that you could get into an interesting literary discussion with a cop. But what he had said bothered me. I wasn't writing literature; just a spy thriller, what Graham Greene called 'an entertainment,' and still only in the early stages of it at that. I resolved to make the thriller deeper, but when I got back to the villa, Anne was waiting, brandishing a letter envelope at me like a subpoena.

"He's a *thief*!" she announced.

"Who is?" Thinking we've been robbed. We'll have to go back to California as failures, our tails between our legs.

"Greg. As in Greg and Janie. He's on the lam," she said.

"When did you learn to talk like a gangster's moll?" I asked.

"Don't be funny," she snapped. "This is serious. Remember I said I did a research project at UCLA with Greg's first wife, Barbara? I wrote to her. She says he embezzled millions of his clients' money. The cops in L.A, are after him. She's called her attorney. He stole money from her too."

"Maybe they'll leave Cap d'Antibes," I said hopefully.

"Don't think so. Apparently, Greg had talked about it. One of the reasons they picked France is because the French rarely extradite to the U.S."

"So he had it planned all along. What do we do?"

Just then the phone rang. Anne picked it up. 'It's Janie,' she mouthed, pointing at the phone. They talked for a minute.

"What's up?" I asked, when she hung up.

"Janie's found some Christmas trees. A lot on Avenue Clemenceau. She said to hurry."

"But what are we going to do?"

"Well, I don't know about you," Anne said, grabbing her coat, "but I've been looking for weeks. I'm going to get us a tree."

Chapter 7

New Year's in Cap d'Antibes

The Christmas tree was pathetic. A forlorn little thing barely three feet tall with sparse pine needles clinging to spindly branches.

"Sure you don't need help carrying it in?" I asked Anne and she began to cry.

"It was the last one," she said, her voice muffled against my chest as I put my arms around her. "It's pretty bad, isn't it?" she said finally.

"Awful," I agreed.

"This is harder than I thought. I want a normal Christmas tree. I want to be able to go somewhere and just get what I need and where everyone speaks English. I want to see Jane Pauley in the morning and drink coffee, not *café au lait,* and watch real TV, not just two crappy channels where all they show are French talking heads and static. I want to shop just once a week, not this business of shopping in ninety-three stores every two hours. I want groceries in a real supermarket where there's parking and room to move and someone else does the bagging! I want to be normal again," she whined.

"Thank you, Private Benjamin."

Anne laughed. "I was good, wasn't I?"

"I'm sorry. Who knew living in a fancy villa on the French Riviera was a form of punishment?"

"It's not. It's just... I don't know."

"Foreign?"

"Yeah. The trouble with France is that it's just so... *French!*"

"Well," I said. "If it's any consolation, I think you're cuter than Goldie Hawn."

We set the tree on a stool in the corner of the salon to make it look a little bigger and so we wouldn't trip over it. We decorated it with little paper and plastic ornaments and a string of colored electric lights Anne had bought and I lifted Justin up so he could put a cardboard star on the top. As night fell and we gathered around a fire in the fireplace and our little Christmas tree with its few colored lights. Justin told Anne it was *"très beau, Maman,"* in his *crèche* French and somehow, that made it all right.

The weather turned cold and clear. We settled back to our routine. Each morning Anne bundled Justin up and took him to the *crèche* and I went down the stairs to what I thought of as my secret room. I would sit at the little table and face the wall, shivering in my sweater. The room was white and empty and icy cold. I had turned the heat off in this part of the villa because we were spending more on heating oil than for rent and fuel prices were going up. Even though we were trying to be careful, the money was going out too fast and I was getting worried.

The shopkeepers in Antibes said it was the worst winter they could remember on the Côte d'Azur. I took their comments seriously until Sally said they say that every year. But there was no insulation in the villa and the heat seeped out no matter what we did.

I began to dread my daily check of the heating oil level with the long pole, watching it drop relentlessly day-by-day. None of it mattered though, once I got started writing. In the book, my CIA agent, Sawyer, had followed a lead to the resort town of Ban Phattaya on the Gulf of Thailand. Sawyer was to meet with a snitch, a strungout heroin addict named Eddie Macbeth. Eddie had been a Marine lieutenant in Vietnam who had gotten his nickname "Macbeth" by supposedly fragging his captain and assuming command of the company. Eddie's company had suffered eighty-five percent casualties to capture a hill near the Rockpile. By the time they took it, Eddie was the only officer left. After the choppers airlifted what was left of the company off the hill, the captain had ordered Eddie to take the survivors and retake the same hill that had been re-infiltrated by the VC as soon as the Marines had evac'd out. Eddie couldn't see the point.

I had based it on a real incident I had come across in my research. The book was set in the early Eighties, just six or seven years after the Vietnam War, and little by little the war was beginning to seep into the thriller. At first, there were just artifacts, passing references to things that belonged to the war, like "Tu Do Street" and "Ruby Queen cigarettes" and "33 Beer," that I had put in for authenticity, but you could feel the war coming.

I wasn't sure how my editors were going to like it – I suspected it wasn't what they thought they'd bought – but my feelings about the war were starting to bubble up. I wasn't sure I could stop it if I wanted to – and I wasn't sure I wanted to. That *commissaire* in Antibes had gotten to me. I knew how to write a spy thriller, all right, but the thought that maybe it could be more was luring me into something else.

I had begun to live in two different worlds: one was the book world of intrigue and treachery in Southeast Asia; the other, my normal world with Anne and Justin and friends and the villa. In a strange way, the two worlds complemented each other and made each other more interesting. As I came up the stairs, I could hear Justin pedaling the kiddie car we had bought him for Christmas around the hall. All of a sudden, he called out, "I found one! I found one, Mom!"

"What did you find, sweetie?" Anne asked.

"A parking space!" Justin called back.

Anne was still laughing at how Justin had picked up on her frustrations at finding a parking space in Antibes and Nice as I came into the kitchen. Afterwards, over dinner, she raised the issue what we were going to do for New Years Eve. We had spent a quiet Christmas, just the three of us, and on the night after Christmas had taken a lonely walk along Gatsby's beach, Justin in his stroller, the lights of Nice in the distance. Winter had begun to isolate us and Anne was feeling the need for people. Max and Sally had invited us to a New Year's party in Monte Carlo. According to Sally, "everyone" was going to be there.

"So we'll go. What's the problem?" I said.

"We don't have a babysitter."

"What about those English *au pairs*?" The Côte d'Azur was filled with young women from Scandinavia, Germany and Britain who came for the sun and hopes of a millionaire boyfriend and who supported themselves working as *au pairs* for the children of the international set. Through Martine, we had found two English girls who sometimes babysat for Justin.

"They have dates. Everyone's busy. It's New Year's Eve." Unlike Christmas, the French made a big deal about New Year's Eve. If you believed Max, there was even a clause in the Code Napoleon that said adultery on New Year's Eve could not be considered cause for divorce. Although Sally said the only place you could find that clause was in the Code Max.

"How desperate are we?"

"Very," she said.

"Bad enough to try Mrs. Trophy Wife?" Janie.

"I already tried," she said glumly. "They have a babysitter, but didn't think it would be a good idea. Sloane doesn't want to play with Justin. He's a boy."

"What about Colette?"

"She's *French*. They've all got parties, champagne, fireworks! She's got some major thing in Nice."

"Maybe some girl from the *lycée*? We could place an ad..." Many of the local shops had all sorts of little *avis* posted on bulletin boards or taped in the store window. *Chien perdu* or *Maître d'anglais et italien; cours particuliers*; that kind of thing. "Or we could run an ad in the local paper. Shouldn't cost much."

"Great! You want me to leave my baby with a potential ax murderer? I'll really be able to enjoy myself!"

"So what can we do?"

"Nothing. That's what I came to the Riviera for. To sit at home and do nothing!" she said stomping off into the kitchen, where I could hear pots being slammed around.

The situation was serious – even a husband could figure that out. The next day, I told her I had to get some hardware for the villa and took the car into Cannes, to the caviar store on the street with the plaque that showed where Napoleon had landed when he had come back from Elba. The caviar store sold dozens of varieties of Russian and Iranian caviar and the pretty *vendeuse*, who worked there and looked like a cross between Leslie Caron and Brigette Bardot and I spent an hour discussing the different types and brands. It was, she agreed gravely, a serious purchase and a matter *très grave*. We were down to a decision between the Sevruga and the Beluga, both extravagantly expensive. I explained that my wife and I had had a disagreement; we were *ne pas être d'accord*.

"In that case, *Monsieur*, one must choose the Beluga."

"Are you sure?" I gulped. The 45 ml. (less than 2 oz.) tin of Beluga cost nearly half a month's rent!

"Your wife is upset, no? *Alors, cela parle en votre faveur* (it will make amends)," she said.

"This has to work, *Mademoiselle*."

"Rely on me, *Monsieur*. I am also a woman," she said, wrapping the can in a gold tissue paper with a hand-tied silk ribbon. After that, came the *cave* near the Croissette for a bottle of Dom Perignon and the *fleuriste*, from which I emerged with a bouquet of flowers. I was spending a fortune, but the marital hurricane flags were flying.

New Year's Eve began badly. The weather was cold and stormy and we hadn't been able to find a babysitter. We listened to the rain rattling on the windows as we sat in the salon, watching TV. Anne smiled when I brought out the flowers and the caviar and the Dom Perignon, but I could tell her heart wasn't in it.

On the TV, a bunch of French men and women were sitting in tuxedos and gowns discussing a very intellectual and obscure movie about French collaborators in Algeria. While the men pontificated in rapid-fire French, the women stared with glazed eyes at the camera.

This TV disaster was followed by a Quiz show, which consisted of watching people write their answers to obscure questions on French history. Five to ten minutes of screen time was actually spent watching them scribble answers to each question. All this for the Grand Prize, announced with enormous fanfare, of an all-expenses paid trip to Tibet! For one! "*Cocorico Boy,*" Anne said, "was starting to look very good."

By this time Justin, who had wanted to stay up for midnight, had fallen asleep on the couch and we were about to call it a night and give up when something wonderful happened. The Quiz show ended and an old Fred Astaire Ginger Rogers movie came on the TV, in English no less!

Suddenly, there were Fred and Ginger dancing "Cheek to Cheek" in an incredible white Art Deco nightclub, with words and music by Irving Berlin, and suddenly Anne and I were dancing, wonderfully, better than we had ever danced before, all around the salon, me realizing for the first time why it was so big, because it was meant for dancing! Which was what we should have been doing all along. Both of us laughing and nibbling caviar and sipping Dom Perignon and dancing cheek to cheek ourselves, falling in love all over again and swearing it was our best New Year's Eve ever.

"We're so lucky," she whispered.

"I know," I said, wishing I had a lucky coin or something to rub, because it doesn't do to tempt the gods, but I didn't have anything. Before the week was out, I'd regret not having that coin.

THE NEW YEAR began with sunshine and good news. Our *cartes de séjour* had finally been approved. We were legal. All I had to do was to pick them up at the *préfecture* in Nice and then show it to the *commissaire* at the police *gendarmerie* in Antibes. The *commissaire* received me in his office.

"*Alors,*" he said. "What is this book you are writing?"

"It's a *roman d'espionnage,*" I said.

"*Vraiment,*" he said, stroking his mustache. "I think perhaps you are CIA, *non?*"

"*Non, Monsieur.* I do a lot of research," not wanting to get into my having been accepted into the CIA's CTP (Career Training Program) with a suspicious French cop.

"Myself I prefer the *roman policier*. Although I don't like it when they are not authentic about police work. There is much the public does not understand."

"What about Simenon?" I asked.

"You like Simenon?"

"Very much."

"*Moi,* not so much. It is not true to life. With Simenon, there is a crime or worse, a crime that has not yet happened but will, and always there are too many suspects. Everyone has a motive and no alibi. *Alors, l'inspecteur* Maigret goes to a zinc bar, of the type one no longer finds in Paris, smokes his *pipe* and *voilà!*, he returns to interrogate the least likely suspect, perhaps the *petite amie* (girlfriend) who was supposedly not in the old crumbling estate at the time but who secretly snuck back in, who confesses all. *C'est trop facile, non!*"

"In what way?"

"True police work is different, *Monsieur*. Most *criminels* are stupid. There is often only one suspect or there are none. In other cases, the suspect is *tout evident, non?* The career *criminel* whose work bears a *signature* or perhaps the money is missing from the accounts and a clerk who owes money has disappeared. The hard police work is not learning who the guilty person is, but capturing him. Still, I credit Simenon with understanding that police work is *un métier psychologique,*" tapping his finger on his forehead. "That is very true. So who are the good American writers of the *roman policier?*"

"Dashiell Hammett, Raymond Chandler, Ross Macdonald, a friend of mine, Rod Thorp, who did *'Die Hard"* and *The Detective.* These are some of the best; there are others."

"This 'ammett. What did he do?"

"*The Glass Key, The Thin Man, The Maltese Falcon.*"

"*Ah oui, Le Faucon...* 'umphrey Bogart. *J'aime beaucoup.* So, which of these are the best?"

"It's not a fair question. They are very different."

"In what way? Setting? Style? Who is their main character?"

"No, the setting is always the same. California. Now that I think of it, the main character is also the same, always a hard-boiled private eye, *un détective privé et dur.*"

"*Enfin,* there is no difference. They are the same. How does one tell which is the best?"

"Hammett was the first. He created the genre of the *détective privé.*"

"So he was the best... *l'original, non?*"

"Hammett was a great storyteller with good, tough dialogue. But Chandler gave you that with a sense of place. Of California as this sunny world of beautiful blondes and endless possibilities that only masked the human corruption underneath."

"So who is the best, your friend? *Monsieur* Chandler?"

"No, for me Macdonald is the best."

"Why?"

"Because his stories give you everything Chandler does, plus something more. Crimes don't just happen because of greed, but because of families and history, your *métier psychologique, Monsieur le Comissaire.* With Macdonald every crime is an excursion into the past."

"You mean into *la condition humaine,* do you not, *Monsieur?*"

"*Oui, Monsieur le Comissaire.* Though I still very much like your Georges Simenon. But if he is not your favorite, who is?"

"In truth, one hates to admit this, but in matters of the *roman policier*, the English are the best. P.D. James, Eric Ambler, *Madame* Christie, who had the good sense to make her *policier* speak French, although it was a mistake to make Poirot *belge* (Belgian)."

"Why a mistake?"

"*Alors*, everyone knows *les belges* are too dull to make a good *policier*. Do you know, one of best of the *écrivains anglais* lives quite near?"

"Really? Who?"

He called out to the other police officer. "Philippe, who is the *écrivain anglais*? The one with a name in English like a color?"

"The *anglais* who lives near Juan les Pins?" Philippe called back.

"That's the one."

"In English, green, I think?"

"Graham Greene?" I asked.

"*Eh voilà!* le Graham Greene," *le Comissaire* said.

"My God, I've always wanted to meet him," I said.

"Truly? Why?"

"Because he did it all. Not just groundbreaking *romans à sensation*, like *This Gun For Hire*, but also serious important books like *The Quiet American, The Comedians* and *The Power and the Glory*. Do you think it's possible? Is he *agréable*?" Unlike English, the term in French meant not merely agreeable, but approachable as well.

"The English sees no one, *Monsieur*. He is said to be ill," he said and I understood I was too late. Graham Greene was ill, perhaps dying and I would never meet him. "I am desolated, Monsieur," and perhaps feeling sorry for me, handed me the orange residents' cards that had taken us so much effort. "Here are your *cartes de séjour*." We were legal at last. "Perhaps you won't come back now for our discussions," he said, a bit wistfully, then brightened. "Do you play chess?"

"Badly."

"*Tant mieux.* We can continue our discussions over the board," he said. As I started to head out the door, he added, "You are friends with the other American, *Monsieur* _____?" mentioning Greg's last name.

"I know him," I said carefully, using verb *connaître*, which denotes acquaintance, but not necessarily friendship.

"What does he do? His *métier*?"

"From what I can tell, very little."

"He bears watching, that one."

"Why?"

"This," he said, tapping the side of his nose.

"I suspect you are a pretty good *policier, Monsieur le Commissaire*," I said.

"And you, *Monsieur*, I believe you may be almost worth reading – for an American," he said.

Chapter 8

Mlle. Onassis Throws a Party

The weather stayed cold and wet, but in the book, it was a steamy night on the Bangkok waterfront. My protagonist, Sawyer, was trapped in a warehouse where three Cambodians with AK-47s were about to execute him. I had gotten him into this fix without any idea of how he was going to get out. And all the while in the back of my mind, the clock on bringing my female lead character onstage was ticking. It was the sixth chapter already and so far she had barely been mentioned. Of course, none of it would matter if I couldn't get Sawyer out of the warehouse. And it had to be real. I couldn't have Sawyer pull off some James Bond super-karate move without breaking the agreement every writer makes with his reader.

"Let me tell you a story," the writer says, with the understanding that the world he creates is coherent. You can have a Middle Earth fantasy with flying wizards and walking trees, but you can't have them communicating via laptop computers without breaking the book's verisimilitude (unless the computers are made of fairy dust or something). There are thriller writers, like Robert Ludlum, Ken Follett, and Ian Fleming, whose books seem pseudo-realistic, but when you cut into them they bear little resemblance to the real-life world of spies; others, like Frederick Forsythe and Tom Clancy, who do a ton of research and whose works read like a cross between a documentary and a technical manual; and those, like Le Carré, whose books seem realistic, but are actually serious novels, character studies masquerading as thrillers. That's where I was aiming the Southeast Asia book: somewhere between Forsythe and Le Carré, but with the pacing of Ludlum and Follett. The realism was part of my contract with the reader; there could be no super-karate escapes.

For two days I was stuck, while the book sat there, waiting for me. I began to dread going down to that cold room next to the garage to spend hours staring at the white wall. The Cambodians had tied Sawyer's hands and were about to shoot him and no matter what I tried, there was no way out. And what about the girl? She had to be brought onstage soon or it would be turning into something by Beckett. I went for a walk in the rain to think it out. I walked by the Heineken estate, raindrops strung like pearls along the barbed wire. From somewhere on the grounds I heard a German Shepherd bark and wondered where the hell I was going with this. I had dragged my family halfway across the world to do this and I was stuck.

I looked out across the bay toward Nice, a distant blur with lights coming on early in the gloom and wondered what if I couldn't come up with anything? What if the book just ended? I went into the restaurant overlooking the Plage de la Garoupe and ordered a glass of Bordeaux. The restaurant was empty, except for a woman behind the bar cleaning glasses. I watched the rain streak the windows and tried to think it through. What was the story about anyway? The original concept had been the love story between the American CIA agent and the Eurasian woman. America and Asia and their tragic seduction that led to the temple ruins in the jungle.

"*Monsieur* is wet," the waiter said, bringing me the wine and a *marc* of cognac I hadn't ordered. "Filthy weather."

"I thought it was supposed to be better on the Côte d'Azur," I said.

"It's true. *Normalement,* one can stroll on the beach now," he said.

"It is the worst winter in fifty years, *Monsieur,*" the woman behind the bar said. "There is no business. We should have closed for the *fermeture annuelle.*"

"I guess it's just our bad luck to have come this year."

"It is not luck," the waiter said, sitting at the next table and pouring himself a *marc* as well. "It is *les américains,* if *Monsieur* will forgive my saying."

"The Americans! What have we got to do with it?"

"Your spy satellites," he said. "The ones in space. All over us. What are they looking for in France? A secret *crème brulée!*? And the TV satellites too."

"How does that affect the weather?"

"The same principle as *la* microwave (pronouncing it the French way, '*meecro*'). All these satellite transmissions in the atmosphere have the effect of a microwave *gigantesque.* And what does *la* microwave do, *eh?*"

"Wouldn't that make things hotter?" I asked.

"It does! They melt the polar ice caps, thus making the ocean colder and bringing the cold and storms, *et voilà!*"

"Pay no attention, *Monsieur.* He's an idiot, this one," the woman behind the counter said.

"The *Monsieur* is an American. He knows I speak the truth," the waiter winked at me and refilled the cognac in my glass.

"The *Monsieur* thinks you are crazy. He understands nothing, *Monsieur,*" she said, referring to the waiter. "You know nothing of climate or satellites or anything else, not even restaurants, *imbécile!*" she snapped at him.

"Not of restaurants run by a woman. That's bad luck, like a ship, no?" he said, winking again.

"And even less about women! *Mon Dieu,* you are *le Einstein* about the satellites compared to what you know about women!"

And just like that the answer popped into my head. I was being too male-centric. Sawyer didn't have to save himself. The woman, Suong, wasn't some passive female sidekick, but a character on her own. She was Asia, beautiful, mysterious, and not innocent. She could save him for her own reasons! Excited, I left the two of them ignoring each other, slamming dishes onto tables and hurried back to the villa. When I got there, Anne was looking worried.

"Martine called. She said we have to leave," she said.

"What do you mean 'leave'? Leave what?"

"The villa. She says we have to get out."

"What are you talking about? The rent's paid. How can she tell us to leave?"

"I don't know. That's what she said."

"What else did she say?"

"I don't know. She was babbling away a mile a minute in French. I couldn't understand a word," Anne said miserably.

"It's impossible," I said, dialing Martine's number.

"*Mon dieu*, what have you done, *Monsieur*? What have you done!?" Martine said as soon as she I got her on the line.

"What did I do?" I said.

"You got a *carte de séjour*!," she accused. "How could you have done such a thing?"

"I thought it was the law."

"What difference does that make!? You think they are going to arrest Americans who spend money in France!? What were you thinking?"

"I thought we should be here legally. What's the problem?"

"You told them *where you lived*," she hissed. "You gave them your address! How could you!?"

"It was on the application," I said.

"Don't you understand? The landlord did not declare the rent on his taxes. Nor did I. We will be investigated by *les fiscs*!" (the dreaded French tax agents), she shrieked. "The landlord demands you leave. You must leave the villa at once!"

"What do you mean, 'leave'? We can't leave!"

"Why not?"

"It's raining. And we have nowhere to go."

"You must go *Monsieur*. The French law is very strict. I beg you."

"*Madame*," I said. "Inform the landlord we are paid till the end of the month. Nothing will happen till then."

"He will return the money."

"I refuse to accept. Tell him we will stay till the end of the month whether he returns the money or not, during which time I will consult a lawyer as to our rights under French law. Are we agreed, *Madame*?"

"I don't know whether the landlord will accept."

"I do not think he has a choice, *Madame*. We are legal residents of France. If he tries anything till we've determined our rights and what to do, I will have my *avocat* notify the *cour de justice*, the *bureau des impôts*, and anyone else we can think of, and we'll give them your name first. Are we in accord, *Madame*?"

"I will tell him, *Monsieur*. But this is not the finish," she said in a threatening voice and hung up.

"My god, what are we going to do?" Anne said.

"I don't know. I may have bought us a couple of weeks, but I think we're going to need a lawyer," I said, thinking there was another expense we sure as hell didn't need.

"Where would we find a lawyer? They don't even have a Yellow Pages in this crazy country!"

While I grabbed the local phone book and looked for an *avocat*, Anne called Sally.

"It's all set," she told me. "I told them all about it. She and Max said according to French law we can't be thrown out. They're meeting us for drinks tomorrow at the Hôtel du Cap."

"Why not lunch?" I said.

"I asked. Sally said no one can afford lunch at the Hôtel du Cap."

The next day, the weather was beautiful. It was as if the universe was taunting us, telling us 'Now that you have to go, I'll show you what you can't have.' We picked up Justin at the *crèche* and drove to the manicured grounds of the Hôtel du Cap not far from Greg and Janie's villa. In the lavish marble lobby, we passed the famous Eden Roc restaurant and headed for the bar overlooking the pool and the Mediterranean. Anne had a Compari and I had a *pastis* while we waited.

Justin wanted to play in a little sandbox near the swimming pool. We told him he couldn't, but at that moment, the *maître d'* happened by and said, "I have a little boy the same age, *Monsieur, Madame*. There are few guests now. He can go. I'll watch him and you can see he's safe from here." That was the thing about the French, I thought. Sometimes they can infuriate you so much you wished the whole country would sink into the sea, but perhaps because we were with a child, they were often wonderful to us.

At that moment, with the sun shining, soft jazz coming from the bar radio, Justin, watched over by the *maître d'*, playing with a bucket and a shovel in the sand and off the rocky coast, sailboats, their sails white against the blue of the Mediterranean, it seemed impossible to imagine a better place on Earth. Except we were being kicked out. This is our Paradise Lost, I thought as Max and Sally came in and we did the ritual cheek *bises*.

"Well, they can't throw you out. Not till May. It's against the law," Max said over a martini.

"What does May have to do with it?"

"French law says that you can't throw tenants out in winter if there is a mother and child, even if they don't pay their rent."

"But we have paid our rent," I said.

"Doesn't matter. You've got him over a barrel."

"It's not our fault he cheated on his taxes," I said.

"Everyone cheats on their taxes in France. It's a form of political expression. It's been calculated that half the gold in the world is hidden in French mattresses," Max said.

"We called Bernard. He says you don't have to go. He gave us the name of an attorney in Nice," Sally said, handing us a slip of paper.

"Who's Bernard?" Anne asked.

"He's a friend, a businessman in Paris. Bernard knows everything," Sally said.

"Everything?" I said. "The cause of war... the formula for diet Coke... Einstein's theory... the purpose of the universe?"

"Everything, except maybe women," Max said, motioning to the bartender for another drink.

"Is he married?"

"Not lately."

"How come he couldn't figure women out?"

"He says that to a man, the mind of a woman is like lead to Superman's X-ray vision."

"He has a scientific turn of phrase."

"Finance, numbers, are his business."

"Speaking of which, how much will a French attorney cost?"

"Five, six thousand."

"Francs or dollars?"

"Dollars, of course."

"That's a lot of money," I said.

"You can't let him get away with it. The idea! Throwing out a mother and child in the middle of winter!" Sally said.

"How much time would it be tied up in court?"

"A couple of years," Max said.

"A couple of years! And this means going to court all the time? In French!?" Anne said.

"Yeah, but you're in the right," Max said. "Unless they rule against you just because you're Americanos."

"Would they do that?" Anne asked.

"Bernard thinks the odds are slightly against it," Sally said.

"But it's a possibility?"

"With the French, there's no telling," Max said.

I watched Justin down by the pool. He was standing barefoot on the stone step, splashing water and babbling something in French to the *maître d'*, who had rolled up his pant legs and stood next to him in the water.

"I'm not sure I want to keep the villa," I surprised myself by saying.

"Why not?" Max said.

"The place is huge. Too big really. And the cost of heating is killing us. It's more than the rent. And no matter how much oil I burn, it's still freezing. Justin's starting to cough all the time."

"It's really far from you guys. We never see you anymore. We never see anyone," Anne said.

"We know. We've missed you too," Sally said.

"It's lonely," Anne said. "Andy's got his work, but I'm alone in that big house and grounds."

"Well, we can fix that," Max said. "That's one of the reasons we came to see you. Aristotle Onassis' daughter Christina is throwing a party."

"Where?"

"On her yacht."

"And we're invited!?" Anne stammered.

"Not exactly," Sally said. "It's Bobby G. and Gaby."

"What do you mean?"

"Bobby G. and Gaby's apartment overlooks the harbor in Monte Carlo. Onassis' yacht is berthed directly below their balcony. Whenever Christina Onassis throws a party, so do Bobby G. and Gaby. Everyone knows everyone. It's a lot of fun," Sally said.

"I don't know," I started to say. It all sounded a bit *chi chi* for us.

"You have to come," Max said. "Everyone will be there. We're sure to find someone who can help you with this mess."

"I've been dying to go out," Anne said, looking at me. "We'll be there."

A FEW NIGHTS LATER, Justin safely ensconced in the villa, watched over by a skinny English girl with spiked purple hair who had babysat for us several times before, Anne and I arrived at

Bobby G. and Gaby's apartment in Monte Carlo. Even before we entered their building, we could hear French rock music blasting out across the *quai*. As promised, the apartment balcony directly overlooked Onassis' enormous yacht, festooned with lights for the party.

Onassis' yacht was bigger than the King of Arabia's and as we entered, a helicopter was landing with a roar on a pad on the stern deck. Guests in evening clothes were chauffeured to the yacht's gangway. People waved from Bobby G. and Gaby's balcony and Onassis' guests waved back. Quite a few seemed to know each other and there was *repartée* shouted between them as to which party they should be coming to. Little did we know that soon we would be the people going to one of Mlle. Onassis' yacht parties.

"Hey pard,'" Bobby G. shouted over the music, handing me a very large vodka martini. "Come meet everybody."

Just then, the doorbell rang and a woman screamed "Billy!" A young man, so drunk his eyeballs were swimming, stood swaying in the doorway.

"Who's that?" I asked.

"Billy Bacardi. Bacardi rum," Bobby G. said. "Hey Billy, I'd like you to meet..."

"I have to throw up," Billy said, staggering past me toward the bathroom. I looked around. Anne and Gaby were deep in conversation. Max was on the balcony, yelling to someone he knew on the yacht to tell Christina Onassis to skip her party and come join us. Sally was talking to a stunning blonde woman in a Dior evening gown, both of them staring right at me.

"Who's that with Sally?" I asked.

"That's Maia. She used to be married to some big Swedish industrialist. He died and left her bazillions," Bobby G. said. Someone grabbed him and the two of them headed to the bar. I took a good-sized sip of the martini and felt it immediately go to my head.

"Why'd you break up with Jean-Pierre?" I heard Chuck ask Eva, the pretty Finnish girl who worked in his office. "Oh, he was so *sérieux*," she said. When I looked up, the beautiful blonde Sally had been talking to was in standing in front of me.

"We have to talk," she said, in a Scandinavian-accented English.

"Me!?" I said.

"You're the writer, yes?"

"Are you sure you want me?" I said, always smooth where attractive women are concerned.

"Please. Can't we go somewhere private? It's a matter of life and death," she said, taking my arm with urgency.

We stepped out onto the balcony, where there was one other couple, waving at someone getting out of a taxi and walking up the gangplank to Onassis' yacht. The view was spectacular. I could see across the harbor filled with yachts to the floodlit Casino and the lights of the buildings on the hills of Monte Carlo. From Onassis' yacht came the sounds of an old French song, "*Quand il est mort le poet*" ("When the poet dies"), which suddenly sounded like a prophecy.

"I need to see you. You must come to my villa," Maia said.

"I don't understand."

"You must come. I'm desperate." I shook my head to try and clear the martini fog. This was getting way out of hand.

"What about my wife?" I said.

"Bring her too."

"That's very liberal of you."

"Only you can help me," she said.

"I doubt that. Surely there's someone . . ."

"I'm in love with Adam."

"Well, I'm sure it'll all work out," I said, patting her hand and starting to leave just as Anne stepped out on the balcony.

"Come, there's someone you have to meet," Anne said.

"This is Maia," I said, introducing them. "She's in love with Adam."

"Adam who?"

"Adam Shaw, the writer's son," Maia said.

"Wait. Irwin Shaw's son?" I asked. "*The* Irwin Shaw?"

"He wants to be a writer too," she said miserably.

"Well, I hope you'll be very happy," I said, trying to edge out of this gracefully and steer Anne back into the apartment, but she shrugged me off.

"What's the problem?" Anne said.

"Writers are difficult," Maia said with a sigh.

"Tell me about it," Anne said.

"Maybe you can help me," Maia said. "I thought if I could get insight into what it's like living with a writer it could help me."

"Absolutely. All us writers are exactly alike," I said, escaping. I stepped back into the apartment, the music louder than ever, leaving Anne and Maia talking conspiratorially like college roommates. As Bobby G. danced by with Gaby, he thrust a fresh vodka into my hand. From across the room, a florid Englishman with white wavy hair called out to me.

"Aha! A fellow scrivener! A companion toiler in the jungle of words!" He pushed his way through the crowd and embraced me. "I'm Nigel, old chap," he said, thumping me on the back. "Surviving our little *soirée*, are we?"

"Barely," I said.

"It's all right, old chap. You and I, we know the secret."

"I do? What is it?"

"Get drunk," he said, draining his glass. "How's Maia? Saw her make a beeline for you."

"She's in love with Adam," I said.

"Everyone knows that," he said. "She's besotted with him. Funny thing, he loves her too. Can't imagine why? Just because she's rich, beautiful, and all things considered, rather nice."

"So where is he?" I said, looking around. I was certainly interested in meeting Irwin Shaw's son. As far as I was concerned, Irwin Shaw had written some of the best short stories in the English language.

"St. Moritz, I think. He's hosting one of these ridiculous ski tournaments. Horrid things. Break your bloody neck. Irwin liked to ski, you know. Had to give it up, though."

"Why's that?"

"Interfered with drinking. Ah, here she is," he said, as Anne approached with an attractive angular woman in a black and white designer dress.

"Who?"

"The ball and chain," Nigel whispered in my ear.

"This is Monika, Nigel's wife," Anne said. "I just found out her mother owns the Cable Car, the souvenir store on Pier 39 in San Francisco. She knows my friend Terry. She's a countess."

"Terry's a countess?"

"No, silly. Monika."

"Hi. What are you countess of?" I said, shaking Monika's hand.

"Austrian, old chap. Related to royalty. The Froggies all kiss her ring as if she were the bloody Pope!" Nigel said as Monika waggled a large jewel-encrusted signet ring at us.

"Don't mind Nigel," Monika said. "He just keeps me around to protect him."

"From what?" I asked.

"His ex-wife and children."

"Horrible creatures. What I ever saw in that harridan and the litter she spawned," Nigel shuddered.

"You don't like your children?" Anne said.

"Worthless lot. Sent 'em to Eton and all they do is take drugs and live off the dole. Never did a day's work in their lives. Never see 'em unless they want money. Told 'em if they needed money they'd have to talk to Monika."

"I give them just enough to keep them away," Monika said.

"Where'd the money come from?" I asked.

"Oxford, dear boy. I wrote the books to teach English to foreigners. Told you we had something in common. Chums at Oxford published 'em. They sell millions of the bloody things to India,

Pakistan, and all the rest of what used to be the Empire. Money rolls in. So who have you met literarily, so far?"

"I wanted to meet Graham Greene. Seems he's sick."

"Dying, poor bugger," Nigel nodded. "Have you met Burgess?"

"Anthony Burgess? *Clockwork Orange* Burgess? Is he here?"

"When Liana lets him out. Catch him sometimes at the Café de Paris. He lives quite near, on rue Grimaldi."

"She claims it's for his own good. Keeping people from interfering with his work," Monika said.

"What about Irwin Shaw? Did you know him?"

"Lovely chap. Wonderful wit. Of course, Max knew him best. Quite a pair, those two," Nigel said, swiping a drink from a passing tray.

"Really?" I said, looking around for Max, who was talking to Eva. Sally was talking to Chuck and Emma.

"He's really close with the Prince, you know," Monika said.

"Prince Rainier – and Max?"

"Mmm. Remember when Princess Grace died?" Nigel said.

"For God's sake!" Monika whispered, looking around. "Not here."

"Right-oh. Mum's the word. Loose lips sink the Titanic," Nigel said.

"I thought it was an iceberg," I said.

"Indeed, and you never know when you might run into one," Nigel said.

Chapter 9

The Princess Intervenes

On Sunday mornings in Antibes, the bicycle riders would gather at the café across from the bus station in the Place General de Gaulle. Amid the smells of *café au lait* and *pain au chocolat*, Gitanes cigarettes dangling from their lips, they would plot their ride on detailed topographical maps.

"*Vous permettez?*" one of them, a young man with a lion's mane of dark hair, asked me. I gestured and he sat at my table. His name was Henri, a meter reader for the gas company. Suddenly, two of the men started arguing. "*Impossible! C'est pas possible!*" one kept saying. The other man shook his finger in the first man's face. "You will see. It will be the end of France."

"What are they arguing about?" I asked.

"The *Tour*," Henri shrugged. "Girard believes Hinault will triumph again. No one has ever won the *Tour* six times, but Girard believes Hinault cannot be defeated. Jean-Louis, on the other hand, says the American, Greg LeMond, will make the Americans dominant."

"I thought the *Tour de France* wasn't till the summer."

"It has nothing to do with the *Tour*. It is a psychological ploy by Jean-Louis. He wishes to make Girard angry so he will break from the *peloton* too soon. This is why I like to ride (*faire du velo*), Monsieur. One can learn all there is to know about life and be a *sportif* too."

"How so?"

"*Ecoutez*," Henri said, leaning closer. "The *velo* is life. Everyone reveals himself. Some are not *serieux*, but only make themselves *sportifs* for show. That one," indicating a middle-aged man with a goatee. "He will start fast and make a break with the early group. For one kilometer, he will lead everyone, but it is all for show. Many times he will not even finish, but will be back here for an *aperitif* before the race ends.

"Then there are the technocrats; Claude, *par exemple*," indicating a curly-haired man with a mustache writing something on a little pad. "They will argue for hours over which type of tubular tire to use, or the advantages of the carbon Kevlar wheel, or what the gearing should be for different road conditions: 55 on the front and 11 on the back, or 53 on the front to 12 on the back. *Oh là là!* And in the end, riders who don't even know what type of tires they are using beat them."

"I thought French *cyclistes* were serious about their sport."

"There are the *cyclistes sérieux*, of course. You see Alain?" indicating a muscular blond man getting up to check the calipers on his bike. "He will stay with the *peloton* for the first eight or nine kilometers, then go with the first breakaway group, always drafting the lead *cycliste*, always calculating. In the end, he will finish at least five or six minutes ahead of everyone. If he does not win, he will not allow himself even to drink a *biere* at the end. For him, it is not about *le sport*, it is about winning."

"But not everyone is *sérieux*?"

"For most types, myself *par exemple*, it is something a little *sportif* to do on a Sunday morning," he shrugged. "We are the ordinary ones who stay in the middle of the *peloton*, in the middle of life, just going along with our jobs, trying to make life easy on ourselves by catching the air draft from the group."

I was impressed. "Henri, you are a philosopher," I said.

"*Regard* Auguste," Henri said, nodding towards a tall thin man. "He pretends, but he is not even a *cycliste*. Three kilometers out of town he will drop out and go to see his mistress at her apartment in Juan les Pins. But when the group returns, he will rejoin the *peloton* just a block from here and his wife never the wiser."

"How do you know all this?"

"I told you. It's my *métier*. A gas meter-reader knows everything about everyone."

"How so?"

"When one reads the *compteur*, one cannot help noticing things. Someone has guests staying over, you see the cars parked and the usage of the *gaz* goes up. You see a makeup compact in the car, or perhaps the scent of perfume and you know that a man who was living with just his mother, now has a woman living with him. Then the usage of the *gaz* goes down and you know that he and the woman are eating out and there is trouble with the mother."

"You should be a detective."

"What for?" he said, getting up. "The *entreprise* takes care of me. When I finish each day, I go home. I ride in the middle of the *peloton*, Monsieur. Life is difficult enough. You don't have to go looking for trouble; it comes to you."

I watched him put on his plastic helmet, get on his bike and ride off with the others towards the *Corniche* to Nice. He was right about trouble. Martine was calling nearly every day wanting to know when we were leaving. I couldn't stall much longer. Either I had to get a lawyer and start spending money to fight the eviction or I had to find us another villa and fast.

The truth was that I had miscalculated. Because of the sky-rocketing cost of fuel oil, we couldn't afford the villa. And now that the winter had settled in, no matter how high I turned the furnace, our rooms were cold and gloomy. Justin was coughing all the time now.

The best thing was to move, if we could find something. Sally had called and told us she had seen an *avis* in a realtor's office window about a villa in Eze. I was to check it out while Anne took Justin to the children's *cour de récréation* (playground) in Juan les Pins.

As I drove to Eze along the *Lower Corniche*, I thought about the book. I had ended my most recent chapter on a cliffhanger, my protagonist, Sawyer, trapped in the warehouse, the Cambodians about to shoot. I had originally planned to end the first part of the book with the cliffhanger, but I needed a way to explain how Sawyer had gotten out of the mess he was in and then get him and the Eurasian woman, Suong, to the heart of the book in the Golden Triangle, a lawless mountainous land where the borders of Thailand, Laos, and Burma came together, where remote hill tribes subject to no government grew opium poppies and every man sat with his gun next to him. Following the map along the coast, I drove through Eze to the real estate office in Cap d'Ail.

Eze is really two separate towns with the same name. There is Eze-sur-Mer, a seaside village about ten miles east of Nice with a pebbly beach, a few shops, a *bistro* and a *petit hôtel* on the *Basse Corniche* and villas on streets winding up the hill, and then there is the medieval town of Eze, high in the mountains overlooking the sea. The medieval town is accessible only via the *Moyenne* or Middle *Corniche*, the steepness of the mountains making any direct road link between the two villages impossible.

A medieval town with a small artists colony, the upper Eze, called "Eze Village," is a popular tourist stop, though less overrun than St. Paul de Vence, to which it bears some similarity. The medieval Eze is perhaps best known for the Chèvre d'Or, a small inn with a famous restaurant with a spectacular cliff-side view of the coast all the way from Nice to Cap-Ferrat.

The real estate office in Cap d'Ail was closed, but thanks to Sally, the agent had taped a note, *Attention Monsieur Kaplan*, with the name and address of the villa, the "Villa Olivia," to the window. I drove to Eze-sur-Mer and away from the beach, up a winding Avenue

Lamaro – the town was small enough that it was easy to find – to number 19. The villa was smaller than the one in Cap d'Antibes, with a worn red-tiled roof and ivy climbing up the walls to the shuttered second floor windows. The villa was surrounded by a low stone wall surmounted by a hedge. Feeling like a thief, I unlatched the wooden gate and walked around the house, unable to peek inside the wooden window shutters. The front yard was bare ground, not the park we had *chez Polanski*, but with enough room for Justin to run around.

At the side of the house facing an overgrown vegetable garden was a small raised stone porch or *terrasse* and a large pile of wood for the fireplace. In back, a wire fence separated the property from a dense forest. This was what we had been looking for from the beginning, I thought. Smaller, more intimate, more us. I was almost ready to take it without even seeing the interior.

Excited, I drove back to Cap d'Ail and slipped a note through the slot asking the *propriété immobilière* to call me, *très urgent*. I couldn't wait to tell Anne, but when I got home, she was upset.

"Justin's sick. His temperature's 104. His breathing's shallow too," she said.

"God, should I call Martine about a doctor?"

"I already called Sally and got the name of one."

Because my French was better, I called the doctor and got her answering service. I gave them our phone number and address, telling them it was *très urgent*, the second time that day I had had to use that term. In an hour, the answering service called back. They told us the doctor could come that evening and wanted to know how we were going to pay.

We had prepaid a year of health insurance before we had left California and were assured by Blue Cross that we'd be fully covered in France. But the answering service told us only French national insurance was acceptable. I looked at Anne. Her face was desperate. I told them again that it was *urgent* and that I would pay cash.

That night it poured, wind and rain hammering on the roof tiles.

Justin was in bed, coughing and limp, his forehead hot and sweating. Anne put cold compresses on his forehead, tried to get him to drink some juice and read to him from his favorite book, Maurice Sendak's *Where The Wild Things Are*.

I put a flashlight and umbrella by the door, ready to go out and open the gate for the doctor. There are few things in life that make you feel more helpless than being the parent of a sick child. You wish you could make a deal with God and take the sickness on yourself instead. Worse, I was feeling guiltier than ever. Justin had been dragged here with us. Coming here wasn't his idea, it was mine. I had seen him coughing, but thought it was just a cold, too absorbed in my own stupid world and writing the book to pay attention. I kept peering out the window. The night was black and my thoughts even blacker. Then I heard a car honking.

I ran out in the rain and opened the gate. Using the flashlight, I led the doctor's car down the driveway to the villa. An elegant woman in a raincoat got out. I led her inside and to Justin's room. She examined him and after a few minutes, motioned the three of us out of his room. She explained it to me and I translated for Anne.

"He has a throat infection and fever, Monsieur. An antibiotic should take care of it. Also, he has the *bronchite asthmatique*. The dampness," she looked around the hallway, "is not good for him. Here," she said, writing a prescription and handing it to me. "There is a twenty-four hour *pharmacie, la Pharmacie Dhèry*, in Juan les Pins." I paid her cash and walked her with the umbrella and flashlight to her car.

"What can I do about the dampness?" I asked.

"Get him out of this villa, Monsieur," she said and drove off. I went back inside.

"He has asthma?" I said.

"She knows what she's talking about," Anne said.

"What makes you so sure?"

"She was wearing an Hermès scarf."

"So?"

"Do you have any idea how expensive they are? It means she's successful – and the only way a woman doctor can be so successful in France is if she's good. Now get the prescription."

I drove through the rain to Juan les Pins. "Blah-blah-blah Hermès scarf," I told myself in an imaginary conversation. "Maybe the only way a woman doctor gets so successful in France is by charging foreigners a lot of money even when they have insurance," aware of how stupid I sounded. The night and the rain and the limited street lighting made it hard to see, forcing me to focus on the driving. The *pharmacie*'s green electric cross was reflected in puddles on the wet pavement. We had to get out of the Polanski villa and fast, I thought, as I waited for the prescription.

When I got back, Anne and I had to hold Justin down to make him take the red liquid medicine. He didn't like the taste and kept yelling and spitting it up. Finally, I had to force his mouth open and pour it down. It was after midnight before he stopped crying and fell asleep. Anne and I slumped in front of the fire in the salon, exhausted.

"Tell me I'm not a lousy parent," I said.

"You're a good father," she said. "He loves you."

"I don't feel like a good parent. Forcing him like that, God! I think I made a mistake coming here."

"Kids are more resilient than you think. Maybe this business with Martine is a blessing in disguise. It's like a sign telling us we should leave the villa."

"Oh, we're leaving all right," I said.

The next morning, Justin was feeling better. I left him playing with his toys in bed and called the *propriété immobilière* in Cap d'Ail about the villa in Eze.

"Is there furniture inside? I couldn't see," I said.

"Of course, Monsieur. Furniture, dishes, silverware, wood for the fireplace, linen for the beds; everything is ready."

"How much?"

"Until June, five thousand francs each month. Ça va?"

Once Upon A Villa

Was it all right? I nearly whooped for joy. It was three thousand per month less than we were paying for *chez Polanski*! "Would you like to see the inside, Monsieur? I can meet you."

"*Oui*. And bring the papers for me to sign, *s'il vous plait*. I'll have the money," I said.

THE NEW VILLA WAS PERFECT, I told Anne, who still hadn't seen it. Though much smaller than *chez Polanski*, it had a *salon* with built-in bookcases, a TV, a large brick fireplace, country Provencal furniture and French doors opening to the stone *terrasse* and garden I had seen earlier. Also a tiny kitchen, a bathroom, and three bedrooms. On the second floor, a small bedroom perfect for Justin overlooked the front courtyard. The bedroom for Anne and me was right next to his and had a large balcony from which we could see over the roofs of houses down the hill to the sea.

There was a bedroom on the ground floor with a table I could use as a writing desk. The table faced a window that looked out to a forest behind the villa. Sitting at the desk, I could make out a leafy path through the trees. In the 1880's, the real estate agent told me, the philosopher, Friedrich Nietzsche, would walk that same path daily during the time he was writing *Thus Spake Zarathustra*. Apparently, author Aldous Huxley had also lived nearby too. Apart from *Brave New World*, I later told Anne, the only thing I remembered about Huxley was that his death had gone unnoticed because he had died the same day President Kennedy was assassinated. Anne said she had been in Paris with her grandmother when Bobby Kennedy was shot and two weeks later had seen the mother, Rose Kennedy, getting out of a chauffeured car on the rue St. Honoré, where she had been shopping. "I couldn't understand how could she go shopping for clothes just two weeks after her son had been killed," Anne said.

"That's a tough family," I said.

I called Martine and told her we would be out of the villa after the coming weekend. That would give us a week to make arrangements and move.

"*Bon*" was all she said and after a moment, "*Bonne chance.*" (Good luck).

So now our problems with Martine and the villa were solved, except as Anne reminded me, for one thing.

"I can't find a *crèche* for Justin."

"What do you mean?" I said.

"I've been calling everywhere. There are no *crèches* anywhere near Eze. The closest ones are in Monaco and they all have long waiting lists. Millionaires can't get their kids in! One of them told me to call next year just to see if I can get on the waiting list."

"I don't suppose there's any chance we could manage without putting him..." The look on Anne's face stopped me cold. "I guess we have to find a *crèche*, don't we?"

"Unless you're planning on doing all the shopping and errands yourself. Forget about writing your book. Apart from shopping and cleaning, you can just spend your time getting stoned like those other great writers, Hal and Greg."

"Speaking of which, how are the Ugly Americans these days?"

"Janie says she met someone who's related to an Italian duke or something. Apparently that's the best she's been able to do so far on the social climbing front."

"Tragic."

"Oh, don't be so condescending. What are we going to do about the *crèche*?" she frowned.

"What about Max and Sally?"

"I called. They didn't have a clue. They suggested dinner, though."

"How does dinner get Justin into a *crèche*."

"I don't know, but Sally has a theory that dinner can solve anything. Besides, there's a restaurant in Nice, Max wants to show us."

That evening we met Max, Sally, Bobby G., Gaby, Chuck,

Emma, Nigel, Monika, Yasper, Betje, and Annette, a friend of Sally's at Michel, a *bistro* near the Place Garibaldi in Nice. Over candles, a good Bordeaux, *paté Campagne,* a *quiche,* and a *tapenade des olives* to start, Betje was telling us about their twenty-year-old daughter's first trip to America. According to Sally, their daughter, Anika, was a blonde bombshell who had already received four marriage proposals from wealthy men.

"She went to New York, Washington, and St. Louis, then California," Betje ticked them off.

"Why St. Louis?" Gaby asked.

"Some man. He owned a baseball team there. He was interested in her."

"I bet he was," Nigel said, rolling his eyes.

"How'd she like it?"

"She loves America. She was thinking maybe of going to Hollywood, but she does not like California," Yasper said.

"Really, why not?" Anne asked.

"She says the problem with America is that Americans have no freedom," Betje explained.

"How so?"

"She says there are too many restrictions. Walk. Don't walk. Don't step on the grass. Don't do this. Don't do that. Everywhere you go: no smoking. No animals in restaurants. You have to show your *carte d'indentité* to prove you are old enough to have a beer or a glass of wine. Who can live this way? She doesn't like."

"Tell them of the swimming pool," Yasper said.

"*Ja,*" Betje said. "She is staying at this motel in Los Angeles with a nice swimming pool. So each afternoon, she is going for the sunbathing. But then she notices something strange. She is the only one there. Yet the moment she leaves the pool area, mothers come out with their children and they jump in the pool. So finally, she stops a boy and asks him and he tells her his mother made them stay inside because of her bathing suit. Just because she had taken her bikini top off. Imagine!"

"I'm trying to," Nigel said.

"She's a cutie," Bobby G. said.

"America is a sexual nuthouse," Chuck said. "That's one of the reasons I left."

"I thought it was the taxes," Sally said.

"That's another."

"It all goes back to the Pilgrims," Max said.

"Wait a minute. You're blaming the fact that a woman at a motel doesn't want her kids to see a young woman topless on the Pilgrims?" I said.

"My ancestors came over on the Mayflower," Anne said.

"Mine too. Except they took one look at America and sailed back to England. Heard they converted the Mayflower into a pub. Best thing for it too," Nigel rumbled.

"I think so many people sailed on the Mayflower, the ship must've sunk ten times over from the weight," Monika said.

"You're missing the point. In order to understand America, one must understand the Puritans," Max said.

"This I gotta hear," Bobby G. said.

"Look, the Puritans in England wore only black. All they ever did was work and spend all day Sunday praying. They banned music even in church, were against dancing, jokes, laughter, fun of any kind. They banned theater, condemned everything and unless you did exactly as they said, you were condemned to burn in Hell forever. Those were the Puritans."

"So?" Gaby said.

"So... the Pilgrims left England and came to America because they thought the Puritans were too liberal!" Max said.

"Bull. Americans like sex too. What about Marilyn Monroe?" Bobby G. said.

"I said it was a nuthouse, I didn't say we were crazy," Chuck shrugged and everyone laughed.

"Sally tells me you are having trouble finding a *crèche* for your son," Annette, sitting next to me, said.

"It's a big problem. It's too far for Justin to continue in Cap d'Antibes and none of the *crèches* in Monaco have any openings."

"Perhaps my boss can help. I can ask."

"Where do you work?"

"The *Societé* for the Prevention of Cruelty to Animals."

"I don't know . . ." I started to say, then glanced at Sally, who was smiling and I got it. That clever little devil, I thought. She sat us together on purpose. "Who's your boss?" I asked.

"Princess Caroline. She heads the *Societé* in Monaco. If you like, I can ask her," she said.

Driving back from Nice to Cap d'Antibes, lights from houses on one side and the darkness of the sea on the other, Anne and I talked about it.

"Sally planned it, all right. Now I know why she was so insistent that we come tonight. I told her we had to start packing for the move, but she insisted we come. Maybe she's right," Anne said.

"About what?"

"Maybe you can solve everything with dinner."

The next day, I had just finished work and was waiting for Anne who had gone to the *École du Cap* to pick up Justin, when the phone rang.

"*Monsieur Kaplan?*"

"*Oui.*"

"*Ne quittez pas, s'il vous plaît. Voici la Princesse . . .*"

Another woman's voice came on.

"Monsieur Kaplan? This is Princess Caroline. I understand you are having difficulty finding a *crèche*," said a voice in perfect English with just a hint of Grace Kelly in it.

"It's been very difficult," I said.

"Have you tried the *Jardin des Enfants?*" she said, naming what Anne told me was the most exclusive nursery school in the south of France.

"They told us there was a three-year waiting list."

"Never mind. You need to call Monsieur Joubert now," she said and gave me the number.

"Excuse me, Princess, but are you sure? Anne said they told her it was impossible."

"I'm in charge of all the *crèches* in Monaco, Monsieur. I assure you Monsieur Joubert is waiting for your call. Please call me if there's anything else I can do."

I didn't know what to say. "Princess . . ." I started, not sure if I should say it. "I'll probably never get another chance to say this. I was crazy about your mother."

"So was I," she said softly. "How old is your son? His name is Justin?"

"Justin. He's two and a half."

"The same as my son, Andrea. Perhaps they could play together . . ."

"We'd like that. And thanks."

"Well, I'm part American too, you know," she said.

I had no sooner hung up then the phone rang again. It was Janie.

"I've been trying to call," she said, "but the line's been busy. Who were you talking to?"

At first I wasn't going to say, as if it was any of her business anyway, but knowing what a social climber she was, I couldn't resist.

"Princess Caroline of Monaco," I said.

"Princess Caroline!! What! How do you know Princess Caroline?!!" she shrieked.

"She's helping us get Justin into a *crèche*."

"She knows about Justin!!! I don't believe this!" she said.

I heard the car honking outside.

"Anne's here. I've got to go," I told her.

"I don't believe this!" she said.

Once Upon A Villa

We planned to leave Polanski's villa that weekend. All that remained was to pack and move our things to the new villa. At the *École du Cap*, they made a little *au revoir* party for Justin. I went to the *gendarmerie* in Antibes to notify the police *commissaire* of our change in address.

"*Alors*, what will your President Reagan do about Libya?" the *commissaire* asked. Over the past few years, there had been a rise in terrorism and hijackings. In October, Palestinian gunmen had seized a cruise ship, the *Achille Lauro* and murdered a Jewish passenger. After Christmas, Palestinian terrorists had massacred twenty people at the Rome and Vienna airports. Now, the U.S. was accusing Libya of sponsoring terrorism.

"I don't know. Bomb the *merde* out of them," I said.

"Typical American response. You are all *"les cowboys."* This Reagan; he's a *cowboy* too, *n'est-ce pas?*"

"I guess. Ronald Reagan rides a horse. He made *des films de cowboy*. He's got a ranch. No cattle, but it's a ranch. I guess he qualifies as a cowboy."

"How can a superpower elect such a *tête de veau* as President?"

"Beats me, but are Mitterand and Chirac so much better? Or perhaps a racist like Le Pen." There was an election coming up soon in France.

"No one takes Le Pen seriously, except the foreign journalists. As for Mitterand and Chirac, at least they can talk without having someone else write every word for them. With Reagan, it's like a *spectacle de marionettes* (puppet show) for President."

"And Mitterand and Chirac have good-looking mistresses," the other *agent* said.

"*Et voilà*," the *commissaire* said. "One should express one's *virilité* with beautiful women, not by bombing people." Only the French would regard a sex scandal as something for a politician to be proud of, I thought.

"Do you like Woody Allen, *Monsieur le Commissaire*?"

"*Oui, le grand* Woody. After Jerry Lewis, he is a true genius."

"There's a line in a Woody Allen movie where he and his New York intellectual friends are discussing how to react to a march by neo-Nazis. His friends want to write a strong letter to the *New York Times*, but Woody wants to go after them with baseball bats. He tells them, 'With Nazis, bats are better.'"

"*Et alors,* your point *Monsieur?*"

"Maybe with terrorists, you need a cowboy," I said.

"*Peut-être.* But even in the *film de cowboy*, when the *chef de la police* goes after the bad guys, he does not go alone. He makes the "posse," no? But you Americans like *le shootout* at *le OK Corra*l too much. We Europeans have learned war settles very little."

"American guns settled a lot in France, *Monsieur le Commissaire.*"

"*Les américains* we do not forget, *Monsieur*, even though at times it seems we do. In any case, how goes the book?"

"It goes well. How is the police business?"

"Always there is crime. That never changes, Monsieur."

When I got back to the villa, Anne was all excited.

"We're throwing a party," she said.

"We are?"

"I wanted to thank Sally and Annette and then we realized that none of our friends had even seen the villa and it's huge, just perfect for parties, we're here for the weekend and well, everyone's coming."

"Sounds good," I said. Later, I recalled thinking those were probably the words of the captain of the Titanic after they told him the sea was calm and if they kept going full speed ahead they could break the Trans-Atlantic record.

Chapter 10

La Bouffe or How Not To Throw a Party in France

The weather forecast should have been a warning. According to the woman on Canal Plus TV with the bizarre *franges oranges* (orange bangs) over her eyes, the Côte d'Azur was due for the worst Mediterranean storm in fifty years. Heavy downpours, flooding, and gale force winds were predicted along the coast all the way from the Camargue to Italy. In Cap d'Antibes, residents near the shore were fleeing inland or sandbagging walls around their houses.

Before the storm, I made a run in the car to haul some of our things from *chez Polanski* to the new villa in Eze. On the way back, Anne and I picked up Justin from his *crèche*. The teachers and kids at the École du Cap had thrown a going-away party for him and Justin came out wearing a cardboard crown. There was something touching in hearing his little classmates calling after him, "*Adieu, Justin,*" and "*Au revoir, Justin*" as we left, the teachers telling us that our son was *très gentil* and *très mignon* and how far he had come from the first days when he didn't understand a word of French and how sorry they were to see him go. One little girl kept waving good-bye until her mother finally dragged her away.

It doesn't matter where you are, France or America, I thought, as a parent you spend half your time wondering if you are doing the right thing. We had thrown him into a school where he was the only one who didn't speak a word of the language. It had to have been hard and lonely for him and just when he had finally made some friends, here I was uprooting him yet again. When I looked at Anne, I could see she felt it too. But by that time, the sky was growing black and the first drops of the forecasted storm began to splatter on the windshield. We drove quickly back to the house, ducked inside, and began closing all the wooden shutters and doors and getting candles and flashlights ready.

That night the gale came ashore. A torrential downpour battered the roof and shutters. The house creaked and shook, the wind keening in the eaves so loudly it reminded me of the Russian poet, Mayakovsky's line, "as though the gargoyles of Notre Dame were howling." The electricity went out, of course. Anne made soup and we ate by candlelight, listening to the house creaking like a ship in the night.

"Welcome to the sunny French Riviera. We were supposed to be sipping wine under an umbrella at the beach. Great planning, Babe. I brought nothing but summer clothes," Anne said.

A blast of thunder like artillery shook the house, making us all jump.

"Daddy, I don't want to sleep by myself in my room," Justin said.

"No problem. You can sleep with us tonight," I said.

We went to bed early, all of us huddled together under the blankets, listening to the rain and wind in the night. The storm continued on through the next day and night.

We stayed inside, the windows shuttered, telling stories and playing Monopoly in front of the fire in the *salon*. We hadn't shopped for food and all that was left for dinner was spaghetti. Anne asked me to light the stove, which I did as always, with a dive onto a cushion by the kitchen door as the walls rattled to the boom of the gas igniting, thinking how strange that this peculiar method of starting the stove had become routine for us.

The morning after the storm, we ventured outside. The villa grounds were blanketed with leaves and downed branches, but incredibly, none of our trees had come down. It didn't look too bad at all and that's when I nearly made a fatal blunder. I decided to try to drive to Eze to move some more of our stuff to the new villa and assess the damage there.

"Be careful," Anne said.

"What about the party? Is it still on?"

She gave me the kind of look that wives use to remind husbands that men are at best, *idiots savants*, vaguely useful for opening jars and fixing things and the like, but who will never understand anything really important. When I left, she was on the phone discussing menus with Sally.

Driving to Eze was a challenge. In Cap d'Antibes, fallen trees had torn gaps in stone walls around the villas and many of the streets were blocked with downed trees and power lines. A strong wind was still blowing.

As I approached the *Basse Corniche*, I saw something extraordinary. The sea had come ashore. It was nearly up to the road. This was getting dangerous. I drove on, watching the waves lapping at the edge of the road out of the corner of my eye. In Eze-sur-Mer, the new villa, which stood on high ground part way up the hill, was untouched by the storm.

Using the key from the real estate office, I unlocked the door and put our things in the closets and bedrooms. I had filled boxes I had found behind the *supermarché* with books and now put the books on the shelves in the *salon*. I stepped out onto the stone *terrasse* and looked out over the neighboring houses and on down to the sea. An older French woman in the garden of the next villa down the hill from ours watched me like a hawk. The two properties were separated by a wire fence.

"*Vous êtes le nouveau locataire, Monsieur?*"

"*Oui, un bon voisin,*" I said, trying to sound like a friendly neighbor.

"*Ne touchez-pas mes tomates!*" she snapped.

Hello to you too, I thought. "*J'ai des tomates à moi aussi, Madame!*" I have my own tomatoes, I replied, but she had already gone inside. So much for meeting the neighbors. I hadn't moved in yet and we were already having a tomato war.

The drive back to Cap d'Antibes was nerve-wracking. The wind had grown stronger and past St. Laurent du Var, the sea covered the *Basse Corniche* for a stretch of several miles. I stopped the car and walked into the water. Right there, it was only a couple of inches deep. I could either try to drive through or I could go back to Nice, go all the way up to the *Moyenne Corniche* and over, then down to Cap d'Antibes; a good two-to-three-hour detour. In my mind I could see the newspaper headline: "*Touriste Américain s'est noyé à la Basse Corniche,*" with the unspoken implication of "Idiot American Tourist drowns on the *Basse Corniche* road because he was too dumb to know not to drive through the Mediterranean Sea, thereby doing us all the immense favor of removing himself from the gene pool." On the other hand, I had a feeling Anne needed me. I decided to risk it.

I drove slowly, the wind whipping the spray from the waves across the windshield, the tires leaving a wake like a boat on the water. Driving that road was nerve-wracking and when I reached the villa I felt like I had survived something. But when I tried to tell Anne what happened, she had no time to listen.

"It's a disaster... we're doomed!" she said.

"What's the matter?"

"What do you mean what's the matter? What kind of help is that? We're having a party, right?"

"So?"

"So I don't see you coming up with any ideas about what to serve."

"We've had parties before. What's the problem?"

"What's the problem?! I'll tell you what the problem is. This is France. That's the problem!"

"I'm missing something here…"

"They're French! Do you understand? French! They're all fantastic cooks used to serving incredible French food. How am I supposed to compete with that?!"

"A lot of them are Americans," I said.

"Americans who live in France. They know what good food is supposed to taste like. It's a disaster. And everyone is coming."

"What do you mean 'Everyone's coming?'"

"I mean everyone. All our friends. Max and Sally's friends. Annette's inviting the Princess."

"Princess Caroline here?!"

"Martine's coming too. Also your friend, the police *commissaire*. Everyone," she said miserably.

"My God, what are we going to do?" Just then I had a horrible thought. "Wait a minute. Don't tell me you invited Greg and Janie. No, of course you wouldn't," I laughed nervously. She didn't answer. "Anne? You didn't?"

"She saw me buying champagne. What could I do?"

"Great! The Princess and the Social Climbers of the Western World. We'll have an international incident! And the *commissaire* will be right there to arrest me! How much more perfect can it get?!"

"It won't matter," she said.

"Why?"

"Because they'll have nothing to eat! I'll never be able to show my face again. What do we do?"

"We could leave the country… Italy's nice."

"We. Can't. Leave," she said through clenched teeth. "Everyone's coming."

"We could have it catered. Some local restaurant…" The look she shot me killed that idea instantly. "So you have to make it. This is some female code of honor?"

"Explain to me again what I saw in you," she said.

"I make cute babies," I said.

"Yeah, well unless we come up with something, that may not be enough. What do we do?"

I decided to try Sally's method. "Have lunch," I said. "Maybe we'll come up with an idea."

We decided to go all out. We drove over to Cannes for lunch at the famous Reine Pédauque on the rue Maréchal-Joffre. It was a Riviera lunch of baked *tomates* stuffed with almonds and roasted peppers, hot oysters *aux poireaux*, and *lapereau aux pâtes fraîches*, which of course, we told Justin was chicken, so he wouldn't think we were horrible for eating a bunny rabbit. As we pushed away our empty plates after an amazing chocolate *mousse*, which in Provence, to Justin's delight, was called a *gendarme de Saint-Tropez*, because the cylindrical *mousse* resembled a chocolate policeman's hat, Anne said, "Never in a million years."

"Never in a million years what?"

"Never in a million years could I cook like this," she sighed.

"Then don't try."

"What do you mean?"

"We're Americans. Cook American."

"Like what?"

"I don't know. How about franks and beans? Or chili? It'll be a novelty for them. They get this fancy French stuff all the time."

"I don't have a recipe for chili. But I do have one for stew," she brightened, grabbing Justin as he was about to bat his balloon into the salad at the next table.

"There you go. Good old American stew. You can feed an army with it and with stew it's hard to go wrong," I said, not realizing that once again I was tempting the gods.

The next day was spent shopping. Bottles of Bordeaux and Loire wine from the *cave* in Antibes, a score of assorted slabs of *pâtés* and a *foie gras* in puff pastry with figs and spiced wine from an *épicerie fine* in Saint Laurent du Var recommended by Colette, two dozen different cheeses, Brie, Camembert, Roquefort, several types of *chèvre* goat cheese, three different *Epoisses* from Burgundy, a *Fromage blanc* from Bresse, and for dessert, several dozen *tartes*, *mille-feuilles*, and *mousses au chocolat* from three different *pâtisseries* in Nice and to top it off, a *Grand Marnier soufflé* from Colette.

Janie lent us a giant pot big enough for a battalion and Anne spent all day preparing the vegetables and beef for the stew. But the ghost of Polanski wasn't done with us yet. That afternoon, as I came back to the villa with the *patés*, the place was rocked by an explosion. I raced to the kitchen. Anne was sitting on the kitchen floor in shock, Justin watched her anxiously from the doorway. I ran over to her.

"I tried to start the stove by myself," she said, starting to cry.

"My God, your face . . ." I stammered.

"My face?! What do you mean my face?!"

"Your eyebrows . . ." I said. They were singed black and smelled of burnt hair. I wet a kitchen towel and wiped her face. She still had eyebrow hair left, but part of them was gone and stubbled. She got up and stared at herself in the hall mirror.

"I can't go to a party like this!" she wailed and raced to the bathroom. I went over to the stove. The gas was burning perfectly now, as though having done its mischief, it was pretending that nothing had ever been wrong. It's a curse, I thought. Some weird Eastern European gypsy spirit that Polanski had left behind and was doing this to punish us for leaving.

I put the big pot from Janie onto the burner, with the uneasy feeling that *chez Polanski* wasn't finished with us yet. When Anne came out, she had eyebrow-penciled in new brows. It gave her a different look, a kind of 1930's glamour.

"I've decided what the hell. It's the best I can do."

"Actually, you look beautiful. Different," I said. She did.

"God, I hate this stove."

"I love you," I said.

"I love you too," she said.

"The stove in the new villa in Eze seems to work," I said hopefully.

"A French stove that doesn't explode. What a concept!" she said and began bustling around the kitchen. The villa was soon filled with the aroma of cooking. Justin and I set out plates and glasses, the *patés* and cheeses, etc. for a buffet on the long oak table in the *salle à manger*. By dusk, the villa and grounds were ablaze with light. Anne still hadn't dressed and was still in her apron, her face intent as she studied her recipe book one last time, then glanced around the kitchen, a general inspecting her troops. For the first time in two days, she almost smiled. Then she said something that changed everything.

"I need you to taste the stew."

"Haven't you been tasting it all along?" I had a sudden horrible presentiment of Polanski's face watching us from a corner as if directing a scene from one of his movies. Here we go, I thought.

"I'm sure it's fine. I followed the recipe exactly. Just taste this," she said, holding up a soup spoon for me.

"YEOOOOOOW!!!!" They must've heard my scream in Italy. I was howling and hopping around the kitchen like a madman, my mouth and tongue on fire like nothing I had ever experienced. It was like biting into a million of the hottest Mexican *chilis* in the universe. My eyes watered, my nose began running, and the pain was so intense I couldn't even talk. I ran to the refrigerator, grabbed a liter bottle of Evian on ice and began chugging it down as fast as I could, the water splashing down my neck and shirt collar, but it didn't help. I needed more ice water, more anything!

Justin giggled and offered me his half-finished orange drink. I drained it, then stuck my mouth under the tap in the kitchen sink and began gulping the water down. The burning was beyond belief. My tongue began to swell to twice its normal size. I grabbed a handful of ice cubes from the freezer and stuffed them into my mouth. Nothing helped.

"Wawa!" I begged with my swollen tongue, unable to even say "water."

"Too hot?" Anne said.

"I thig I ned t'go da hobital," I mumbled through the melting ice cubes.

"What?!!"

"I THINK I NEED TO GO TO THE HOSPITAL!"

"OK, so it's a little spicy. It's supposed to be," Anne said.

"Are you crazy? You can't serve that!"

"Don't be a baby. It can't be that hot."

"Anne, human beings can't eat that."

"People like it a little spicy," she said, a little defensively.

"Anne, people from southern India can't eat that! Mexicans who live on red-hot chile peppers can't eat it. What the hell did you put in there?"

"Nothing."

"Well, it must've been something. Mexican jalapenos or what?"

"Nothing really. Just a little pepper and cumin. But I followed the recipe."

"What recipe? The recipe from Hades?! How much cumin did you put in?

"Look, you're over-reacting. Try another taste," she said, holding up the spoon.

"Please, no!!! No way!"

She started to cry. "What are we going to do? I don't have anything else." She glanced at her watch. "Oh my God! They'll be here in half an hour!"

"Daddy, jump around again," Justin said, grinning.

"Daddy needs to help Mommy, Justin. You can laugh at Daddy later," I said.

"What can we do?" Anne said.

"Can we order something? Anything?"

She shook her head.

"What about thinning it out, so it's not so spicy?" I asked.

"How?"

"I don't know. Water?"

Anne filled the water pitcher and poured about a glass' worth into the giant pot. I grabbed the pitcher and poured it all in. She gave me a look, then stirred and stuck the spoon in and held it out for me.

"No, you try it," I said.

"I'm afraid," she said.

"So am I."

"Please..."

I tipped the spoon leaving only a drop of stew, then readied a glass full of ice water. I tasted the drop, immediately gulped down the water, and hopped around the kitchen cursing with my blistered tongue. Justin giggled. He thought it was hilarious. I grabbed another ice cube and sucked it for all it was worth.

"Any better?" Anne said, plaintively.

"A touch. There must be a better way to make it less spicy. How about flour?"

"Does that help?"

"I don't know. We've got to do something." Anne brought some flour and heaped a cup into the pot. Then she added more water and stirred.

"Are you ready?" she said, holding out another drop of the stew on the spoon.

"Here's the glass, Daddy," Justin said, handing me another glass of water.

I tasted it. Tears came to my eyes again, but it was merely as hot as an unbelievably spicy Indian curry. I only sipped the water to Justin's disappointment.

"What do you think?"

"Better. But it's missing something."

"What?"

"I don't know. What else can we throw in?"

"Wine?"

"Absolutely!"

We grabbed a half-full bottle of red Bordeaux and Anne poured in a shot or two. Then she looked at me, took a swig from the bottle, shrugged and poured half the bottle into the pot. We tried the spoon again.

"Well...?" she asked.

"It's still spicy, but you know, it's not half-bad."

Anne poured another slug or two of wine into the pot, stirred and tasted. Her eyes immediately started to water.

"Yikes! Holy crap that's hot!" she said.

"No, that's mild. Before, it was hot," I said, wiping my brow. I was sweating up a storm.

"So how are we going to sell this? If someone asks about the stew, what do I say?"

"Just tell 'em it's American. We like things spicy. They won't know the difference."

"Maybe regional... what's spicy regional American?"

"I don't know... Creole... Cajun? My great-aunt Ida lived in Mississippi. Gulfport. It's not Louisiana, but it's near New Orleans."

"That's it! It's your great-aunt Ida's Cajun stew. Old family recipe," Anne said, glancing at her watch. "Oh my God! I've got to change," she said and ran off. Justin and I looked at each other.

"That was funny, Daddy," Justin said.

"Glad you're having fun, Justin. Everyone likes parties. I hope," I said, pouring myself another glass of water.

PRINCESS CAROLINE SENT HER REGRETS, Annette told us. Something about a charity affair Prince Rainier couldn't make and she had to fill in at the last minute. Colette had brought Freddie and her husband, Jean-Claude, bringing with them their dashing good looks and charm and the unmistakable whiff of Parisian *chic*. Max surveyed the salon, crowded with people. Justin and his babysitter, the English *au pair* with the bizarre spiked purple hairdo, watched from a doorway.

"So this is where you've been hiding," Max said. "Nice."

"I heard you were close with the writer, Irwin Shaw," I said.

"We used to hang out. Can't believe it's almost a year since he ... you know. He did it all. Hollywood. Producers used to come out here. Women, too. Boat loads of women. He told me he introduced Hemingway to his fourth wife, Mary. Irwin said she was his girlfriend first during the war. Mary Wells her name was then. Irwin liked to ski. Said that's why he moved to Switzerland. Personally I figured he just wanted to be closer to his money."

"Was he a good skier?"

"Hell of a skier."

"Hell of a writer, too."

"You jealous?"

"Absolutely. There's a line in one of his post-war stories where a German major tells the American that he wasn't a Nazi, he was just a middle-class person with a wife and three children, and the American says, 'I'm getting very tired of your wife and three children.' I'd kill to write a line like that."

"Doesn't make it easy on Adam," Max said, nodding toward Adam Shaw and Maia, talking with Anne and Sally.

"No, that's got to be a tough act to follow."

"The girls like him though. Who's that?" Max said, looking over at Freddie, babbling away in French with Martine and someone I didn't know.

"She's married," I said.

"That isn't what I asked."

"Yes it is."

"*Touché*," he laughed. "Have you met Mark?" indicating a tweedy Englishman talking to Yasper and Betje.

"No, should I?"

"Absolutely. Best yacht parties in Monte Carlo. He's got this incredible one-hundred-and-fifty-footer. Acres of mahogany and brass. Wait till you see it. Mark," he called, motioning the Englishman over.

"Mark, Andrew is an American. Very talented," Max said.

"Delighted. Do you know anyone who wants to buy a yacht?" he asked me.

"Why are you selling?" I asked.

"Buying a bigger one," he said. "Absolute necessity."

"Why is that? I heard this one's a hundred-and-fifty-footer. What would you need a bigger one for?"

"Share it with the wife. The more space between us the better. Sure you don't want to buy it? I'll make you a lovely price."

"It's a bit out of my league. As a matter of fact, it's an entire universe out of my league," I said.

"Well, we'll have to have you out then. You're not opposed to getting sloshed, are you?"

"Not in the least."

"Good. There's an incredible thirty-year-old single malt I'd like your opinion on," he said, patting me on the shoulder.

"In the interest of science?" I asked.

"No, just in the interest of idle drunkenness. We're British, you know. We've lowered our expectations. Who's the beauty?" indicating Freddie.

"She's married," Max said.

"Of course she is. Your wife's a lovely piece too," he said to me.

"She's married too," I said.

"So am I, come to that," Mark said, wandering off. He grabbed Nigel. "Hello Nigel, do you want to buy a yacht?"

Just then Betje came over. She looked upset.

"I've never been so insulted in my life," she said.

Bobby G. came by waving a bowl of stew and his spoon. "Great Cajun jambalaya, Bub. Gaby's dying to get the recipe."

"It's my great-aunt Ida's," I said and turned to Betje. "What happened?"

"He called me an addict. He asked if I drank more than two glasses of wine and when I said yes, he said I was an alcoholic. What kind of people do you know?"

"Who did?" I said with a sinking feeling.

"Him!" she declared, pointing at Greg, who had wandered into the *salon* with a nervous-looking Janie. He started to say something to Chuck and Emma and they just walked away.

"Don't mind him. He's the winner of the Ugly American of the Year Award," I said.

"*Ah oui*, tell me more about this *américain laid*," the police *Commissaire* said, coming up behind me. "We suspect he's selling *les drogues*. This tells me," he said, tapping his nose. "*C'est vrai?*"

The *commissaire* had placed me in an awkward moral dilemma. On the one hand, I despised Greg and wished him no good. But on the other, I didn't like the idea of being a snitch on a fellow American, nor could I personally swear that he was dealing. "It's possible, Monsieur le Commissaire."

"What does he want, this *type?*"

"He says he wants to go to Aspen," I said.

"Perhaps we can encourage him to follow his desires. The sooner the better."

"Well I'm leaving. I refuse to be around such persons," Betje declared. "Though I must say, your wife's *pot au feu au style Cajun* is incredible. Everyone is talking about it. No one expected such a miracle of *cuisine américaine*. And she looks wonderful. Her eyebrows. She looks like *la* Garbo."

"Precisely what I was telling Monika," said Nigel, coming over. "Who's this?"

"*Je suis le Commissaire des Polices d'Antibes-Juan les Pins.*"

"Excellent. If you ask me, this place is thick with *voleurs*. That one over there, Inspector, is a real *type sinistre, n'est-ce pas?*" Nigel said in a conspiratorial manner.

"That is *mon auxiliaire, Agent Leclerc*," the *Commissaire* said stiffly.

"Yes, well I'd keep an eye on him. You can never tell. I say, don't suppose you could arrest my ex and her brats? A pack of thieves, the lot of 'em," Nigel said.

"On what charge, Monsieur?"

"Well, they're British."

"Alas, that is no longer sufficient grounds, Monsieur," the *Commissaire* said, then pulling me close, whispered, "*C'est un opéra bouffe,* (comic opera) *ces types-ci.* You should associate more with us French, Monsieur."

"Colette is French," I said, pointing Colette out.

"I knew her father in the *Maquis,*" the *Commissaire* winked. "In those days, we knew what to do with *les parasites.* Today, one cannot touch them. They are the basis of the French economy. *Dites-moi,* how goes the writing? Where is your *espion* now?"

"He's headed for the Golden Triangle between Burma, Laos, and Thailand."

"A lawless land."

"Very."

"Like Corsica," the *Commissaire* said. "I'll have to read it, even if it is American."

"You honor me. What would Voltaire say?"

"That all human history is merely a record of crimes and follies. Literature too, I suspect."

"Of all the things here, I shall miss you, *Monsieur le Commissaire.* I wish we didn't have to move."

"I too, Monsieur. I still have to beat you at chess. And tell your wife her *pot au feu au style Cajun* was a *surprise exceptionnelle* from the New World."

"You have no idea," I said.

"*Pardon?*"

Max came by. "We need to throw that idiot out," indicating Greg, in the middle of a noisy crowd. "He's managed to insult almost everyone."

"It's not possible. He's only been here a few minutes."

"Don't be so sure. Talent will out," Max said.

"Permit me, Monsieur," the *Commissaire* said and the next thing I knew, he and *Officier* Leclerc were leading Greg outside.

"My fault, old chaps," Nigel said. "Told him Monika was a countess. Like throwing meat to a starving hound. Literally saw him salivating. Absolutely Pavlovian."

Anne came over. "Greg insulted Monika. Said she couldn't be a countess from America. Then he insulted Freddie. Offered a thousand dollars to sleep with her."

"Outrageous! She's worth more than that," Nigel said.

"Do shut up, Nigel," Monika said, and to us: "Pay no attention. The British upper classes are notorious for their bad manners."

"How's Adam Shaw?" I asked Anne.

"He's gorgeous. Dark curly hair, intense. No wonder the girls are nuts about him. He wants to meet you. Says you're a real writer. Oh God, Janie's coming back," Anne said and rushed off.

Just then Annette, who worked for Princess Caroline came up. "Your wife's *ragôut* is *incroyable*. But she won't give me the recipe."

"I'm not sure we could recreate it if we tried," I said.

"*Je ne comprend pas.*"

"I know. It's very Zen. But please, thank the Princess for us. I don't know what we would have done without her help."

"She'll be sorry she missed your wife's *ragôut*. It is, how you say, *un* 'blast.'"

I thought of the exploding stove. "You have no idea," I said.

The party went on into the morning hours. Someone turned on the stereo and everyone drank and danced to American Rock n' Roll. Around four in the morning, Max and Sally led a caravan of cars to a place by the *marché aux puces* in the port in Nice, where we had *café au lait* with Armagnac and an enormous stack of *tranches dorées*, slices of French toast, fried to a luscious golden color and covered with powdered sugar. As the sun broke over the port, even Martine agreed that our little *soirée d'adieu* had been a success. A farewell, *comme il faut*, to Cap d'Antibes.

The sun was well up by the time we got back to *chez Polanski* to pack for the last time. I asked Anne what Janie had wanted.

"She wanted to know if we could still be friends even though her husband's an asshole."

"What did you tell her?"

"I told her I would, but I don't think she believed me. It's sad."

"Why?"

"The trophy wife shine is starting to wear a little thin for both of them," she said. "Personally, I suspect they're running out of places to hide."

PART 2

Eze sur Mer

Chapter 11

Zarathustra's Path

The weather continued cold and windy. From our bedroom in Eze-sur-Mer, we could see beyond the balcony and the trees to the sea. During the day, the sea was gray and choppy and at night we could hear the trees swaying in the wind.

Mornings, we would have *pain au chocolat* and *Nescafé* and Anne would take Justin to the new *crèche* in Monte Carlo. Except for a few Monagasques, she was the only mother who brought her own child. Most of the children came from aristocratic or extremely wealthy families and were brought by nannies or *au pairs*, often in limousines with bodyguards. After dropping Justin off, Anne would make the rounds of shops, the *charcuterie*, the *épicerie*, the *boucherie*, the *boulangerie*, and the *supermarché* in Cap Ferrat. After the second day, she refused to shop in Eze-sur-Mer, coming home before noon, slamming the door and turning on the music on the radio as loud as it would go.

"I'll never go there again. Never!" she snapped.

"Go where?"

"The *boulangerie* at the corner on the *Corniche*. That girl... she refused to wait on me. She waited on everyone else, gossiping away a mile a minute and deliberately ignored me and finally I said, 'S'il vous plait, Mademoiselle,' and she just looked at me and said that I spoke French so badly I wasn't worth talking to. I told her I would take my business elsewhere and she just shrugged and said, "*Tant mieux*" and something else in French that made her stupid girlfriend laugh and I'll never shop there again, I'd rather starve! Only what are we going to do for bread? I hate the French!"

"*Vache sale!*" I said.

"What?"

"'Dirty cow.' It's what you should've called her. Do you want me to come with you and insult her?"

"I'm never going in there again."

"Are you sure? There are some dirty French words I've been saving up because I didn't want Justin to pick them up."

"You can't insult them. They don't care. They're just stupid... what do you call them... *vaches*?"

"*Vache sale! Laid comme un pou!* Ugly as sin. She won't like that. The French don't mind being called 'nasty,' but they go bananas if you call them 'ugly.'"

"Except they had really good *baguettes* and *pain au chocolat*. Justin loves their *pain au chocolat*. What are we going to do?"

"We'll find another *boulangerie*. It's France. The one thing you can find in this country is a decent *baguette*."

In the mornings, after Anne left with Justin, I went to the small downstairs bedroom to write. Through the window I could see the forest behind the villa. I was writing about the hill country in the Golden Triangle, so I described the jungle with its thousand shades of green and the way the light filtered through the overhanging trees as I saw it through the window. In the book, my agent, Sawyer, and the Eurasian woman, Suong, had bribed an opium trader named Toonsang to guide them to a powerful warlord who might be involved with Parker's (the CIA agent who had disappeared) mission. But the opium trader was a problem, eying Sawyer's goods, trying to buy the woman from him, and calling Sawyer, "younger brother," an insult. It was becoming clear to Sawyer that he might have to kill Toonsang.

Sometimes I would take a break from the writing and walk up the road to the top of the hill, then down Nietzsche's path through the woods. Near the top of the path was a lone tree, winter bare and twisted. I thought about the tree in *Thus Spake Zarathustra* and how Zarathustra tells the boy while a man cannot bend the tree, the wind does and that it is by invisible hands that we are bent.

The day was cold and I could see my breath. According to Stefan Zweig, Neitzsche was utterly alone and friendless in Eze. About the tree on the mountain Neitzsche had written that it was high and alone and that it was waiting – waiting for lightning! And of course, for him the lightning struck with a vengeance.

First the failure of his book; then madness, death, and after his death, his idea of the *Übermensch* that he had first conceived right here in this same silent wood almost exactly a century ago, would be perverted by Adolf Hitler into the Holocaust. I shivered and hurried down the path, glad I wasn't Nietzsche and that I had Anne and Justin to come home to. By the time I got back, for the first time in fifty years on the Riviera, it was snowing.

The snow dusted the trees and the roofs and tops of the stone walls of the villas. The hills were white and beautiful and a layer of snow perhaps a quarter-inch-thick coated the yard. Being a southern California kid, Justin had never seen snow before and he was excited. Anne bundled him up in a sweater, waterproof pants and jacket and a blue wool cap and he and I went out to play in the snow. We made snowballs and thew them at each other and jumped around in the snow. There wasn't enough snow on the ground for a proper snowman, but we built a small one, about six inches high on a stone step in the yard that led to a locked gate to a neighbor's property.

"It's wet, Dad," Justin said, watching the snow melt in his hand.

"Snow is water, Justin. That's all it is," I said.

"Then how come it's white and you can make it into a snowball?"

"Because it's solid. It's just a different form of the same thing."

"How can that be, Dad?"

"That's just how things work." I thought about Neitzsche and the tree. "Things aren't always how they seem."

"I like snow, Daddy. You can fall in it and it doesn't even hurt."

"It's pretty, isn't it?"

Justin looked around at the yard and the snowman and the villas on the hillside. "Everything's pretty, huh Dad?"

"You bet," I said. We went inside. Anne had a fire going in the fireplace and we had hot spiced cider and read *Where The Wild Things Are* and a French comic book based on a Jules Verne-ish French TV cartoon show that Justin loved called *Les Mondes Englouties* ("The Engulfed Worlds").

One of the advantages, now that we were living in Eze, was that we were closer to friends and places we liked. There were Maria and the Chef's, the La Caravelle and La Frégate restaurants on the *quai* in Villefranche, Edmund's in Cap d'Ail, where whenever we drove up, the Italian waiter immediately ordered Justin's favorite, *spaghetti Bolognese*, even before we got out of the car and that he never let us pay for. Also, Le Bateau Ivre in the marina in Beaulieu-sur-Mer, where we met the Robot Man.

Beaulieu was a seaside Riviera town that featured white wedding cake hotel-casinos like the Réserve and the Métropole on the Boulevard du General-Leclerc. They were the casinos you would see in a James Bond movie and by the marina, the Le Bateau Ivre (The Drunken Boat) restaurant, that some owner with a poetic turn of phrase had named after the poem by Rimbaud, where you could sit and look out at the masts of the sailboats and the rigging lights reflected on the water.

The first time, when we walked in, we had thought the Robot Man, dressed in a white tuxedo and derby, was a statue until just as Justin passed, he tipped his hat and smiled, nearly scaring Justin to death. All during dinner, Justin watched him like a hawk, but the Robot Man never moved, or even it seemed, blinked or breathed.

At first Justin was afraid, but he was also fascinated and after he finished his *moules marinières*, he ran up to the Robot Man and yelled "Boo!" But the Robot Man understood children and never moved. It was later, as we were finishing dinner that the Robot Man made his rounds of the tables, moving with the jerky movements of a mechanical man as he proffered his derby to customers for his *pourboire*. When he came to our table, I gave Justin a ten-franc note and Justin put it in as quickly as he could, jerking his hand back and squealing with delight when the Robot Man tilted his head as a way of saying *merci*.

"Did you see, Daddy?" Justin said.

"I saw."

"Is he a real person?"

"Yes."

"I don't think so, Dad."

"I'm pretty sure, Justin."

Every time we went back, which was often enough because Le Bateau Ivre served an exceptional salmon and an even better *loup grillé au fenouil* (grilled sea bass with fennel), Justin would stand for the entire meal staring at the Robot Man, waiting for him to move.

Meanwhile, Anne had made two discoveries that changed her life. The first came the day after Le Bateau Ivre, when she came home with a basket with three *baguettes*.

"Taste this," she said, ripping off a piece of bread. I did. It was the best bread I had ever eaten in my life, warm and smelling of wheat, with a perfect crunchy golden crust that flaked in your mouth. We grabbed butter from the refrigerator and polished off all three *baguettes* in a few minutes.

"That's the best bread I've ever eaten. Who needs dinner?" I said.

"Where did you get it?"

"You're not going to believe it. It's this old *boulangerie* in Eze

Village right on the *Moyenne Corniche*. There's this old woman, all by herself. She's got to be at least eighty, with an ancient brick oven, huge, must be a couple of hundred years old. I saw a line of people at the door and decided to try it. That's all she does is bake bread. No *pâtisseries* or anything. It's incredible. I mean it's a long way out of the way. You've got to go all the way up to the *Moyenne Corniche*, but my God!"

"It's worth it. It's worth a hundred-mile detour. This is incredible," I said.

"I spoke to one of the old Frenchmen waiting. Me with my lousy French. I asked him how long he had been coming and he said since he was a *petit garçon*. What if she were to retire or something, I asked. He said she was in the hospital for weeks two years ago and no one in the village ate bread. It was like the whole village went into mourning. People wouldn't speak to one another. He said if it happened again, people would consider it the death of the village."

"I can believe it."

"I'm going to take a couple of *baguettes* to Sally," Anne said. "Finally, something I can give back to her."

The next night, Max and Sally called. Everyone was talking about the *baguettes*. We must have passed some kind of test, because we were informed Stuart and Glenda wanted to have us out to their country place for lunch and we had to be sure to bring *baguettes*.

"Who are Stuart and Glenda?" I asked.

"Apparently, we're about to find out," Anne said.

Anne's second great discovery was the California Terrace, a new fitness center and spa in the Hôtel de Paris, the classic grand hotel located next to the Casino in Monte Carlo (Eze-sur-Mer is about two miles west of Monte Carlo). The fitness center overlooked the harbor and Anne began going two or three times a week for a workout and a yoga class after dropping Justin off at the *crèche*.

Things at the Villa Olivia began to settle into a new routine. Around noon, after I had worked on the book and Anne had done her shopping or worked out, she picked Justin up from the *crèche* and we would go for lunch in Cap d'Ail or Roquebrune or Cap Ferrat, or Villefranche. Afternoons were spent exploring the hill towns or shopping in Nice, Menton, or Monte Carlo.

At the *cinq à sept* cocktail hour, we would meet Nigel, Monika, Max, Sally, and whoever else might be around for drinks at the American Bar in the Hôtel de Paris in Monte Carlo. All was going well till the second week, when Anne called to tell me she was being kidnapped.

"My God, what's happening?"

"I'm being kidnapped by three Jewish doctors' wives from Brooklyn," she laughed.

"Doesn't sound like your typical kidnap gang," I said, breathing a sigh of relief. In the background I could hear women chattering in New York-ese. "What's going on?"

"I met them while I was working out at the spa. They're all staying at the Hôtel de Paris and they want to go shopping in Italy. When I mentioned I had a car, they glommed onto me and said I was taking them to San Remo or else."

"Or else what?"

"Or else they won't buy me lunch. I think I'm in too deep. They've already bribed me with a *glace au chocolat*."

"What about Justin?"

"We're taking him with us. Blossom says it'll be fun."

"Who's Blossom?"

"I told you. She's this doctor's wife. Wait..." The phone was yanked away and a female voice with a strong Brooklyn accent came on the line.

"Mr. Kaplan. Your wife is a darling. Listen sweetheart, we're stealing her just for the afternoon, but I promise to bring her back, OK doll? And don't worry, we know about the baby. Between the three of us we've got eight kids and five grandkids."

Anne came back on the line.

"I just picked Justin up from the *crèche* and we've already bought him a new toy truck to play with. Can you fend for yourself for lunch?"

"Anne, don't bother about that. But watch out for Justin. You know what I mean?" Recently, there had been a rash of high-profile kidnappings of children of wealthy parents in Italy.

"We'll be careful. We're just going shopping for the day."

"But you don't know your way around San Remo. How will you know where to go?"

"Blossom says not to worry. Her son told her she'll know when she gets there... They're pulling me away. These women seriously want to shop..." she said and was abruptly gone.

That evening, over dinner, I got the rest of the story.

"I've never seen anyone shop like these women," Anne said. "It was like watching a military maneuver."

"How'd you get shanghai'd in the first place?"

"They wanted to go to San Remo. Blossom said they could find amazing bargains at Gucci's and the other Italian designer shops, but they were afraid to go by train. They'd heard stories about thieves on the trains that ripped off tourists coming back with all their expensive stuff, especially women. I happened to mention I had a car. That was all I had to say. They were all over me, begging me. I told them I couldn't. That I had to pick up my two-and-a-half-year-old from the *crèche*. They said to bring him along, that the second he got tired, they would all come back. What could I do?"

"How was the border crossing?"

"You would have been proud of the Italians. The second the border guards saw Justin, they made us go through two checkpoints, not just one like everyone else. Then they double-checked everything, made me open the trunk. They didn't care about the rest of us, but they wanted to check Justin's passport and make sure he was with me. They're very protective of children."

"So how'd you find the way? You've never been there."

"It was unbelievable. We saw a sign to San Remo, but when we got to the outskirts of the city we had no idea where to go. I just kept driving down what looked like a main road. I told them I was lost and Blossom said not to worry. When we stopped at a red light, she opens the window and screams out in English in the loudest, brassiest New York voice I've ever heard, 'WHERE'S GUCCI'S?!'

"I was never so mortified in my life. I literally cringed. People in the street stared at us. Then all at once some man dashes up to the window and says, 'Americans! I love Americans! Gucci's is not far. Just go straight for three blocks and turn right at the light. You can't miss it!' And just like that we were parked outside Gucci's."

"So that's all it takes to find anything in Europe? No maps, guides, satellite positioning. You just have to yell it out?"

"Apparently."

"Might not work for us. We don't have that Brooklyn tone of authority."

"Believe me, everything they did was like no one else. I've never seen women shop like this in my life."

"Why? What'd they do?"

"They ran to all the good shops. Gucci's, Ferragamo's, Bottega Veneta, Versace's, Fendi's. They picked out the most expensive stuff: handbags, shoes, scarves, belts, whatever. But they didn't buy them. Instead, they just wrote down the price in these little notepads. Then they ran and compared their notes to things in the other shops, scribbling away a mile a minute. It was amazing. It was like watching a well-oiled team of accountants or something. Finally, I told them Justin was getting tired, which was true, and they said, No problem. They'd be done in twenty minutes. And sure enough, they compared notepads, found the best buys on each thing, each one ran like crazy from shop to shop and in twenty minutes they had bought enough to equip half the women in Manhattan. They piled into the car and we were back in France in less than forty-five minutes."

"Well, I hoped they thanked you."

"Apparently if we're ever in Brooklyn, we've got free medical care for life."

"At French medical prices, that might not be so far off," I said.

The next day, Anne had another surprise.

"It's all set. We're spending the weekend with Stuart and Glenda."

"Who's Stuart and Glenda?"

"Sally says Stuart owns George's. It's the super cool pub in Monte. Everyone hangs out there. Well, the Brits and the Aussies, anyway – and the Scandinavian babes interested in them. Max and Nigel practically live there."

"Monte? We're calling Monte Carlo 'Monte' now?"

"Well, you want me to get with it, don't you? We're part of the in-crowd now. Stuart wants to show us his *mas*" (farmhouse).

"Why do I want to see Stuart's *mas*?"

"So we can get to know them. Only we're not allowed to ask them what they do. Sally says we've been guilty of a bad *faux pas*, asking people what their occupation is. She says only Americans do that and in Europe that's a no-no."

"Why is it a *faux pas*? In America, everyone judges you by your profession. If Americans didn't ask people what they did, we wouldn't know what to say to one another."

"Well, with people with money, it's considered terrifically *gauche*. Such things are supposed to be beneath them."

"Well, they're not beneath them when the rent is due," I muttered.

"What was that?"

"Nothing. What does one wear to a weekend at a *mas*? I hope we're not shooting foxes or something equally stupid that people with money pretend is fun."

"I don't know," she said. "I'll have to ask Sally."

That Saturday, Justin in tow, we drove to Mougins, north of Cannes, where we met Sally, Max, Stuart and Glenda for lunch at the Ferme de Mougins near the town square. It wasn't Roger Vergé's famed Moulin de Mougins, the Guide Michelin three-star restaurant that people came from all over the world to try, but a local place with solid bistro food that

Stuart and Glenda liked, for which we were grateful, since a lunch at the Moulin would've blown our entire budget for months. We ate at an outdoor table under the trees while Justin played with the owner's dog.

"So how do you spend your time?" Anne asked. Having been warned against asking people what they do, she thought this would be a good way to get around the topic. Sally rolled her eyes.

"Right now, I'm fixing up this *mas* we just bought," Stuart said. "Also, I've been thinking about some business investments. There's a hotel in Roquebrune I've been eying. Right on the water. What do you think?" he asked me.

"I thought the tourist business was down this year," I said.

"That's a concern," Stuart agreed. He was an easy-going older type in an English country gentleman's flannel shirt with sandy-colored hair. He was originally from Philadelphia, he said. His wife, Glenda, was astonishing. We had first seen her from the back. She was wearing white short-short hot pants, knee-length white leather boots and had long blonde hair that she wore in a ponytail. She had an amazing figure and looked for all the world like a sexy NBA cheerleader till she turned around and you realized that despite a face-lift that she had to be in her fifties at least.

"What about the money? I hear prime property in Roquebrune is pretty expensive," I said.

"When I was eighteen I inherited $60 million," he said.

"That was clever."

"Not really," he shrugged. "When I was twenty-five, I inherited real money."

"So you're like rich as anything?" I asked.

"Pretty much. It's not all it's cracked up to be, you know."

"Actually, I don't know. But I'd like to."

"That's what everyone says," he said.

"So why the pub in Monte?" I asked, trying to be with it by calling Monte Carlo 'Monte.' "It wasn't for the money."

"Just wanted a place to hang out. Actually, it's doing very well," he said. "Don't know if I'll keep it though. Might want to spend more time out here once we build the *mas*."

"How'd you two meet?" Anne asked, indicating him and Glenda.

"Hong Kong," Glenda said. "I had just come home."

"How's that?"

"Horrible long story," Glenda said. "You don't want to be bored by it."

"Of course he does," Anne said, indicating me. "He's a writer. He'll eat it up, then steal it and use it in a story."

"How'd you get to Hong Kong?" I asked.

"From Manchuria. My family were White Russians, you see," she said, and began telling me of her childhood in Manchuria and Shanghai, where her parents had fled during the Russian Revolution. "All very Doctor Zhivago," she said. "When the Japanese came to Manchuria, we fled to Hong Kong. I was just a little girl."

"How'd you like growing up in Hong Kong?"

"I loved it. After Russian, Cantonese and English were my first languages. I would chatter away in Cantonese with my *amah*. Hong Kong then was an amazing place for a kid. All the little shops and markets with their exotic smells in these narrow crowded streets, the old men taking their caged birds for a walk and of course, proper etiquette schools for girls that my parents insisted upon. We always wore white lace gloves. There were wonderful parties on the Peak, with cakes and Chinese orchestras and dancing to American music and kumquat trees on the terraces and fireworks over the harbor. Then came Pearl Harbor. My father sent my mother and me out on the last ship, her jewels sewed into her dress, the Japanese planes bombing and strafing overhead. My father had to try and save the business and transfer money for us. I remember it was just before Christmas and I asked him to bring me my Chinese dolls that I had to leave behind. He said he'd try though I could see by his face that he was worried about more than dolls. Father said he'd be out on the next flight, but we never saw him again."

"Then what happened?"

"We were on this ship to Australia, but it was sunk. A Jap submarine. We were in lifeboats for weeks and finally got picked up by an Aussie fishing boat. I'll never forget the smell of fish from the hold. It smelled awful, but I've loved the smell of fish ever since because Momma said it meant we were going to live."

"How'd you like Australia?"

"The Aussies were wonderful; they took us in. You can still hear it in my English. But after the war, Mother wanted to go back to Hong Kong and try to find Father. She never did, but we stayed on and then Stuart came along. We met at the Governor's Ball and that was that."

"She was pretty hot looking," Stuart said.

"I still am, darling. Don't you think?" she said, laying her hand on my arm.

"When I first saw you, I thought you were twenty," I said, trying to avoid Anne's eyes.

"You see. White Russian women stay sexy forever. My mother lived to almost ninety and the men were still after her," Glenda said.

"So when are we going to see the famous *mas*?" Max asked. "I've heard it's quite a property."

"Just wait. And don't forget the *baguettes* we've heard so much about," Stuart said to Anne.

We formed a three-car caravan that followed Stuart up N85 and then on country roads for miles into the countryside. We arrived at the iron gate of a property surrounded by hedges and a wire fence that seemed to extend for miles. Instead of unlocking the gate, Stuart rang a large brass bell that tolled like a church bell across the hills. After a few minutes, a short Frenchman with narrow eyes and a weathered beret unlocked the gate.

"This is Hivert. He looks after the place for us," Stuart said, getting back in the car and driving up a long gravel road to what seemed like the main structure of a stone *mas*, but which we soon realized was only one of three large two-story *mases* in the process of construction. The three buildings formed an open "U" shape and were connected to each other by scaffolding. While Glenda, Anne, Sally and Justin went inside the central structure, Stuart insisted on giving Max and me a complete tour of the property, which extended for what seemed like several miles in every direction.

"When it's built, it'll have everything. Swimming pool, cabanas, a gym for working out, tennis courts, a theatre for screening films, satellite TV in every room, a separate studio in the woods for Glenda to do her painting, everything," Stuart said.

In a large grassy area bordered by tall oaks, two pretty teenage girls were sunbathing on beach lounges. "That's where I'm going to put the pool," Stuart said. "Have to get rid of those oaks, though."

"*Ils sont fous, les gens riches,*" Hivert muttered.

"*Pourquoi?*" I asked him.

"Because these trees are *chênes des truffes*. Cutting them down is *une follie*. To attempt such an *acte d'infamie* is an invitation to *sabotage*, eh?"

"Doesn't the *patron* know about the oaks and the truffles?" I gestured toward Stuart, who was talking with Max as he paced out the dimensions of an Olympic-size pool.

"I told him, but he said it doesn't matter. But at night, Monsieur, one sometimes sees lights and men with *les cochons truffiers,* the pigs with the good noses for the truffles, always around. This is asking for trouble, *je crois.*"

Stuart introduced us to his daughters, Genevieve and Solange.

"How do like your new country house?" I asked them.

"It's boring. There's nothing to do here," the older, Genevieve said.

"That's the whole idea. A place to get away for peace and quiet," Stuart said. "There are no clubs, no *jeux de video*, no boys. It's stupid," Solange pouted. "I want to go back to Monte."

"You'll like it when you're a bit older. You'll see," Stuart said.

"I'll never like it. It's too far. No one will ever come out here," Solange said, chin quivering.

We tramped through thick woods and fields where Stuart

planned to plant a vineyard. "Kids," he said. "I don't know. Glenda likes it. She thinks they spend too much time with these rich kids. A lot of drugs, fast cars, too many boys. She thinks maybe bringing them out here will give them an appreciation of something else."

"They're at the wrong age for this," I suggested.

"I know," Stuart shrugged. "But I love it out here. Otherwise, I'd sell it. Anyone want to buy a *mas*?"

"Why do I get the sense it's out of my price range? Max?" I said.

"It's a huge property. Get it going, you could feed half of France," Max said.

That evening, after a huge *pot au feu*, with a thirty-year-old Grand Cru Burgundy from Stuart's cellar, caviar from Glenda's favorite *épicerie fine*, and our *baguettes*, we drove back to Eze.

"I don't see those girls wanting to stay out at the *mas* on weekends," I said to Anne as we drove on the *Moyenne Corniche*, the lights of the coast barely visible in the darkness below.

"I know. It's hard not to spoil them."

"I guess being poor has its advantages. At least we don't have to worry about that with Justin."

"We're not poor," Anne said. "We don't live poor. We live like millionaires on the French Riviera, for God's sake."

"I don't know how we manage it."

"And don't be too sure about not spoiling Justin. He's growing up with these same kids. Most of the kids in his *crèche* arrive by limousine or helicopter. What kind of values do you suppose he's picking up?"

"We'll have to watch it, I guess."

"Not just Justin. All of us," Anne said and all at once, I thought of Neitzsche and Zarathustra's tree in the woods in Eze and wished I had a piece of wood to knock on for luck. Instead I rubbed an American quarter that I had kept in my pocket since we had left California, a talisman that somehow connected us to home.

I made the turn from the *Moyenne Corniche* and drove down the dark winding road to the *Basse Corniche* and Eze-sur-Mer. Princess

Grace, the former movie star Grace Kelly, had been killed in a car crash three years earlier on this same road. Neitzsche had said that the tree was waiting, waiting for lightning and I suddenly sensed that something was coming. What I didn't know was that it would be unexpected and soon – and that like lightning, it would come from the sky.

Chapter 12

A Falling Star

I was sitting at a table in the Café de Paris, the restaurant-café catty-corner to the Casino and directly opposite the Hôtel de Paris in Monte Carlo. I had finished my morning's work early and was waiting for Anne to bring Justin from the *crèche* so we could go to lunch. During the lunch and dinner hours, the Café de Paris was crowded and tables were hard to get, but in the mornings the outdoor tables under the awnings were nearly empty and you could sit over a *croissant* and a *café au lait*, looking out over the flowers in the plaza in front of the Casino with the just-washed smell of the street and sidewalk hosed down by the waiter and read the latest news in *Nice-Matin*, the main newspaper in our part of the Côte d'Azur.

The front-page story was the cancellation of the *Carneval* in Nice this year because of the bad weather. The French and British governments had finally agreed to build a tunnel under the English Channel; some were calling it a "Chunnel." In a smaller article, it said that NASA's Voyager 2 spacecraft was approaching the planet Uranus, the first space probe ever to do so. Apparently, it had found evidence that Uranus had ten moons that no one had ever known about. I sipped my *café au lait* and thought about the book.

In the current chapter, I advanced the intrigue with a secret meeting in the jungle ruins of Angkor Thom between the Shan warlord, Bhun Sa and Son Lot, a character I had patterned after Nuon Chea, the Khmer Rouge's murderous "Brother Number Two," who together with Pol Pot had ordered the killing fields of Cambodia. Hidden in the moonlit ruins were nearly four thousand tons of morphine base, the result of virtually the entire year's opium production of the Golden Triangle, enough to supply the entire world with heroin, enough to finance Son Lot's war. The problem I had to deal with in the chapter was what would stop Son Lot from just having his Khmer Rouge troops take the morphine base from the warlord Bhun Sa by force. I decided to have Bhun Sa have the place rigged with *plastique* explosive, so if Son Lot or anyone else tried to use force, the morphine would be destroyed.

At that moment, a blond young man with a three-day stubble sat down at my table.

"Please excuse," he said in a good, but accented English, "but they won't stop following me." Near the table were two young women in bikini tops and shorts who couldn't take their eyes off the young man. "If we pretend we are talking business, maybe they go away," he said.

"They're pretty. Most young men your age wouldn't complain," I said.

"That's what I used to think. Now they won't leave me alone. If I go to the W.C., they are outside waiting."

Suddenly I recognized him. "Wait a minute. You're Boris Becker. You won Wimbledon. No wonder they're after you."

"Everyone wants something. I did not expect all this," he said, looking down.

"Do people think it was a fluke? You beating someone unseeded, like Curran, instead of Jimmy Connors or McEnroe?"

"That's what the sportswriters say. What do you think?"

"On grass, with that serve and those diving shots. I think you'd 've beaten Connors and McEnroe anyway. And I'm an American."

The waiter came and Becker ordered a Warsteiner beer. Out of the corner of my eye, I saw the girls whispering to each other.

"So what are you doing in Monte Carlo?" I asked.

"I'm a resident now. The taxes," he said. "All is about money. I had to get a financial manager and everything."

"How old are you?"

"Eighteen."

"*Vorsichtig auftreten*," (Watch your step) I said in German. "They'll all want a piece of you."

"I know," he said.

"Already?"

He nodded. "So, what do you do?"

"I'm a writer."

"I wish I could do something creative like that. Do you believe, already in Germany they want me to write my life story? I'm eighteen. I play tennis. That's my life story."

"I wish my tennis was good enough to even be able to practice with you."

"Come. I let you practice with me."

"It'd be a waste of your time. I shouldn't be on the same court with you. You know, they're still waiting," I said, indicating the two girls.

"Let them wait. It isn't about me anyway. It's about famous. They don't know me."

Just then, a bushy-haired man with a large mustache approached. Becker stood up. "My manager. I have to go," he said, shaking my hand. "Perhaps we talk again. Come see me play."

"I will," I said, watching him go off with the mustached man, both of them trailed by the two girls, as Anne and Justin came and sat down.

"Who was that?" Anne asked.

"Boris Becker, the Wimbledon champ."

"Really! Nigel and Monika were there last summer. They said he was amazing."

"He is. He's a nice kid, but he's going to have a tough time."

"You mean against McEnroe and Lendl and those guys?"

"No, the tennis he'll handle. It's everything else," I said. "So, where are we going for lunch? Edmunds?" Edmunds, with its red awning on the *Basse Corniche* in Cap d'Ail was one of our regular places.

"Yes, Daddy," Justin said.

"Well, in that case, I guess someone's going to have spaghetti Bolognese," I said. Justin giggled.

"We need new people," Anne announced at Edmunds over a *lapin au moutarde*, that as usual, we told Justin was chicken, so he wouldn't think we were eating a bunny rabbit, and a white Côte du Rhone wine. "Apart from Colette, the only people we know are Sally's crowd."

"What about the doctors' wives from Brooklyn. You guys have been hanging out a lot."

"They're heading back to the States tomorrow. Although Blossom did come up with a great business idea for us."

"Oh, what's that?"

"Pets for tourists. You know, rent out little poodles for women tourists to take into restaurants like the French women."

"She might be on to something. Sometimes I feel naked in France, dining without a dog."

"Doesn't have to be dogs. The Chinese take birds for walks," she said.

"Cocteau had a pet lobster. Maybe we could try one of those on a leash."

"He'd just end up in a pot as somebody's lunch," she said.

"What's all this about new people?"

"There's this organization, 'The American Club of the Riviera.' They're having a lunch tomorrow. You never know, we might make some contacts. You said you wanted to meet other writers. You know, the literary life, discussing life and Sartre at sidewalk cafés. Minus three-year-olds," she said, pulling Justin away from a woman's pet Schnauzer, growling at him from under the table.

But first I had to open a new bank account, one closer to where we lived than the bank in Antibes. Sally had suggested we open an account in one of the many banks headquartered in Monaco. While Anne took Justin to the flower market in Monte Carlo, I walked along the Avenue de la Costa, where most of the banks were clustered. My first stop was the Credit Suisse, its hushed marble interior and mahogany desks exuding solidity and the Swiss connection promising privacy.

I sat at a desk and a banker in a tailored suit and impeccable English asked me if I wanted to open an account in francs or dollars. I needed francs for paying bills, like the rent or the electric bill, I told him. "One could do *"francs convertibles"* to take advantage of the exchange rates," he suggested. That sounded good, I said, handing him my passport and beginning to fill out the paperwork.

"And how much does Monsieur wish to deposit to start the account?" he asked.

"How about four thousand... dollars," I said, which was a sizeable chunk of our disposable cash. The rest I kept in travelers' checks denominated in Swiss francs which I had purchased back in L.A.

Suddenly his handsome smile disappeared. "I'm sorry, Monsieur," he said, pulling the papers away and handing me back my passport. "We have a minimum deposit requirement."

"Oh, what's the minimum?" I said, thinking I might have to use the extra two thousand I was holding in cash dollars in reserve.

"A quarter of a million, Monsieur."

"Ah... of course ... Francs or dollars?" I muttered, as if it mattered.

"Dollars."

"That's a wee bit more than I want to deposit," I said. "Is there another bank in Monte Carlo – with a lower minimum perhaps?"

"I doubt it, Monsieur. I believe there are banks in Nice for that sort of thing," he sniffed, tossing my papers in the wastebasket and walking away. I had to admire the way he did it. I had rarely been so thoroughly snubbed. I walked outside and not sure what to do, realized I wasn't far from Bobby G.'s souvenir factory. I walked down the street and around to the back entrance to Bobby G.'s place. One of his souvenir stamping machines was going full blast and the place smelled of chemicals. Bobby G. was showing a workman something as I walked in.

"How's business?" I asked.

"You look like you could use a drink," he said and pulled a bottle of Stolichnaya vodka from a refrigerator and poured us both full glasses.

"*Santé*," I said.

"Mud in your eye," he said. "What's going on?"

I told him how I'd been snubbed at the Credit Suisse.

"Yeah, they're good at that," he said. "You should try Barclay's Bank on the Boulevard Princesse Charlotte. Wait, I'll make a call."

He got on the phone and when he came back, told me "It's all set. Just ask for Jean-Philippe."

"Thanks. How's business?"

"I'm negotiating for a Disney license for Bulgaria. What do you think? Mickey Mouse for kids in Bulgaria?"

"Why Bulgaria?"

"The license is available. It's not too expensive. What do you think?"

"Disney's good. Pretty international. People'll always spend money on their kids."

"That's what I think. By the way, Gaby wants to throw a party. Kind of welcome you guys."

"Sounds great," I said, feeling woozy from the vodka. I suddenly became extremely conscious of the rotation of the Earth. "What time does the bank close?"

He consulted his watch. "You better run. I'll tell Gaby about the dinner."

I somehow staggered to Barclays's Bank and quickly opened an account with a deposit of a thousand dollars.

"What about a *'francs convertibles'* account?" I slurred to the bank clerk, Jean-Philippe, barely able to sit upright as the room whirled around me.

"*Pas de problème*, Monsieur."

I met Anne and Justin window shopping outside Bulgari's. Good, more stuff I can't afford, I thought. She took one look at me and said, "I'm driving."

Once in the car back to Eze, she said, "I have just one question. How the hell did you manage to get drunk in a bank?"

"It's Monaco. They have their minimum requirements," I said thickly.

"Well, it's a good thing you only opened a checking account and not a savings account too or we'd have to scrape you off the floor," she said.

The American Club of the Riviera met for lunch in Nice at Le Méridien on the Promenade des Anglais in a dining room overlooking the port. All the members were dressed to the nines in suits and dresses and except for the waiters, we were the only ones in the room under the age of eighty.

"I feel like a teeny-bopper," I whispered to Anne, as a hostess guided us to a table of eight. One of the older women with an oddly border Southern accent, wearing an estate-style necklace and bracelet with diamonds the size of marbles, introduced herself as a Texan and told us she threw the best parties on the Riviera. "Everyone comes, hon'. Even all the little princes and dukes and things. You'll have to come." Her husband, a former U.S. ambassador to Uruguay tried to say something and she told him to not interrupt.

"We seem to be the youngest ones," I said to the man next to me. He was a dignified white-haired man with a trim mustache, dressed in a Savile Row suit that looked like it came from another era.

"We're all retired. Welcome to Eternity's waiting room," he said and his wife nodded as we introduced ourselves.

"Don't be shy. The food's good here," the Diamond Lady told us as the waiter served a salmon *mousse*, which he announced as a *mousseline de saumon au coulis de crustacés*.

"Why did you retire to the Côte d'Azur?" Anne asked the man in the Savile Row suit.

"My wife's French," he said. "I was with the State Department. My last posting was Paris. Her mother lived in Cannes. Seemed a good fit."

"What about you?" Anne asked the Diamond Lady.

"Oh hon', after the post-War years in Paris, Houston was common as a fart at a bean contest."

"Interesting metaphor," Anne said.

"You come see me, darlin'," the Diamond Lady said, jangling her bracelet. "I got a million of 'em."

"So you're a writer," the Savile Row man said. "I knew a writer once. Remember David, dear," he said to his wife as my heart sank. The worst thing about telling someone you are a writer is that they always know someone who is a writer, who it turns out, is an amateur friend halfway through a TV script they hope to sell, or a cousin who has written a cookbook of Croatian recipes or something, or worst of all, the ones who say, 'My life would make an amazing story. What say I tell you about it, you scribble it up, and we'll split the royalties?' like they're doing you a favor.

"Who?" his wife said.

"You remember, David, when we were in Germany."

"No, I don't. Should I?"

"Of course you do," he said. "I was the American consul in Hamburg and he was something or other at the British Consulate. We'd see him at embassy things there and in Bonn. As a writer he did quite well, you know."

"Did he?" I said.

"I think so. Hated his job. Couldn't wait to get away. Just wanted to write. Finally sold a book and absolutely the next day he quit his job, packed up the family and moved to Crete. Book didn't sell, of course."

"That happens a lot," Anne put in.

"So I gather. The second or third one though did quite well. Something about a spy catching a cold or something. Cornwell, that's it! That was his name. He didn't write under it. Used a *nom de plume*, as it were. Something French. Can't remember it though."

"*Le Carré?* John Le Carré? Was that it?" I asked, not quite believing what I was hearing.

"That's it. John whatever. Do you know him?" he said.

"He's the reason I became a writer of spy novels. He made it possible for a spy thriller to be taken as a serious novel, not just entertainment."

"Well, there you go," he said, gently patting me on the shoulder. "Perhaps there's hope for you too."

"You never know," his wife said, patting her lips with a napkin. "You never know."

That night, Anne and I stayed up late, sipping tea and talking in front of the fireplace. I was coming to love the Villa Olivia, its big brick fireplace and book-lined walls in the *salon* with its French doors to the stone *terrasse* and garden. I liked waking up in the morning to the distant blue of the sea through the balcony door of our bedroom and I loved sitting with Anne that night imagining the possibilities. Le Carré, who was the best thriller writer, had done exactly what I had done. He'd taken his chance and gone for it and maybe it could happen to me too. The Southeast Asia book was about a third done and I was liking what I was doing with it.

"It's really good," Anne said. She'd been reading the chapters as I finished them. "I think it's the best thing you've ever done."

"So do I," I said. "Whatever happens, they can't take that away from me. Maybe they won't know the difference, but I will."

I woke up the next morning filled with resolve that if anything, I would write even better. Through this old retired diplomat at the

American Club, I had somehow caught a glimpse of the real thing. Writing that mattered.

I was writing the next chapter. Sawyer, Suong, and the opium trader, Toonsang's group, had pulled off the trail to avoid a Thai army patrol. Toonsang had detected advance warning of their approach by the scent of gasoline fumes from their jeeps. It reminded my protagonist, Sawyer, how the Viet Cong would get advance warning of American patrols in the dense jungle by the smell of the Americans' after-shave lotion. Sawyer cursed himself for being rusty in the jungle. He was telling himself he would have to do better, when Anne knocked on the door and came in, something she never did when I was writing.

"Something awful's happened," she said.

"Justin?!!!" I started. She shook her head.

"It's the Challenger," she said and for a moment I didn't connect what she was saying and just stared blankly at her.

"The space shuttle. The Challenger."

"What about it? Wait a minute. Wasn't that teacher on it? What is it?"

"It exploded. They're all dead."

"It can't be," I said. "All of them?"

She nodded. We ran out to the *salon* and stood there, transfixed, watching the television. On the screen was a shot of a trail of smoke in a blue sky that split into three tendrils and a radio-transmitted voice saying in understated NASA-ese that there had been "a major malfunction." The French news channel broke in and the announcer said that the space shuttle *américain* had blown up some seventy-three seconds into the flight. All seven *des astronautes* were presumed dead.

The shuttle mission had attracted a lot of attention because of the diversity of the crew: two were women, another was an Asian-American, one an African-American; also because it was launching a special probe to study Halley's Comet, due in March, and because one of the women astronauts was a New Hampshire schoolteacher,

Christa McAuliffe, who had been selected in a nationwide contest and who was going to teach school lessons from space.

"My God, her children watched it happen," Anne said, reading my mind.

"You mean kids from her class?"

"The kids from her school, her own children, kids from all over the world were watching. They watched her die. How could it have happened?"

"I don't know."

On the television, they replayed the launch of the space shuttle, its fiery ascent into the sky and then the explosion and those splitting trails of smoke we were to become so familiar with as the scene was replayed again and again on television over the next week.

"What could cause such a thing?"

"Probably some stupid part that costs a buck that somebody skimped on to save two-bits. Or some asshole who didn't torque a bolt to tolerance because he was too damn stupid or lazy and the guy who was supposed to double-check got yanked to do something else. It's always something stupid," I said angrily, not sure why I was so angry, but I was.

That night we went for dinner to Maria and the Chef's in Villefranche. Although the restaurant was crowded, it was quiet. Conversations were subdued. People glanced at us and looked away and once or twice I heard someone say we were *américains*. When it came time to pay, Madame Maria and le Chef came up to our table and refused to accept our money.

"*Nous sommes américains aussi, Monsieur.* We are with you," Monsieur le Chef said, tears streaming down his face and before I knew it, we were all crying, Justin too, not knowing why, just because Anne and I were. As we walked out of the restaurant, someone behind us in the restaurant shouted *"Vive l'Amérique!"* and others echoed it.

'Boy, the next time someone says something about the French," Anne said, choking. I took her hand.

"I know," I said, thinking again about good luck and bad luck and how you can never tell which you are getting. Christa McAuliffe, the schoolteacher, had been the lucky one. There had been a nationwide contest. Thousands of teachers had tried for it and finally they had narrowed it down to two and they picked her and I wondered how the other teacher, the one who came in second and who hadn't gotten to go felt now.

I thought about Boris Becker flaming like a new star in the tennis world and wondered if winning Wimbledon at seventeen was really good luck or not and about us and how if I hadn't broken my foot we never would have come to the Riviera or felt what these French people felt for us. I thought about Zarathustra's tree and how lightning strikes and how sometimes stars fall out of the sky and explode. It was a mystery, all of it, and Anne's and Justin's hands in mine seemed very fragile as we walked back to the car under the stars over Villefranche.

Chapter 13

Le Sporting Life

It was Adrian who introduced us to *Le Sporting Club* in Monte Carlo. Normally, it was a nightclub popular with the international set, but on Monday nights they would show an American movie in English and sometimes on weekends, there were sporting events. I had met Adrian through Bobby G. and Gaby, who told us that he was a fan of my book, *Scorpion*, and wanted to meet me. For a writer, having someone who likes your work is a terrific basis for friendship with people with whom you might otherwise have nothing in common. Adrian was head of operations for Europe and the Middle East for a large American oil equipment company whose European subsidiary was headquartered, for tax reasons, in Monaco. Adrian lived in an apartment above the Boulevard des Moulins, the main street in Monte Carlo, though he rarely spent time there because he traveled so much on business, he explained in his French-accented English.

After drinks at his apartment, we had dinner at Monsieur Zizi's, a restaurant on the Avenue St. Charles. The owner Zizi was a jazz fanatic. We listened to John Coltrane on the sound system as we sampled the best Vietnamese spring rolls Anne and I had ever tasted.

Monsieur Zizi, a well-groomed Vietnamese man in a tan suit, came over to our table and Adrian introduced us after congratulating Zizi for having just gotten out of jail.

"*Une affaire absurde*," Zizi sniffed. "A trivial dispute over finances. The *Monagasques* are too *sérieux* on issues of money," he confided.

"You like jazz?" Anne asked, listening to a Miles Davis solo that echoed out to the street. With the restaurant windows brightly lit and the street dark outside, being in Zizi's felt like being on a ship at night.

"*J'adore le jazz américain*. It is everything, every emotion, in life," Zizi said.

"Jazz and the martini are America's two great contributions to world civilization," Adrian pronounced.

"How many languages do you speak?" Anne asked.

"Only eight," Adrian said.

"Only! I can barely manage French – and not very well at that. They make fun of me," Anne said.

"*Pas de bêtises*! You are a beautiful woman and the fact that you even try to speak French already makes you more *charmante* than most other Americans," he said, snapping his finger and motioning for the *garçon* to bring her more wine. "So, what did you think of Reagon's speech?"

President Reagan had made a television speech about the Challenger tragedy. It had ended with a line about the astronauts that was being quoted around the world. How they had waved goodbye "and slipped the surly bonds of earth to touch the face of God."

"It was sad," Anne said. "I keep thinking about her own children and her pupils watching her blow up."

"I thought it was a good speech. The thing is, every time I hear a politician make a speech or come up with a line everyone quotes, I always wish they'd have credits like a movie, so you know who really wrote it. I mean maybe Ronald Reagan did write that line – and more power to him, but let's face it. He's an actor, not a writer. Just once, I'd like to see the writer get credit," I said.

"I understand. Mind you, I think we American expatriates are more patriotic than the stay-at-home variety," Adrian said.

"That's something I don't understand," Anne said. "If you're an American, how come you speak with a French accent?"

"My father was an oil man with Socony, this is before it became Standard Oil. That was something I identified with in your book, *Scorpion*," he told me (in the book the title character, codenamed 'Scorpion,' grows up among the Bedouin in Arabia when his father, an American oilman, is killed). "Only I grew up in Turkey, going to the French schools in Izmir and Istanbul, not Arabia like your Scorpion."

"What was it like back then in Turkey?"

"It was amazing for a kid. A different world then. Very international, very sophisticated. Germans, French, British, Italians. The parties, the cafés, the bazaars, the baths, the Golden Horn and ships from all over the world, businessmen in fezes, spies from Russia and the Balkans, sailors on leave, the men in the coffee houses with their hubble-bubbles, the call of the water sellers in the streets and all the different quarters, Greeks, Kurds, Jews, the sin quarters with their *fin de siècle décor* and American jazz, the *luxe* hotel bars in Istanbul, where uniformed boys with signs would call out your name for a phone call and everyone would know how important you were. It was Europe when it was still Europe and the exotic East all at the same time, until the war of course."

"What happened?"

"Turkey was always too close to Germany. My father said we had to leave. We eventually made it to Egypt. From there, we caught a freighter to the States. That was a trip, I can tell you. Dodging German U-boats in the Mediterranean and the Atlantic. Never thought we'd make it. I'd been with the Office of War Information, the forerunner of the OSS in Istanbul, plus my languages. Naturally, I thought they would send me to Europe or the Middle East, but of course, the American Army, in its infinite wisdom sent me to the Pacific instead," he laughed. "I was at Leyte Gulf and Okinawa. After the war, Texaco sent me to the Belgian Congo. Of course, trouble followed me there too."

"I know. I was in Katanga Province in the Sixties, a young pup trying to write freelance articles," I said. In the background, Monsieur Zizi had put on an Ornette Coleman track and the saxophone squeaks were like a musical track bringing back New York and Africa and that Jack Kennedy time.

"I thought I felt an affinity in your writing, that our paths had crossed before," Adrian said. "Speaking of which, Andy, there's been something I've been meaning to ask you ever since I read *Scorpion*."

It always made me uncomfortable when people asked me about my work. It made me feel like a magician talking about how he did a trick. There was a sense that no matter what you said, part of the magic was about to be lost.

"Oh?" I said.

"When were you in Bahrain?"

"Why do you ask?"

"I'll tell you. I go to Bahrain at least three or four times a year for the past twenty years. I know Bahrain like the back of my hand. After all, it's not a big place. And yet, you know Bahrain better than I do. You have things in that book even I didn't know."

"Adrian, I've never been to Bahrain in my life."

"*Pas possible!* I don't understand. How is that possible?"

"I don't know. I did a lot of research. It's amazing what you can dig up if you're serious."

"I don't believe it. You make it so authentic. It's accurate down to the very streets and little *souks*. And in the Middle East, believe me, it's hard to get things right. Amazing."

"Thanks. You've made my evening. That and Zizi's food and the jazz," I said, munching one of Monsieur Zizi's spring rolls wrapped in a lettuce leaf. "What's this about your daughter having married a billionaire?" I said.

"Ah, that would have been clever," Adrian said.

"No, merely practical," Anne said.

"It's not my son-in-law. It's his brother, Arthur, who's the billionaire."

"Only one brother rich? That's got to be an interesting family dynamic. Can't be inherited," Anne said.

"No, friendship."

"Must be quite a friend."

Adrian leaned close. "Khaddafi," he whispered.

"Libya's Khaddafi?" How did an American become friends with Khaddafi?" I asked.

"And make money out of it?" Anne added.

"From what I'm told, he went to Libya as an engineer for an oil company. Khaddafi was a junior officer at the time. They became friends. Arthur taught him English. When Khaddafi took over, he insisted only on dealing with Arthur. Anyone who wanted to do business with Khaddafi, oil, arms, anything, had to go through Arthur. They've done very well by each other."

"And the other brother. Jealous?" Anne said.

"That's not my affair. But now that I know your secrets and you mine, perhaps you'd join me for a little escapade?" Adrian asked, as Zizi served us a *poulet au citron* accompanied by Vietnamese sauces.

"Not Bahrain?"

"No, the fights. There's a Junior Welterweight World title bout this weekend at Le Sporting Club. The champion, the Argentine, Sacco, versus the Italian challenger, Oliva."

"I don't know," Anne frowned. "Fights aren't my thing."

"Please, you'll be my guests. Besides, if you don't do *Le Sporting*, what do you do on weekends?" Adrian said.

"We play tourist. We're still new," Anne said.

That was true enough. We were still exploring the Côte, starting in St. Tropez. The last time we'd gone, having lunch under the trees at Le Café on the Place des Lices, I spotted Brigitte Bardot, barely recognizable in sweats, sunglasses and a headscarf, picking over some fruit in front of the *épicerie*. I pointed her out to Anne.

"She was the sexiest woman on the planet," I said.

"What are you talking about?" Anne said.

"That's Brigitte Bardot."

"Really? She was famous. My parents never let me go to her movies. Back then, French movies were considered *risqué*," Anne said, turning to look.

"For teenage boys of my generation, she was the stuff that sexual fantasies are made of."

"I'm not sure I want to hear this."

"Nowadays, all the actresses try to be sexy. There's a kind of sameness. But Brigitte, trust me, if you were male, you couldn't look at her and not think of sex."

"What's sex, Daddy?" Justin asked, looking up from the truck he was playing with.

"It's a game Daddies and Mommies play," I said.

"How do you play?"

"Don't ask your Dad. He's still trying to figure it out," Anne said, then to me, "You're lucky we live in France."

"*Vive la différence*," I said.

Then there were the artistic villages in the hills, Biot, in the hills northeast of Antibes, where we bought Leger-inspired blue vases, Vallauris, between Juan-les-Pins and Cannes, where Picasso learned to do ceramics and founded the pottery industry, with dozens of shops with their *art modern* pottery, La Turbie, with its massive Roman monument erected by the soldiers of Caesar Augustus, and Cagnes sur Mer, where we visited the Renoir house, with its view and its olive trees and large *atelier* with Renoir's bed in it, so even near the end of his life, he could still work, that seemed familiar to us; "*très déjà vu*-ish" as Anne said, because it had all been described to us before by Dido Renoir.

We had met Dido, widow of the legendary French film director, Jean Renoir (*Grand Illusion, Les Jeux Sont Fait*, etc.) in Los Angeles through Norman and Peggy Lloyd. Norman was a well-known character actor and at the time, he had a starring role as one of the doctors in *St. Elsewhere*, a hit TV show. Dido invited us to lunch at her house in Beverly Hills.

At first, when we drove up, we thought we were at the wrong address. It was a small, even nondescript, ranch-style house; more San Fernando Valley than Beverly Hills, but when we walked inside we couldn't believe our eyes. The walls were covered with Renoir paintings, dozens of them. Hanging on the wall behind the faded couch were more Renoirs, two Cézannes, a Van Gogh, a Monet, and two Gauguins. There were Chagalls, Braques, Picassos, and a Utrillo painting of houses and trees half-hanging out of a broken frame in the hallway. Dominating the living room over the fireplace was a large painting Renoir had done of his son, when Jean was about twelve, in a blue hunting outfit. It was astonishing! This ordinary house, inhabited by a lone woman in her late eighties or nineties and without any kind of security or alarm system, had a better Impressionist collection than any museum in America.

Dido gave us tea and cookies. I offered to get the Utrillo frame fixed for her. "I'm too old to bother with it," she shrugged and told us how she and Jean had visited his father, the painter, when he was sick in the house in Cagnes-sur-Mer. That's where they were heading when the Germans marched into Paris. They fled south in a tide of refugees, rolling up all the paintings we saw around us and stuffing them in the trunk of the car. Dido told us how they had to jump out of the car and hide in a ditch a number of times when German planes had strafed the road. It wasn't until they finally got down to Cagnes that they unrolled the paintings and saw that luckily none of them had been hit by bullets. "At least we kept the paintings. For Jean they were important, not like the Gauguin children," she sniffed. "They sold theirs off anytime they needed a few francs."

She described the *atelier* in Cagnes and how they would wheel Auguste outside in his chair under the olive trees, till he was too ill even for that, so that when we lived in Eze and came to see Renoir's house like tourists, it was like visiting a place we knew.

Another favorite place was the Jean Cocteau fisherman's chapel, the Chapelle St. Pierre on the quai in Villefranche. Before this, I had never been a fan of Cocteau, finding his art too *Parisien*, too affectedly stylistic, until we went inside the little church built for the fishermen and for their women to pray for their safe return from the sea back in the days when Villefranche was still a real fishing village.

Every inch of the small church, the walls, the ceilings, the nave, was covered with the most wonderful Biblical scenes and angels, done by Cocteau with obvious love and devotion for the fishermen whose church it was. Anne and I fell in love with it and I always thought of Cocteau differently after that. In a way, it was like going into the Sainte Chapelle in Paris and being overwhelmed not just with the beauty of the stained glass, but the power of the religious belief that had created it. The Cocteau chapel was an expression of love and Anne and I walked out onto the cobblestones of the *quai* holding hands in awe of what we had seen.

But the place we loved best, and kept going back to, was Saint Paul de Vence, with its cobblestone streets and artist studios, its medieval walls and fountains. We would always go for lunch in the garden inside the walled Colombe d'Or, near the *boules* court in the Place de Café. Instead of ordering *le déjeuner*, we would get the dozens of assorted *hors d'oeuvres* that were more than enough to fill us up.

The walls of the inn's restaurant and garden were hung with Matisses, Braques, Roualts, Legers and Picassos, all of whom had been patrons. We also liked the outdoor bar with its arch looking out toward the garden where the barman Auguste told us stories about the celebrities, Yves Montand, Simone Signoret, Jean-Paul Sartre, Simone de Beauvoir, the American writer, James Baldwin, and others who used to hang out there and the painters, like Chagall and Picasso, who would sometimes pay for their dinner with a painting or a drawing if they were short of cash.

"Picasso used to drink here?" Anne asked.

"He liked pretty women. He would have liked you, Madame," the barman, Auguste, said.

"You think he might have given me a drawing?"

"Unquestionably. He would've wanted to paint you."

"You know," Anne said thoughtfully. "It almost might have been worth it."

"I'm an artist too," I said.

"Sell the book, buster."

"I already have," I reminded her.

"Still, a Picasso," she teased.

Afterward, we would wander the alleyways and shops of the medieval village to browse among the tourists and stop at the Musée du Fondation Maeght, to view the Giacometti sculptures, the Chagalls, Braques, and Miros. We were standing in front of a Miro sculpture that looked like a piece of metal with a big fork and Justin pointed at it and exclaimed "Mickey!" and I realized he was referring to a drawing in his favorite book, Maurice Sendak's *Where The Wild Things Are*, where the boy, Mickey, chases the monsters with a pitchfork. It was a revelation. Suddenly, I was seeing Miro through the eyes of a three-year-old and for the first time understanding that that had been exactly Miro's intent. Sendak's genius was to show children that *they* are the real wild things and that even as children that they have power over the monsters of their imagination. And Miro was showing us the same thing, the reality of the world as seen through the untarnished eyes of children, only if you are not lucky enough to be with a bright little three-year-old as I was, you might not see it.

"I'm so glad we came," I told Anne.

"So am I," she said and I knew she was talking about more than St. Paul de Vence.

That weekend, we went with Adrian to the prize fight at Le Sporting Club. The arena was sold out. Many Italians had come across the border to cheer for the challenger, Oliva. Adrian got us seats near the ring.

"You've been working. I can see it," Adrian said.

"I have," I said. I had just written a scene in which the opium trader, Toonsang, and his men and Sawyer, had caught two Kuomingtang deserters about to rape a Lisu woman in a jungle clearing.

"Up to your eyeballs, weren't you?"

"So deep I need a snorkel to breathe," I said. In the scene, Sawyer fears that Toonsang will use the cover of killing the deserters to have his men kill him off too and take the woman, Suong, for himself. It was a tense action scene, Sawyer's mission becoming with each step, a journey into darkness like Conrad's *Heart of Darkness* and I was right in the middle of it.

In the stands, a fight had already broken out between two men, shouting at each other in Italian. A pair of Monagasque policemen moved in quickly to break it up.

"Pretty lively crowd. I've never been to a fight before," Anne said. "Is the crowd always so rowdy?"

"Sometimes the fights in the stands are more interesting than the one in the ring," Adrian said. The Italian, Oliva, came out draped in the green-white-red colors of the Italian flag and the Italians in the stands went wild, cheering and waving signs and scarves. The announcer introduced the fighters in French and the bell sounded. The two fighters touched gloves and as soon as the Italian, Oliva, dropped his hands, the Argentine, Sacco, hit him in the face with two quick jabs. The Italian lunged after him with a big right hook and Sacco kept his left hand in the Italian's face, blood splattering from the Italian's nose. The Italian went wild, throwing right and left hooks and when the bell rang, they were furiously trading punches, the crowd cheering like crazy and urging the Italian on.

"Good fight," Adrian commented.

"I hadn't realized it was going to be so bloody," Anne said. "It's not how it looks on TV."

"That's what makes it interesting," I said.

"You mean that it's so primitive?"

"No," Adrian said. "That it's real."

The fight went on, the Italian battering Sacco with lefts and rights to the body and the Argentine keeping his left in the Italian's face till it looked like raw hamburger. In the last round, someone draped an Argentine flag over the rail and there was pushing and shoving that ended in a fistfight in the upper deck. The police rushed up, took one look at the crowd of screaming Italians, some of them brandishing wine bottles like clubs, and started to arrest the Argentine. "No, no! It was a German!" the Italian shouted in French. The Argentine, his eye blackened, shook his head. He and the Italian nodded at each other and everyone cheered.

"Why'd they say it was a German?" Anne asked.

"Everyone still hates the Germans. They get blamed for everything," Adrian said.

The fight ended in a flurry of punches from both boxers. The judges declared that the Italian, Oliva, was the new champion. It was a popular decision for the Italians who had come over the border for the fight and who began screaming and waving Italian flags. They poured out into the street, cheering and singing the Italian national anthem. Afterwards, the fight having inspired an Italian sort-of mood, we went to La Polpetta on the rue de Paradis for pasta.

"So what did you think of the fight?" Adrian asked Anne.

"Too bloody for me," she said. "I don't understand what men see in it."

"Well, it's a sport. One likes the action. It's like when people stop to look at a traffic accident. You can't help watching. What about you?" he asked me.

"Actually, I learned one of the most important things I ever learned about writing from a Mexican boxer," I said.

"How so?"

"When I first came to L.A, I had this friend, Stan, a newspaper man. He was doing an article on the Olympic Gym for the L.A. Times and he got to know a top welterweight named Carlos Palomino."

"I remember him. He lost the title to Wilfred Benitez. What about him?" Adrian said.

"They became friends. Now Stan was a big guy, six – three, six - four. He had been an amateur boxer. In fact, he had been the Ivy League Heavyweight Champion, when he was at Columbia. One day, he and Carlos got into one of these stupid arguments we men get into. Stan was saying Carlos was a much better fighter, but he was no slouch. He'd been a top amateur, was still in pretty good shape, and was a heavyweight. He was twice Carlos' size. He said, sure Carlos would outbox him and cut him up like crazy, but sooner or later, he would only have to tag Carlos one time and that would be the end of it. And Palomino kept telling him, 'You don't understand, *amigo*. You're an amateur. I'm a professional. You don't stand a chance.'

"Well, there's only one way to settle this kind of a argument. So they got into the ring."

"You men really are idiots, aren't you? It's all about whose is bigger, isn't it?" Anne said.

"I thought women already knew that about us. French women anyway," Adrian said. "So what happened?"

"Stan asked if I wanted to come, be his second. I said sure. They get in the ring, spar for about a minute and all of a sudden Palomino hit Stan with a left hook in the midsection and Stan went down like a felled tree. That was it. He was done. I had to help Carlos drag Stan back to his corner and after about a couple of minutes, Stan was finally able to talk.

"'How'd you do that?' Stan asked.

"'What do you mean?' Carlos said.

"'What kind of punch was that? I mean, I've been hit plenty of times, but I've never been hit like that in my life. How'd you do that?'

"'It was just a left hook,' Carlos said.

"'No, come on. I really want to know. What kind of punch was that?'

"'I told you, I'm a professional. Listen,' Carlos said. 'When you aim a punch at a man's midsection, where do you aim?'

"'I don't know,' Stan said. 'Somewhere around here,' pointing at his solar plexus. 'Why, where do you aim?'

"'When I hit a man in the midsection, I aim for his backbone,' Carlos said. 'That's the difference between an amateur and a professional, *hombre*.'"

"So what did you learn?" Adrian asked.

"I'm a professional writer, Adrian. This isn't a game for me. When I write, I aim for the backbone too," I said.

Chapter 14

Lunch Italian Style

Fridays were market day in Ventimiglia, the Italian city across the border from the French town of Menton. The main *piazza* was filled with farmers' stalls selling fruits, vegetables, cheeses, local wines, olive oils and pottery along with rows of wooden stands and tents filled with designer clothes and goods, some genuine, most knock-offs. There were discounted seconds and hard-to-detect fakes of Louis Vuitton, Ferragamo, Gucci, Bottega Veneta, Ted Lapidus, Armani, and such and men at folding sidewalk tables selling shiny Rolex and Piaget watches for thirty dollars.

After browsing and shopping, a bunch of us, Max, Sally, Bobby G., Gaby, Nigel, Monika, Anne, Justin, and I, would have lunch at Nanni's on the Via Mil Ignoto across from the *piazza*. Nanni herself did the cooking. She brought us our *antipasti* and fish, while the waiter would open a bottle of Gavi di Gavi wine and an iced *limonata* for Justin.

"Only the Italians know how to live," Max said.

"Providing someone else does the work, you mean," rumbled Nigel.

"Not true," Bobby G. said. "In France, everyone goes on strike. In Italy, it's only the Communists who strike."

"What makes the Italians so great?" Anne asked.

"Because they lost the war. In losing is the beginning of wisdom," Nigel said.

"By that logic, the Palestinians would be the smartest people on Earth," I said.

"Ah, but first you have to have created a civilization. You have to appreciate what you've lost. The Italians have learned the great secret," Nigel said.

"Which is?" Monika said.

"It's all nonsense, all of it. So you might as well enjoy life as best you can," Nigel said.

"Well, it *is* an old culture. They care about beauty," Sally said.

"And food," Max said.

"It's wonderful," Anne said. "Nanni is amazing."

"Nanni *is* amazing," Max agreed.

"And the wine too," Bobby G. said, signaling the *cameriere* for another bottle of Gavi.

"The French care about food and wine, too," Anne said. "Sometimes I think it's all they care about."

"Not all," Max said. "Though it tops the list. There's also cars, sports, politics, sex – extramarital, of course – for the French, there's a whole structure, a kind of cultural hierarchy."

"Like Maslow," Anne said.

"What's that?" Gaby asked.

"He was a psychologist," Anne explained. "He developed this theory that we do things to satisfy needs, only some needs are more important than others, so he arranged them in a hierarchy."

"Anne's a school psychologist," I explained.

"No, this is interesting. Go on," Gaby said to Anne.

"The way it works is you have to satisfy a more basic need before you can go up the pyramid to the next. The most basic needs are Physiological, like food, water, sleep."

"Yeah, you gotta have that," Bobby G. said.

"Once those are satisfied, there are Safety needs. Like if someone's out to hurt you, you need to deal with it. Once Safety is taken care of comes Love needs, like family, friends…"

"Mistresses," Max put in.

"After Love comes Esteem, like why people drive fancier cars than they can afford and then finally, when you've satisfied all other needs, Self-actualization, like why someone becomes an artist or a Mother Teresa or seeks enlightenment in Tibet, or something," Anne said.

"God, that sounds so hopelessly American. The French hierarchy is completely different," Max said.

"British too," Nigel said.

"Oh, what's the British hierarchy?" Sally asked.

"Well, the most basic British need is not physiological or other such piffle."

"What is it then?"

"Fear of being embarrassed. By far the most basic. One would rather die, actually, than make a *faux pas*."

"Amazing! That doesn't even exist for the French. In fact, they go out of their way to be obnoxious or ridiculous," Gaby said.

"Okay, what is the French hierarchy?" Anne asked.

"Food, of course," Max said.

"That's physiological, like Maslow."

"Not at all," Max said. "It has nothing to do with a need for food to survive. It has to do with food as a social statement, an art form, combined with a way of showing off. It's really about a sense of superiority. Your Esteem thing."

"With food, for the French it's not just the taste," Sally said. "It's the whole ritual, the style, like beginning with a clever *amuse bouche*, the look – the *présentation* on the plate, the order of dishes and which wines accompany which sauces. Not to mention, a Frenchman wants not just his food, but to *faire à sa guise* (get his own way)."

"That's true," Gaby said. "A true Frenchman can spend a half hour discussing with a waiter how he wants something cooked. Never mind that everyone else is waiting."

"In fact, it's even better if you keep other people waiting," Max said. "It shows that one has that uniquely French combination of *supériorité* combined with the *savoir-faire* to carry it off. That's the French ideal."

"It's true," Monika smiled. "For the French, it's not enough to show off; you also have to show others up."

"So what's next in the French hierarchy beside food?" Anne asked.

"Wine, of course," Sally said.

"Looking good. Clothes, *chic*, that kind of thing. Then sports. Actually, the two are related. The French don't care whether they win or not, so long as they look good doing it," Max said.

"Not sex?" Anne asked.

"Ah, they'd like you to think so. But it isn't even fifth, which is politics. After politics comes snobbery about French culture, and then, maybe only then comes sex," Max said.

"Actually, it's not even sex. It's seduction; it's *cherchez les femmes*," Sally said. "There's always this element of flirting, of *séduction*, in every conversation, even if it's a meaningless encounter at the *épicerie* between a young Frenchman and a woman old enough to be his mother."

"It's not just the men, the Frenchwomen are always seductive. Watch even the grandmothers, how they play coyly with their pearls when a young man walks by," Monika said.

"They're not great lovers, they just think they are," Gaby said.

"Ah, but what about the Yanks?" Nigel asked.

"For Americans, everything is about their jobs; work," Max said. "They define themselves by their occupations and they work harder than Chinese coolies. Why the first thing an American asks someone is 'What do you do?' because unless they know someone's profession, they literally don't know how to think about that person."

"Well, if sex comes in around sixth or seventh for the French, where does it come in for the Americans?" Anne asked.

"Dead last," Sally said and everyone laughed.

"At least we have it. What about the Brits?" Monika put in.

"Doesn't exist. Not after public school, anyway," Nigel said.

"It's got to be somewhere," Anne said.

"Well, I suppose if one counts flogging and strange leather goings-on and things of that sort," Nigel said.

"So let me see if I've got this straight. For the French, the priorities in life in order of hierarchy are:

1. Food, *la présentation, bien sûr.*
2. Wine
3. Looking chic.
4. Sports.
5. Politics.
6. Bragging about French culture.
7. Sex

"Then what?" I said.

"Family, and only then maybe, maybe work," Max said.

"What about the Americans?"

"Work, work, work, and big cars," Max said.

"And making everything bigger. Bigger food, bigger houses, fancier toilets, everything is too big," Gaby said.

"And buying stuff we don't need," Monika added.

"And getting things done," I said, thinking about Voyager 2 and its images of Uranus.

"And helping other countries when they're in trouble," Bobby G. said and everyone grew quiet.

"What about the Italians?" Anne asked.

"The first priority is food, same as the French," Max said.

"No, *la familia, sempre* the family," Nanni overhearing, said.

"You see. Europe is not homogenized yet," Monika said.

"I like the Italians," Anne said.

"Everyone likes the Italians," Sally said.

"What about the Germans?" Gaby asked.

"Number One is war. And marching. It's in the blood," Nigel said. "They can't help themselves."

"No, I lived there. It's more complicated. For the Krauts, it's all about order, *ordnung*," Max said.

"Tell them about the ticket," Sally prompted.

"One time in Munich, I had to go to the post office. I had to get something off in a hurry and there was no parking space, so I parked in the *Parkplatz Verboten*, the 'No Parking' space. I figured it would only take a minute and anyway, Sally was sitting in the car. When I came out, a *Polizist* was writing me a ticket. I tried to argue with him that it was an emergency and I was only there a minute, but he said he wasn't giving me a ticket because I had parked in the 'No Parking,' but because I had not locked the car doors as required by law. 'But it's a convertible! What's the point of locking the doors of a convertible?!' I said. But he gave me the ticket anyway. In Germany '*Mein Herr*,' he explained, 'the rules are the rules.'"

"What were you doing in Germany?" Anne asked, trying to find out something about Max's mysterious past.

"Having less fun than I do since we moved to France," he said, motioning to the waiter that we were going to *fare alla romana* (split the check).

A few days later, we met Nigel and Monika for drinks at the American Bar in the Hotel de Paris in Monte Carlo. Justin was lining up the peanuts from a glass jar on the table like toy soldiers. An attractive blonde of *un certain age* wearing diamonds that made the Diamond Lady at the American Club look like a beggar in Calcutta, came in with another woman and a handsome young man. She nodded to Nigel and Monika as they went by our table.

"Who was that?" Anne asked.

"Madame Bacardi, of the Rum Bacardis," Monika said.

"Where's Mr. Bacardi?"

"Oh, she doesn't need him now that they're married," Monika said.

Justin knocked over one of the peanuts.

"*Merde*," he said, picking it up.

"Justin! Where did you learn that word?" Anne asked.

"*A la crèche*," he said, eating one of the peanut soldiers.

"Who in the *crèche* talks that way?"

"Everyone, Mommy."

"That's some high-class joint. Remind me to thank Princess Caroline," I said.

"It's everywhere. You can't get away from it," Anne said.

"You can't," Monika said. "I went to this finishing school in Switzerland with some of the richest girls in the world and they all cursed and whored around worse than sailors."

"Well, it's good to know he's getting an education," I said.

"What did you think of the lunch in Ventimiglia?" Nigel asked.

"Nanni is great," Anne said.

"Yes, everyone loves Nanni. But you know, it's just an urban *trattoria*, really. You haven't had a real Italian-style lunch till you get out in the country," Nigel said.

"We'll have to do something about that," Anne said.

A few days later, we picked Justin up from the *crèche* and followed Nigel and Monika's car across the border to an inn in Dolce Aqua, a hillside village above Ventimiglia. Earlier that morning I had received a call from my agent, June, in London, wanting to know how the book was going. I had been expecting a call, expecting the jerk on the chain sooner or later and dreading it, because I didn't know how to explain where I was or where it was going. Then too, I hated talking about a work in progress. The very act of talking about it could alter it. Of course I understood that they were getting nervous. All they had seen was a chapter, not the more than two hundred manuscript pages I had done and they hadn't heard a word since, so they hadn't a clue just how compelling it was becoming. Still, it felt like a kind of invasion. For me, the book was my own private world and suddenly others were reminding me that they had paid money for it and it was theirs as well.

"It's coming along pretty well," I told her.

"So you're pleased with it?"

"I think they'll like it."

"Um, how far along are you?" she asked carefully.

"Hard to say. It's not a small book," I hedged. "About 60%, maybe a bit more," I lied. I was little more than a third of the way through and had absolutely no idea where the trail in the Golden Triangle jungle was leading me or how long it would take.

"Well, that's jolly good. So perhaps another month or two should do it?"

"I don't know. There's lots more, plus rewriting. A bit longer than that, I would think," I said, stalling desperately.

"Well, there's lots of interest," she said. "One bit of news. You've got a new editor." This was disastrous news. I'd been through this before and it had always worked out badly. New editors often inherited books about which they had little enthusiasm and inevitably the book would suffer. Or even if they liked it, they had other priorities, or less clout within the publishing house, or any one of a dozen other things that could doom the book's prospects.

"Oh? I thought there was a lot of interest. They told me God was interested, remember?"

"I don't think you should worry. She's one of their top editors and she quite likes the first chapter. But they do need to do some planning for their release schedule (she pronounced it "shedjool"). Just get it here as soon as you can. By the bye, do you have a title yet? They need to start thinking about cover art and all that."

"No, I'm still working on that too," I said. Actually, I had been wracking my brain for months, had made a list of about a hundred possible titles, and still hadn't come up with anything I thought would work. "Maybe we could just call it 'The Southeast Asia Spy Book,'" I joked.

"I'm sure you'll come up with it. Keep up the good work," she said, the false cheer obvious in her voice, leaving me utterly depressed as she hung up.

The day was warm and sunny. Our cars stirred up the dust of the bare ground in front of the inn as we pulled up. The restaurant was a white building with a red tile roof and an outdoor *terrazza* with an overhead arbor hung with grape leaves. The inn had its own gardens of flowers and vegetables and its own vineyard and from the stone entrance was a view of brown fields with vines. Beyond the fields were the hills of Liguria, green from the recent rains. When we went inside, the owner and his wife greeted Nigel and Monika as old friends. They pressed chilled glasses of Cinzano with *acqua gassata* into our hands and invited us to wander around the grounds while they made lunch ready.

Anne and Monika explored the gardens, while Justin tossed pebbles into a pond. Nigel and I explored the vineyard, the vine leaves dusty in the rising heat. Nigel carried the bottle of Cinzano with him and kept refilling his glass.

"So, how's the scribble-scribble, old chap?" he asked.

"That's what my agent wants to know. She called me this morning."

"Keeping tabs, eh? Not all bad, you know. Shows they're interested."

"They changed editors on me."

"Is it serious?"

"Listen, the first book I ever wrote was a fable called *The City of the Sun,* about an Indian boy and his llama in Peru during the time of the Incas, before the Spanish came. The only things like it were Jiminez's *Platero y Yo* and Exupéry's *The Little Prince,* both books ostensibly for children that are really for adults. I sold it to Holt, Rinehart. The editor who bought it and their Children's Books senior editor, both wrote me that everyone "just loves this book" and believes it'll be around for a long time. Jiminez's book won the Nobel Prize; Exupéry's has been in print ever since it was published. Then both those editors left and the new editor dumped it along with everything else they had bought. She even demanded I return the advance money. I was never able to sell it. It's never been published; yes, it's serious."

"Ah, but do *you* like what you're writing?"

"I think it's the best thriller ever written. It's like a cross between James Bond and a Joseph Conrad adventure. There are layers and layers to it and it's in this exotic Southeast Asia world of warlords and jungle tribes that no one has written about, with echoes of the Vietnam War. And now I'm afraid it'll be for nothing," I said.

"You know, I bet it's not bad, *pas mal*, as the Froggies say when it's as good as it gets. Bugger it all, have another Cinzano," he said, refilling both our glasses. "Do you know how it ends?"

"The book? Pretty much. What I don't know is how I'm going to get from where I am now to the ending." I watched him drain and refill his glass again.

"You're a pretty serious drinker," I said.

"I'm an alcoholic, old chap."

"There's a lot of it going around."

"Monika's been trying to save me for years. Hopeless, of course. Only proves women are nature's optimists. I just try to time it so I don't become too ill or obnoxious. If not for her, I'd 've been dead already."

"I suppose you've tried to do something about it."

"Dozens of times. Whenever Monika threatens to leave, I promise to stop. For a while I do. I don't know why she puts up with me. Love, I suppose. Tell me, have you ever seen me sober?"

"I suppose not."

"Good thing, too. Sober I'm boring. Duller than a BBC documentary, than which there is nothing duller. Drink too much and I become belligerent. Rather silly for a man of my age and health. Most of the time I just try to keep from falling on my face in public. Actually, I envy you."

"Why?"

"At least you're trying. You care about what you're doing."

"Don't you?"

"Not really. All I've ever wanted to is to enjoy myself. At least that's something we can all do, eh? Let's see what they've cooked up for us," he said as we caught up with Anne, Monika and Justin.

We sat in the shade of the outdoor arbor as the owner and the *signora* brought out the *antipasti misti* served *al carello* from a wheeled food cart, beginning with steamed *cozzi* (mussels), followed by *bruscetta* and tomatoes, *prosciutto* with melon, *fagiolini all' agro* (green beans with oil), and a *buranella della Casa* of boiled shrimp, mussels, squid, clams with olive oil and lemon juice, all washed down with a very good Pinot Grigio. This was followed by the soup, then the fish, a delicious Florentine-style sole, served with a local Valle d'Aosta wine, followed by the pasta. For Justin, *spaghetti Bolognese*, of course; for the rest of us, *ravioli* filled with eggplant and ricotta accompanied by a superb Brunello di Montalcino wine, followed by the main course, *saltimbocca alla romana* (veal cooked with ham and sage) and for Nigel, a *grigliata di cervo* (grilled venison), served with a truly world-class Barbaresco wine.

"Now *that's* an Italian lunch!" Nigel declared as the rest of us sat there in a daze, so full we were sure we would never be able to eat again.

"God, I've never been so full," Anne said.

"You can't be. There's still dessert," Monika said as the *signora* served us *tiramisu* and a *torta di nocciole* (hazelnut cake), with a light dessert wine and chocolate *gelato* for Justin. This was followed by the *formaggi*, a wooden platter with a dozen cheeses and slices of Tuscan bread. As we sat there, literally unable to move, the owner brought out a tall narrow bottle of his homemade *grappa* with some kind of a branch and leaves inside and sat down to share it with us.

"*Salute*," he toasted.

"*Chin chin*," we replied. The *grappa* was a bit medicinal, but good and warm going down. We had another round and I began to like it more. It was addicting.

"*Il signor* is an English lord, *padrone*, but one of us, *si?*" the *possessore* said, indicating Nigel.

"I don't know about the 'Lord' part, but when it comes to *grappa*, we are all *camerata* and sinners under the skin. Like the Colonel's lady and Judy O'Grady, as it were," Nigel winked.

"Nigel," Monika said warningly.

"Quite right. Getting on the downside. One more *grappa* and we're off," Nigel said. The owner refilled our glasses and we left a pile of lira on the table for the check.

"You're right. This was definitely the real 'lunch Italian style.' I may never move again," Anne said.

We finished drinking and got into our respective cars, Justin in his car seat, Monika and Anne, who had drunk less, driving.

"What were you and Nigel talking about in the vineyard?" she asked. She followed the winding road down toward the *autostrada* to the French border. As we descended toward the coast, we caught distant glimpses of the sea in the gaps between the hills.

"I told him about my new editor."

"What'd he say?"

"He said from what I told him, the book doesn't sound, as the Froggies say, too bad. What were you and Monika talking about?"

"About how hard it is to be a woman here. Did you know she got her law degree from Stanford?"

"No. Why is it so hard being a woman here?"

"It's easy for you. You're the big shot writer. Everyone pays attention to you. I was the school psychologist for the second largest high school in the U.S. We had street gangs, thousands of kids on triple tracks with eighty-seven nationalities and fifty-six different languages and there isn't one person here who gives a damn or thinks I'm worth talking to. I'm just the wife. In France, women are meant to be seen and seduced, but never listened to and certainly not taken seriously. You don't know what it's like."

"You're right, I'm sorry," I said, suddenly reminded of a book that had been big in the 70's, called *Zen and the Art of Motorcycle Main-*

tenance by Robert Pirsig. It's about a cross-country journey he and his son take on his motorcycle. Only near the end, in an argument with his son, he suddenly realizes that his son has been riding the whole trip on the back of the bike. He hasn't had the same open view of the road and the countryside as the driver; mostly just a view of his Dad's back and Pirsig suddenly realizes that even though they've been together on the same motorcycle, their experience of it has been completely different. Had I done that to Anne too?

"It's not your fault. You're not like that. It's just the culture here. And I don't speak French the way you do," she said.

"It is my fault. I'm sorry. All I think about is the damned book. Would language lessons help?"

"No," she laughed. "I'd rather be ignored."

"What else were you guys talking about?" I asked.

"What do you mean?"

"When we first caught up to you to go into the restaurant, Monika's eyes were red. You were talking about something else, weren't you?"

"Nigel's drinking. She can't stand watching."

"Why doesn't she leave?"

"She loves him. She knows if she leaves, he'll die."

"He said he envied me. All these people we know with tons more money than us and I'm beginning to believe we're better off than they are."

"I think they like us," Anne said.

"I think they do."

"Nigel was right about one thing. That was an unbelievable meal. I don't think we'll have to eat again for a year."

"It was incredible. Maybe we should have come to Italy instead?" I said.

"I don't think so," she said, slowing down for the French border crossing. "Things where we are are getting interesting."

Chapter 15

Yachting with the International Set and Mlle. Onassis

"We're invited to a party on Mark and Rachel's yacht," Anne said, showing me the invitation that had come in with the mail. We were sitting on the stone *terrasse* at our villa, looking out over the garden, where Justin, dressed in a Zorro mask and cape, was fencing an imaginary opponent with his plastic sword. French TV was showing reruns of the old black and white Guy Williams *Zorro* television series and children in France had gone Zorro-crazy.

"Who?"

"You remember Mark, the Englishman. He was at our party, tried to sell you his yacht. Rachel's his wife. According to this, Rachel has a special announcement," she said, showing me on the invitation.

"I thought they didn't live together."

"According to Sally, they spend a month together every year on the yacht."

"Interesting approach to marriage. We're not going, right?"

"Of course we are. I've never been to a fancy yacht party. Besides this is our *entrée* into the 'International Set.'"

"Maybe I don't want to be a member of the 'International Set,'" I said.

"Don't be ridiculous. Besides, we have to go. Everyone will be there."

"Then, they won't miss us. Besides, I get seasick."

"It's in the harbor," she said.

"It can get choppy in the harbor."

"God, you're such a wimp. I can't believe I married someone who gets seasick. My parents had a sailboat. I grew up sailing. I loved it. If I had known you got seasick, I'm not sure I would've married you. Besides, don't pretend you're not going when we both know you are."

"What are we supposed to wear?"

"This is going to be something. It says, 'evening wear,'" she said, tapping the invitation.

"Well I'm out. I don't have a tuxedo," I said.

"You can wear your Navy-Blue suit. You can get away with it. You're a writer. You're considered eccentric by definition," she said. "And I've got my black dress. You know, the one with the lace. Should work, providing it doesn't get too warm. God, I wish our summer clothes were here."

Since we had been unable to bring all our clothes with us from California, we had prearranged for a friend to ship us our summer clothes that we had left boxed-up. She had shipped it out to us more than two months ago and it still hadn't arrived.

The next day, while Anne made arrangements for Chuck and Emma's latest *au pair* to baby-sit Justin along with Emma's kids since Chuck and Emma would be at the party too, I was in my office, looking out the window at Nietzsche's forest path, working on the showdown that had been building between the opium trader, Toon-sang, and my agent, Sawyer. They had come to a village raided by the Kuomintang. Riding in, by the light of campfires they see the bodies of Kuomintang raiders hanging from the village gate, left as a warning by Bhun Sa, the Shan warlord Sawyer was trying to find. The idea was to up the suspense by letting the reader know how dangerous the Bhun Sa character was.

The tension in the scene was building and I was reluctant to tear myself away that night as we dropped off Justin at Chuck and Emma's lavish Monte Carlo apartment. Chuck and Emma had already left. Anne spoke with the *au pair* while Emma's two boys, both older than Justin, ran around the house cursing in French.

"I don't like this," I said.

"Neither do I," she agreed. "We'll make it an early night." She left the *au pair*, a nineteen-year-old Swedish blonde with a thick accent, strict instructions to call her on the yacht if there was the slightest problem.

"Do you think she understands enough English?" I asked as we left.

"She better," Anne said.

As we parked by the *quai*, we could hear Rock music blaring from the yacht, a huge boat with a sleek white hull and superstructure, strung with lights for the party. Max and Sally had also just arrived. They waited for us at the foot of the gangplank and the four of us boarded together and entered the main salon. Our hostess, Rachel, an attractive brown-haired woman in a sheer white evening gown, greeted us by pulling open her see-through top and exposing two tanned and perfect breasts. She declared, "What do you think, darling? I just had them done."

"Spectacular!" Max said and he and Sally did the cheek-kissing thing with her.

"Very nice," I said, holding out my hand to shake hers.

"Here, do you want to feel them?" she asked, pulling my hand to her breasts.

"That's all right. They look terrific. Very natural," I babbled, pulling back and shaking her hand instead, trying to avoid Anne's eyes as we entered.

The salon was very long and filled with mahogany furniture and brass fixtures. Waiters in white jackets circulated with glasses of champagne and trays of *hors d'oeuvres* and a small band played in the corner, with loudspeakers blasting the music all over the boat. A cluster of people in tuxedos and gowns were around a woman I couldn't see that someone said was a French film star.

Sally pointed out Niarchos, the Greek shipping magnate in a small group that included Gianni Versace, the Italian designer in a silk tuxedo of his own design, and a Saudi billionaire in a white gold-embroidered robe. Nigel and Monika were talking with Madame Bacardi and a handsome man in a white dinner jacket half her age. Bobby G. and Gaby waved to us from a couch. Mark, also in a white dinner jacket, came over and escorted Anne and me to the bar.

"Here's that thirty-year-old single malt I promised you," he said, motioning for the bartender to pour me a large Laphroaig whiskey. "Islay, of course."

"Scottish isles, I believe," I said, doing my best James Bond imitation.

"Too bloody right." Mark said. "Have you seen my wife's new knockers?"

"Very impressive," I said, swallowing a large gulp of whiskey.

"I know. Almost makes me want to have a go at her myself," he said. "Though, mustn't get too carried away. Do you know everyone?"

"Is that Prince Albert in the corner with Max?"

"It is. Have you seen his date?"

I shook my head.

"Over there," nodding toward a spectacular redhead in a low-cut mini-dress that barely reached her thighs. "Heard she was a porn star. Have you heard the latest about Papa Doc?"

"I heard they threw him out," I said. According to the TV news, after weeks of riots, the Haitian dictator, Papa Doc Duvalier, had fled Port au Prince to seek asylum in France.

"Guess where he's staying?"

"Oh my God! Not the Côte d'Azur?" Anne said.

"It'll be in the papers tomorrow," Mark said. "The French government found him a villa. They're such whores, the French. They talk principles, but let someone with cash show up and their skirts go up faster than a five-pound slut in Soho. Guess where?"

"Where?" I said, praying, please not Eze. An exiled Third World dictator with his Tonton Macoute thugs next door was the last thing we needed.

"Mougins," he said.

"Poor Roger. Could be the end of the Moulin," Chuck said, coming up with Emma. The Moulin de Mougins was one of the most famous and expensive restaurants in France. People came from all over the world to sample Roger Vergé's cooking.

"How were the kids?" Emma asked Anne.

"So far so good," Anne said.

"It's time you and I had a talk," Chuck said, taking my arm. As we went outside and climbed a stair to the upper deck, I heard Emma asking Anne how she managed to keep Justin so well behaved. Chuck and I gazed out over the lights of the harbor and Monte Carlo. He offered me a Cuban cigar and when I shook my head, lit one for himself.

"Max's told me all about you. Is it true?" he asked and started grilling me about my technical background. "A writer who understands technology and speaks languages is something I could really use. We need white papers, marketing, also some deals you could help me with, all kinds of stuff." Chuck owned Global Systems; headquartered in Monte Carlo, it was at that time one of the largest computer companies in Europe.

"I'm not looking for a job, Chuck," I said.

"No, of course not. You've got your book and all. But still, if you ever want to make some money, let me know. I'm talking real money, Andy. Speaking of which, you know you're throwing a lot of it away."

"Really? How?"

"Taxes. You pay American taxes, right?"

"'Fraid so."

"That's what I'm talking about. I make a lot. Millions. And I pay nothing. Want to know how?"

I listened to the music from the salon and looked at the lights of the city and the boats reflected in the harbor. There were people on the *quai* looking out towards the yacht and I wondered if they envied us or were just curious.

"I'm an American too. Served in the U.S. Marines, but paying taxes is a fool's game. All you need is a residence in Monaco and you're completely tax-free," Chuck said.

"An American citizen still has to pay taxes no matter where he is," I said.

"That's why I gave it up. Became an Irish citizen. Ireland's a member of the EU. As an EU citizen with a residence in Monaco, you've got all the advantages and none of the disadvantages. My kids are already enrolled for Eton in England when the time comes. Make tons of money and keep every penny. Heard you were going to make some money from your book. Be a shame to give it away to the government. Think about it."

The lights from the boats reflected on the water reminded me of something for the book. In Thailand once a year, people gather on the banks of the rivers and canals to sail tiny boats made of banana leaves, each of which carries a burning candle. It's called the festival of Loy Krathong and the Thais believe that by doing this they cast away their sins. On Loy Krathong, the waterways in Thailand are filled with thousands and thousands of lights floating in the darkness and suddenly, I knew the scene that would end the book and even the last line. Now all I had to do was write it.

"I don't need to think about it, Chuck. No offense to you, or Ireland, but I got to tell you, it'll be a cold day in Hell when I give up being an American to become an Irishman," I said. I left him with his cigar and went down the stairs to the salon, where Rachel was dancing with Prince Albert of Monaco, Madame Bacardi's young man was dancing with Prince Albert's redhead. Bobby G. was with Gaby. Max, Nigel and Monika were talking with another couple and Anne, Emma, and Sally were sitting on a couch sipping champagne. I went over to join Max, Nigel and Monika with the new couple.

"This is Prince Maximilian and his friend," Max said. The Prince clicked his heels and shook my hand.

"We were talking about Papa Doc. I think there is agreement that he will not be received anywhere," the Prince said in a German accent.

"He was a ruthless thug," Max said. "It's a pity the Frogs took him in."

"Probably have voodoo tom-toms at the Moulin de Mougins next," said Mark, coming over.

"Speaking of vich, I hear zere's a new Brazilian club in Monte," the Prince's female friend with a strong German accent, said. "Ve should all go."

"That's it, Brazil. Bossa nova," Mark said, plucking my sleeve. "I say," he whispered. "Your wife is a lovely piece."

"She won't show you her boobs," I said.

"More's the pity," he said, heading over and saying something to the band, which started to play a Bossa Nova. I went over to Anne and took her hand and we started to dance.

"You're being romantic. You know I love Bossa Nova," she said.

"Actually, I don't want Mark hitting on you."

"Well, what was that with Rachel asking you to feel her boobs?"

"Honestly, Babe, I don't think I'm cut out for the International Set," I said.

"Actually, I don't think Emma thinks we belong here either," she said.

Just then, Mark stood up on a chair and tapped a spoon against a wine glass for attention. "*Attention!* Everyone up on deck, *s'il vous plaît*. And don't forget your champagne," he added.

We crowded onto the upper deck and suddenly fireworks began shooting into the sky from a small barge moored to the *quai*.

"Here's to Rachel's new pair!" Mark shouted, raising his glass.

"To Rachel's new pair," everyone toasted and drank as Rachel curtsied to all directions, bowing low and spreading her arms wide to share the view. Anne and I sipped champagne at the rail.

"I don't know how we'd ever explain this at home," she said, leaning against me as we watched the fireworks explode over the harbor. "Still, the International Set does have its moments."

A couple of weeks later, we were finally invited to a yacht party on Christina Onassis' yacht, which she'd inherited from her father, Aristotle Onassis and which he'd named after her. Max and Sally had arranged it. We got the English *au pair* babysitter, drove to the Monte Carlo harbor and walked up the gangplank, where a uniformed attendant checked our names off a list.

The Christina was long and sleek and nautical; lots of mahogany paneling and brass fittings. We peeked into the dining room, which had a long white-linen covered formal dining table set for a formal dinner for twenty-four, even though no dinner would be served that evening. The indoor salon was large, with plush comfortable sofas and armchairs and tables and chairs for card games and through the windows, the lights of Monte Carlo and the royal palace lit up at night. Black-liveried servants walked around with drinks and trays of hors d'oeuvres.

There were two bars. An intimate semi-circular indoor bar; very mahogany and polished brass nautical, with an engraved marble map of the world on the wall and also a circular white outdoor bar in an outdoor area on the stern that had a large mosaic of a lion embedded in the wooden deck.

Back in the indoor salon, Max was talking with a dark-haired young woman in a white gown and a dazzling diamond and sapphire necklace and matching earrings whom I took to be Christina Onassis. She had a gentle smile and the saddest eyes I had ever seen. I'd heard she'd divorced her fourth husband a few years earlier when she found out he'd had a child with his Swedish mistress. Max called us over and introduced us. Turned out she was a fan of my *Scorpion* novel.

"Are you going to write another Scorpion? You must," she said.

"I'm writing a new one. Not a Scorpion, but you'll like it," I said.

"What's the title?"

"I wish I knew. Don't have one yet. It's driving me crazy," I said.

"I can't wait," she said like she meant it. The celebrity at the party was a chunky older woman in a blue dress who wore her hair styled in a straight bang like a medieval monk. She was a famous French New Wave film director, Agnes Varda, whose most recent film, "Vagabond," had taken the Golden Lion at the Venice Film Festival. I'd read in *Nice Matin* that she'd been a close friend of the late rock singer Jim Morrison of The Doors, who'd died in Paris. Someone pointed me out and she came over.

"*Vous êtes l'écrivain,*" she said.

"*Je suis un écrivain,*" I said.

"*Bien sûr vous travaillez sur quelque chose de nouveau?*"

"*Un roman à suspense d'espionnage. Pas votre metier peut-être.*"

"*Mon metier est le monde. La vie.*"

"*On me dit que vous étiez une amie de Jim Morrison.*"

"*Pauvre Jim. Maintenant, ils font des histoires, mais à ses funérailles, nous n'étions que quatre.*"

"Perhaps we could get together sometime?" I said.

"*Quand vous êtes à Paris. Appelez-moi,*" she said as people surrounded her. She gave them and then me a look I understood instantly. Everyone wants to be in the movies.

I looked around. Sally was with Nigel and Monika, the only other people we knew there. Anne and I grabbed some wine from a passing waiter's tray and went over.

"What did Agnes Varda say?" Sally asked.

"She said when Jim Morrison died in Paris, only four people came to the funeral."

"Wow! Now there are always crowds and flowers at his grave in Père Lachaise."

"What do you think?" Nigel said, gesturing at the salon. "Wealthy people are the most boring people on the planet. All they can talk about is the latest plane, boat, impressionist painting, or whatnot they've bought. Deadly."

"Is it me or is *Mlle*. Onassis *un peu triste?*" I asked.

"Depressed," Monika said. "With all the pills she takes to lose weight, she probably hasn't slept in a year."

"She wants to be liked," Anne said. "What do you call people who need to be liked?"

"Politicians," Nigel said.

"The problem with being one of the richest people in the world is that no one will ever feel sorry for you," Monika said.

"*Bonjour tristesse*," I said and they laughed.

Chapter 16

Visitors, Part One: The Budapest Express

One of the absolute certainties in life is that if you live in a part of the world that people put on travel posters, sooner or later you will get visitors. When I got the news, I was in Madame Finot's garden, where she was teaching me how to prune tomatoes, French-style. She was the old woman who had scolded me about not touching her tomatoes when we first moved in, but the early snow and bad weather had damaged her plants and she was replanting the ones that survived and advising me how to plant our garden as well.

She replanted her tomatoes in rows of wooden stakes, each about one and a half meters high, with a single tomato vine tied to each stake. The vines were tied at intervals to its stake with strips of colorful Provencal cloth, because in France even vegetable plants have to look pretty.

"*Le secret des tomates*," Madame Finot explained, was not simply to prune the small shoots from the main stem of the vine. Any *imbécile*, even foreigners like us and *les estivants* (summer people down from Paris) knew that much. The important thing to understand was that the quality of the flavor was determined by the foliage. The more foliage, the better the taste. Thus, one should prune not only the shoots, but also the budding fruit, so there was only one or two *tomates* per vine. Only this and the use of chicken droppings for fertilizer, would allow the true flavor of a *tomate de Provence* to develop. We were amputating tomato buds with the ruthlessness of surgeons when Anne called me from our *terrasse*.

"Your wife is *gentille*, very nice, but she does not speak French," Madame Finot said. "Just '*bonjour*' and '*ça va*' and such. Not even a discussion of the weather."

"It's French, *de l'école*, high school French. It's difficult for her," I said.

"Lonely, I should say. One wants *un peu de commérage* (a bit of gossip) with one's neighbors."

"I'm not sure she knows any. And she's busy with our son." I suddenly realized she was gently suggesting that Anne might be feeling isolated, lonely.

"*Le petit garcon, il est très mignon,*" saying Justin was cute.

"*Merci, Madame,*" I said. I asked her if she had children of her own.

"My daughter and her children are in Nice. I had a son, but *il y a longtemps de cela* (that was long ago)," she said.

"*Il est mort?*" He's dead? I asked.

"*En Algérie,*" she said and suddenly, the shadow of Algeria was across the garden, reminding me that France is an old country and if you dig deeply enough, you will find bones. "If you need someone to *faire du baby-sitting,* bring him to my villa. When one gets older, one tends to appreciate *les enfants* more."

"*Merci, encore,*" I said, opening the gate and crossing back to Anne.

"I just got off the phone. Guess who's coming to visit?"

"Ron and Nancy Reagan. He's looking for a part in a French movie. He'll be the one in the black socks," I said.

"No, silly. Kathy and her daughter, Rebecca. They're coming from Budapest. George's doing some sort of documentary there."

"For ABC?" I asked. George was a reporter for ABC television news.

"I don't know. But it'll be fun. Justin will have someone to play with."

Anne and Kathy had met at a fertility clinic in Los Angeles only to discover that Kathy had been a teacher at the same high school where Anne had started as a school psychologist. Kathy became pregnant a month or so before Anne and the two women kept tabs and exchanged stories during their pregnancies. As it turned out, Justin was five weeks premature and Rebecca came three weeks late, so Kathy was still pregnant and big when Justin was born. Kathy had come to the hospital and cried to Anne, "You're done! How could you do this to me?!"

"Where are they going to sleep?" I asked.

"There's the bed in your office," she said. I had my papers, books, and research material spread out on the bed in the downstairs bedroom that I had turned into an office.

"Where am I going to write?"

"You can take a couple of days off," she said.

"Maybe I don't want to take a couple of days off," I said, going to my office and shutting the door. The problem with guests, I thought, is that they burst into your routine. Even when guests are well-behaved, just the fact that they are on holiday while you are in the middle of normal life, throws things out of joint. But that wasn't what was bothering me. Something Madame Finot had said had brought up something I couldn't quite put my finger on, something just on the edge of memory.

I stared out the window at Nietzsche's path in the woods. The day was cloudy, not like that hot sunny day in Algiers, suddenly remembering a conversation I'd had long ago with a French Foreign Legion officer, during the Algerian War for Independence. We were in a café in the Belcourt *quartier* near the Jardin d'Essai, the botanical garden. There were rumors that the DeGaulle government was going to open talks with the rebels, the FLN, though there were still bombings every day and you never boarded a train or a tram or went to a cinema without thinking about it.

I had just turned 20 then and after dropping out of college and completing my U.S. Army service, I had boarded an Icelandic Airlines flight, in those days the cheapest way to Europe, and went to Paris. I wasn't sure why I was going. All I knew was that all the writers I admired, Hemingway, Fitzgerald, Faulkner and in later generations, James Jones, James Baldwin, Saul Bellow, the Paris Review guys, they'd all gone to Paris. I didn't know what it was that you got from Paris, but figured that when I got there I would find out. Eric Hawkins, an old-time editor at the *International Herald-Tribune* in Paris who was sympathetic to upstart young writers, told me he'd buy something freelance if it was worth printing and suggested I try Algeria, where the war was still generating stories and they didn't have any reporters down there to cover things after Salan and the Army revolt had been put down.

The café was hot and we brushed away flies as the French captain and I downed Kronenbourg beer from sweating bottles. I remember the shadow of the building on a neighboring wall that was blinding white in the sun. The *capitaine* was a veteran of Dien Bien Phu and I remembered asking him which was worse, Algeria or Indochina, which was what the French called Vietnam back then.

"For the politicians, *l'Algérie* is worse because it is a *département* of France herself. Especially now, when everyone fears DeGaulle is going to give it away. But for soldiers, *L'Indochine* was hell on earth," he said.

"Why so bad?"

"The climate. You think the desert is hot. This is nothing. There it is a worse heat, not to mention the jungle, the dust that gets into everything, the insects, the monsoon. And *les bombes* and mines and *les objects piégés* (booby-traps) everywhere. In the cafés, *les bordels* (brothels), on the jungle trails, the rice paddies, you could even step into a river and step on a mine disguised as a rock. It got so you were afraid to take a step anywhere. And the fighting was much worse. The Viet Minh have guns, artillery, and soldiers who can live in the jungle forever on a handful of rice. We killed a million of them and it wasn't enough. You think because they are *asiatiques* they are stupid, but no. They are smart. Smart as any Frenchman, maybe smarter. Twice as smart as an American," he laughed.

"The Americans are starting to get involved in Vietnam now."

"They'll be sorry," he said. That was the connection, I thought. Why it was bugging me. The Vietnam War was seeping into my book like the sun into Madame Finot's *tomates* and for a thriller set in the present I should limit it, but I didn't know how. Anne knocked on the door and came in.

"Don't you like Kathy?" Anne asked.

"Sure. I like her fine. And Justin'll have someone to play with. It's the book."

"Do you want me to tell her not to come?"

"No, don't," I said. "The break might do me good. I think I'm becoming obsessed."

The next day, we picked up Kathy and her daughter, Rebecca, at the train station in Nice. Somehow we fitted the car seats for both kids plus Kathy, luckily she was thin, into the back seat of the Renault. They had been misled into thinking that food wasn't available on the train and had brought awful sandwiches from Hungary that they got rid of, so they were hungry. We took them to the Nice flower market for *pain bagnats* and cold drinks. The market was pedestrian-only and we sat under table umbrellas as we ate, watching Justin and Rebecca squealing and chasing each other around the market stalls.

"God, this is the best sandwich I've ever had. I feel like we've been on deprivation. What is it?" Kathy asked.

"It's a *pain bagnat*. It's the hot dog or slice of pizza of the Côte d'Azur. You can get them anywhere," Anne said.

"It's delicious. What's in it?"

"It's just a French roll, or even better an olive oil *petit pain*, and inside tuna, tomatoes, sweet onions, green pepper, olives *Niçoise*, salt and olive oil. Basil too, I think,"

"That's it?"

"That's it," Anne said. "I'd make them, but it's easier to just pick them up somewhere when you're in a hurry."

"So how's Hungary?" I asked.

"Awful. We stayed at the Hilton, but there was some kind of international conference. Secretary of State Schultz was there and Primakov from Russia and all kinds of security people. They were at the Hilton too. It was like being in prison. And the accommodations in Eastern Europe leave a lot to be desired. And the weather was bleak. This is wonderful," Kathy said, looking around at the flower stalls and the vegetable stands in the sunshine, surrounded by the buildings of the old *quartier*.

"So what's this film George is doing?" Anne asked.

"Some Hungarian guy. He was a Communist official, but then he spoke out against the Party and he had to leave during the Revolution in '56. George is doing a documentary about him going back after all these years, seeing the changes and what hasn't changed. But it's turning into something different. Apparently, this guy had some personal conflicts with some people who are still around. When it's done, it should be interesting. But George was working non-stop; he really didn't have any time for us."

"What's Budapest like?"

"Cold, rainy. Buda's hilly. Pest is flat. The Danube isn't blue and after you've seen the Chain Bridge and taken the *funicular* to Kiralyi Palace and seen the statues in Heroes Square, that's pretty much it. There's a lot of porn and prostitution, though," she whispered. "You can order it from your hotel room."

"What did you like?" I asked.

"My favorite place was Vorosmartz Square on the Pest side. It's got sidewalk cafés and street musicians. It reminded me of France," she said wistfully.

That night we took them to the Bâteau Ivre in Beaulieu-sur-Mer, where Rebecca and Justin peeked through their fingers at the Robot Man. The next few days were spent sightseeing. We took them back to Cap d'Antibes to show them our old villa and Gatsby's beach at La Garoupe, to the *cour de récréation* in Antibes where the kids could run around and let off steam on the see-saws and the hand-turned *carrousel* and then to show them how the other half lived, to the Hotel du Cap, where the *maître d'* remembered us from the last time.

"Who stays here? Is it only millionaires?" Kathy asked him.

"We have many famous guests, Madame. From America, your Monsieur Cosby comes every year."

"Bill Cosby? The TV star?"

"*Ah oui.* You are from Los Angeles. You know Monsieur Cosby?" he asked me.

"Not personally."

"Of course. Los Angeles is a big city," he said.

That evening back in Eze, Kathy called George in Hungary.

"It's not going well," she reported, joining us by the fireplace in the *salon*. "There's all kinds of interference and this Hungarian guy is not cooperating. George's afraid they're going to go over budget. God, I'm so glad I'm away. You guys don't know how easy you have it."

"Well, it's not that easy. There's bureaucracy here too. It's been two months since they were shipped and we still don't have our summer clothes. And they make fun of my French," Anne said.

"That's one good thing about Hungary. Nobody expects you to speak Hungarian. Sometimes I wonder if the Hungarians even speak it among themselves," Kathy laughed.

The next day we drove up to Eze Village, the medieval town with its wonderful view of the coast. But what the kids loved best was climbing up to a barred wrought iron gate and pretending they were in jail.

Anne and Kathy decided to go shopping in Monte Carlo. I was to watch the kids. There was a good children's zoo in Saint-Jean-Cap-Ferrat that I had taken Justin to once before and decided it would be a perfect morning outing, though both Anne and Kathy looked a little worried.

"Are you sure you can handle both kids by yourself?" Anne asked.

"Piece of cake," I said. "You guys go have a good time."

The zoo was on the Cap Ferrat peninsula, not far from Villefranche. It was in an attractive natural setting, shaded by eucalyptus and palm trees, and in addition to the typical zoo animals, it also had farm animals, like goats and sheep, for a petting zoo.

I wasn't too concerned about handling a pair of two-and-a-half year-olds. The zoo was rarely crowded in the mornings and there was only a single entrance and a single long oval path to all the animal enclosures, so it would be easy to keep track of them. I parked in the dirt parking area and as we paid and went in, I told them, "Now let's stay together," but the words were barely out of my mouth when Justin took off running in one direction and Rebecca in the other. They were running fast and I wasn't sure which one to go after. I decided Justin would most likely be headed for either the little playground or the petting zoo; I had no idea where Rebecca was going and decided to go after her first. I caught up with her after about a fifty or sixty yard chase, when she stopped to look at the flamingoes. I grabbed her hand and hauled her after me in the opposite direction to go find Justin.

"What was that all about?" I demanded.

"I don't like boys," she said.

"You will," I said, feeling a stab of panic about Justin, who was nowhere to be seen. We finally caught up to him climbing a log ladder in the playground.

"Come down, " I called up to him.

"No," he said, refusing to budge.

"I'll buy you a *glace à la vanille*."

"No."

"OK. Then I'll either feed you to the crocodile or let your Mother punish you for disobeying. Which would you prefer?"

"You wouldn't," he said.

"No, but I will tell Mom," I said. Justin was going through the stage when boys prefer their mothers and I hoped that would work.

He slowly climbed down and let me take his hand. I told them they had to behave themselves and stay with me, that if I had to run after them again, we would leave immediately.

"You wouldn't feed us to a crocodile?" Rebecca wanted to know.

"I don't know. Let's have a look at him and see how hungry he is," I said as I led them giggling with delight to the crocodile pond. Unfortunately, the crocodile didn't move. He was under the water and all they could see was the tip of his snout and part of his tail. All in all, he wasn't very impressive.

"He's not scary," Justin said.

"Don't be so sure. They can wait like that for hours and then some poor unsuspecting little kid comes walking by and whomp!" I said, using my hands to simulate a crocodile's mouth snapping shut.

"I'll punch him," Justin said.

"So will I," Rebecca said.

We walked around the zoo, petting the goats and sheep, watching the zebras, the kangaroos, the yak, the wild boars, the tiger sleeping in the shade, and the bear. The zoo was the perfect size for kids. They liked the two-headed snake and the pythons best.

We sat in a tiny theatre and watched the monkey show, with the monkeys jumping on seesaws and riding on bikes and when one of the monkeys tried to shake Rebecca's hand, she squealed and jumped back, squeezing herself behind me for protection. Afterwards, I bought them ice creams and cold drinks at the little restaurant. They went back and played in the little playground and by time I got them back to the car, they both fell asleep in their car seats.

Anne and Kathy came back excited. They had gone to the La Condamine Market on the Place d'Armes in Monte Carlo, window-shopped at Bulgari's, Chanel, Hermès, and Yves St. Laurent, had lunch at the Café de Paris, and picked up souvenir Monte Carlo coffee mugs from Bobby G. Rebecca and Justin told them how much fun the zoo was and how the best part was when they tried to run away in opposite directions and I had to catch them both.

"Nice going. I thought you could take care of them," Anne said.

"I think they planned it, like one of those prison movies. Don't underestimate those two criminals," I said.

"How was it really?" Kathy asked.

"Actually, except for the brief moment of panic when they took off in opposite directions, it's the best time I've had in a while," I said.

The next day, we took Kathy and Rebecca to the train station in Nice to go back to Budapest.

"I don't want to go," Kathy said. "You guys are so lucky."

We waited while they boarded. As the train pulled away, Rebecca stuck her hand out of the window and waved goodbye.

That night, Justin asleep, Anne and I sat in front of the fire with our wine. She asked me how I felt about having a break from the writing.

"It's all right. Not thinking about it was good. The kids were good too. They got along," I said.

"They're thinking about adopting," Anne said. I didn't respond. We both wanted another child and so far, nothing had happened. "We're not there yet, are we?" she said.

"Not yet," I said, putting my arm around her.

"You're sure it was OK, Babe? The inconvenience? Playing tourist," she said.

"It probably helped the book." I had decided that the treacherous Toonsang was simply too good a character to kill off too soon. I also wanted to ratchet up the suspense, to make it clear to the reader that the war that my agent, Sawyer, was sent to prevent was about to start.[1]

Chapter 17

Bottled in Bond, James Bond

All the eating and drinking we'd been doing was beginning to put pounds on me. After lunches with Anne and Justin, I decided to spend an hour every day at the fitness center in the Hotel de Paris in Monte Carlo. After a workout, a swim in the saltwater pool, and a shower, I would head down to the hotel's American Bar for a drink. I never knew which of our friends might be there, but there was usually someone and you could usually count on Nigel to be parked at his regular table, a bottle of Scotch at his elbow.

"Working out, eh? How goes it?" Nigel said, as I sat down. He seemed drunker than usual.

"Not bad. I feel better when I do it."

"Don't care for exercise myself. Makes the ice cubes jump out of my glass. How's the scribbling?"

"Took a break. We had guests for a few days."

"Bloody nuisance, people. Reason we moved away from England was to get away from people. Of course, now that in certain circles I'm *persona non grata*, I no longer have that problem."

The white-jacketed waiter came over with a bottle of Evian water and a glass for me.

"Well, these were friends from home. Very nice," I said.

"They're the bloody worst. It's like feeding a stray dog. One can't get rid of them. And I notice, you didn't answer me about the scribble-scribble," he said, pouring us both another drink. I mixed mine with the Evian water.

"It's coming along. I'm a little worried that too much of the back story is getting into the thriller part."

"Why is that a problem?"

"It's the Vietnam War. The publishers consider it box-office poison, although I hear there's a new movie, *Platoon*, that's coming out. Maybe that'll change their mind."

"What makes you so sure they won't like it?"

"After Dell published my first spy thriller, *Hour of the Assassins*, they wanted to know what I was going to do next. I had an idea for a Vietnam novel. My new editor – of course they switched editors on me – asked for an outline, which I sent. She called and told me they couldn't sell Vietnam, nobody wanted to read about it, but they didn't want to lose me. They liked my work. She offered me a deal. They would buy the book and I could set it in Vietnam – the story was a combination spy thriller-love story set in Saigon in the 60's – but on one condition: I couldn't mention the war!"

"What'd you do?"

"Told her I wasn't that talented," I said, as a group of German businessmen and women, two of them good-looking enough to be models, came in and sat at a nearby table. They were talking loudly and laughing and one of the men called out to the waiter for Beck's beer.

"Bloody Kraut bastards," Nigel muttered.

"Take it easy," I said, as one of men glanced over at us.

"You're a baby. But some of us are old enough to remember," Nigel said.

"Let's finish up," I said, signaling the waiter. But as he started over, Nigel waved him away.

"*Prosit*," the Germans toasted. One of them raised a glass toward us.

"This is a good bar. Why do they want to ruin it?" Nigel said.

"*Was sagen Sie?* What do you say?" one of the bigger German men said.

"He doesn't mean anything," I said.

"The hell I don't! Bloody Nazis!" Nigel said.

"What are you saying?" the big German said and stood up.

Suddenly, Nigel stood up and started singing the Horst Wessel song, the Nazi anthem. I recognized it instantly, as anyone who has ever seen any old World War Two documentaries or movies would. The Germans stared in shock as Nigel sang loudly:

"*Die Fahne hoch die Reihen fest geschlossen*, you bloody Nazi bastards!"

The big German started toward Nigel. I stepped between them, my hands on both their chests.

"*Er ist getrunken. Am Morgen wird er alles vergessen haben,*" I told the big German, using the German I'd picked up from my days as a reporter for the *International Herald Tribune* in Berlin, just as Nigel took a wild roundhouse swing at him, missed and nearly toppled over. I wrapped my arms around Nigel and pulled him out to the pillared lobby by the bronze equestrian statue; the one with the horse's knee shiny from a century of people rubbing it, because there is a superstition that rubbing it brings good luck at the Monte Carlo Casino next door.

"Why'd you bloody stop me?" Nigel slurred.

"He was in better shape and twice your size. He'd 've clobbered you," I said.

"Well, better to die fighting the Hun than in bloody inches."

"Better to live," I said.

"He was a bloody Nazi."

"He was too young. He was probably only a little kid in the war, if that."

"Don't you believe it. They're all bloody Nazis at heart," he said thickly. He pushed me away and staggered outside. It was getting dark. I watched him weave his way up the Place du Casino toward the Avenue de la Costa in the direction of his apartment. Just then, Anne showed up with Justin.

"Was that Nigel?" she asked. I didn't say anything. "Are we going for a drink or dinner?"

"Not here," I said. "Let's go someplace we like. Let's go see Maria and the Chef."

"Daddy, can I feed the fish?" Justin asked; he loved feeding breadcrumbs to the little fish attracted to the lights in the Villefranche harbor.

"Sure," I said, watching Nigel's figure grow small and indistinct in the twilight.

That night, after dinner, we walked the cobbled streets of the medieval section of Villefranche, lit by old-fashioned lamplights so you felt you were in another century. Justin ran ahead, but not too far and kept us in sight. I told Anne about Nigel.

"It's sad," she said. "I really like them."

"So do I."

"Bobby G. and Gaby have invited us to an outdoor dinner party. Maia's *au pair* will baby-sit. She's desperate to talk to you."

"Why me?"

"You're the writer."

"She'd be better off with you. You're the psychologist."

"She thinks you'll help her understand Adam. Apparently, they've had a falling out."

"I feel like Humphrey Bogart. Solving the problems of the world is not my business, Sweetheart," I said in a Bogart voice.

"I like you like Bogart. It's kind of sexy," she said, kissing my cheek.

The next night, we dropped Justin off at Maia's villa in the hills overlooking Monte Carlo. The living room looked out to the villa's infinity swimming pool and the lights of Monte Carlo below. She led us into the *salon* and even in a casual dress, she was very pretty.

"Adam's back in Switzerland. He won't talk to me," she said and began to cry.

"What happened?" I asked.

"He submitted his novel to five publishers and they all turned it down."

"Believe me I know the feeling," I said. "Then what?"

"I called him from Florida. I sold some property there my late husband had had that I didn't really need. Made a profit of $850,000. I thought he would be pleased. Instead he said, 'Some people can't sell anything. Others make $850,000 just like that,' and hung up. I don't understand."

"I do. He felt like you were rubbing his face in it."

"I don't see that. I just wanted to let him know he didn't have to worry about money. We have plenty. Besides, he can just write another book."

"Look, Maia. I don't know if you can understand this, but you don't just write another book," I said. "Writing a book is a like having a baby. When people reject it, you don't just forget about it. It's a very personal failure and the last thing you need is someone you count on flaunting their successes in your face while you're mourning."

"That's not success. Selling a property is nothing compared to writing a book. He's very talented. Why won't he take my calls?"

"Give him time," Anne said, getting up.

"Don't worry about Justin," she said. At that moment, Justin along with her two kids, and the *au pair*, a red-haired English girl, were watching French cartoons on TV.

"Make sure the girl keeps him away from the swimming pool," Anne said, looking at the pool as if it were a loaded gun.

We drove into Monte Carlo, parked in the Avenue de la Costa parking structure and took the public elevator down to the little beach by the harbor. Gaby had set up a table with white linens and candle lamps within steps of the water. Max, Sally, Nigel and Monika were already there. Bobby G. poured champagne and we raised our glasses.

"Here's to welcoming Anne and Andy moving from Cap d'Antibes back closer to us," Bobby G. said.

"And Justin too," Gaby added.

"This is for us?" Anne said.

"Gaby did it," Sally said.

"We're very touched," Anne said.

"You've added to our lives and we wanted you to know it," Gaby said, passing around a delicious *oeufs tapenade* (chopped hardboiled eggs mixed with anchovies and olives) with pieces of *baguette* as a starter, followed by a choice of *pâtés* and a vegetable *terrine*.

"It seems you speak German. I'm beginning to think you are CIA," Max said to me.

"Nothing so James Bond. My grandmother spoke Yiddish, very little English. German and Yiddish are similar languages. When I went to Germany as a young reporter, it came very naturally to me."

"Ironic, that," Bobby G. said. "Jewish and German being so similar."

I glanced at Nigel, but he only nodded and sipped his champagne as if the other night hadn't happened.

"You know, being a reporter is a classic CIA cover. I don't know about this guy," Max said, indicating me.

"Don't confuse the writer with his characters," I said.

"You're the one who lived there," Anne said to Max. "Tell us about *your* CIA adventures."

"Nothing to tell. Had to bump off a few KGB types, of course. Steal secret plans, play hide and seek with the STASI. Escaped across Checkpoint Charley chased by the *Vopos*. Nothing really," Max said.

"I can never tell when he's lying," Monika said.

"Neither can he," Sally said.

Gaby dished up the main course, *brochette de moules* (mussels on skewers) and asparagus with *vinaigrette* sauce, followed by a seafood *tarte*.

"So do we ever believe a word Max says?" Monika asked.

"When in doubt, yes," Max said.

"When in doubt, no," Sally said and everyone laughed again. We talked on into the night. Dessert was *crème brulée*, followed by a cheese tray with more *baguettes*.

After dinner, we rolled up our pants and waded in the water, still sipping champagne by candlelight. It was late when we picked Justin up from Maia's and carried him, sleeping on my shoulder, back to the car.

"They're lovely people," Anne said as we drove back to Eze.

"Yeah, but Maia doesn't get it about writers, does she?"

"No, she doesn't, Babe. Writers aren't easy," she said, taking my hand.

"I guess not," I said.

A week later, Adrian called. He was back from his latest trip to the Middle East and asked us to join him for an evening at the Casino in Monte Carlo. We told him we hadn't been inside.

"You're joking," he said. "You live just a few kilometers from Monte Carlo and haven't been inside the Casino?"

"No, really."

"Well, tonight you will," he said. It wasn't an accident that we hadn't been inside. Though we lived among millionaires on a daily basis and though it sometimes seemed that we lived like millionaires, we never forgot that we had to keep track of every franc. What made it even more urgent was that no matter how careful we were, the money was going out faster than I had anticipated. Although, thanks to the move to Eze and the improving weather, our heating costs had dropped, unexpected expenses like babysitters and the fall of the dollar against the franc had us concerned about money.

Still, we weren't about to give up a chance to see the world-famous Monte Carlo Casino. Sally volunteered to baby-sit Justin. Max was out of town on some deal or other. For the occasion, I put on my blue suit. Anne wore her black dress and pearls. For dinner, we met Adrian for dinner at Rampoldi's, one of Monte Carlo's most fashionable restaurants, which we could never have afforded if Adrian hadn't offered to treat. I had fifteen hundred francs (about $200) in my pocket that I felt we could afford to risk at the casino.

After dinner, we went to the Hôtel de Paris for a quick drink at the American Bar and to rub the horse's knee for luck, then marched over to the Casino. One's first impression of the world-famous Monte Carlo Casino has to be disappointment. The outer *salle* was like a small second-rate Las Vegas casino, where locals in everyday clothes played slot machines and *vingt-et-un*.

But then we went through a door to a cashier's cage, where Adrian and I paid one hundred francs per person for admission to the private *salles*. We handed our tickets to the uniformed guard at the door and walked into the large baroque-styled Salle Europe. The large room was surrounded by curtained alcoves of the various *Salons Privés*. This was a different world, very James Bond. Everyone was chic, elegantly dressed, and the soft murmur of conversation mingled with the smell of cigarettes and Cuban cigars, the tinkle of cocktails, and the voices of the *croupiers*.

"What's your pleasure?" Adrian said.

"What about those?" Anne asked, pointing to one of the *Salons Privés*, where men in suits and tuxedos accompanied by attractive women in diamonds were playing *chemin de fer* so that it really was like a James Bond movie. We went over.

"*Entréz, Messieurs, Madame*," said a man in a tuxedo, drawing the curtain aside for us to enter.

"*Et on peut faire un pari le moins de quoi?*" I asked.

"*Le pari le plus petit est de cent mille francs, Monsieur*," he said.

I stepped back, nearly bumping into Adrian who was laughing at my reaction to the hundred-thousand franc or $15,000 per bet minimum.

"*Ma femme préfère la roulette*," I told the man, beating a hasty retreat.

"*C'est normal. Ma femme aussi, Monsieur*," he said with a little head bow and I appreciated that he didn't smile as he said it.

"Roulette is an excellent suggestion," Adrian said and we went over to the roulette table in the ornate Salle Europe. It was crowded with well-dressed Europeans putting down their chips as the croupier called out, "*Faîtes vos jeux, Messieurs, Mesdames. Faîtes vos jeux.*"

"God, this really is like a James Bond movie," Anne whispered.

We gave the assistant croupier our money for chips. I leaned over and put 500 francs down on black. Adrian bet 1000 francs on the first *douzaine*. It came up black, but Adrian lost. I now had 1000 francs on the table.

Adrian redoubled, putting another 2000 francs on the first *douzaine*. Twenty-eight had always been a lucky number for me and I moved my 1000 francs to the first column. Seven came up. Adrian was even and I now had 3000 francs.

"*Faîtes vos jeux, Messieurs, Mesdames. Faîtes vos jeux,*" the croupier called. I decided to go for it. As Adrian calmly bet 1000 on the second *douzaine*, I pushed the 3000-franc stack of chips on a four-number play of 25, 26, 28, and 29. I felt Anne grip my arm as the ball rolled around and around the wheel before finally settling on 29 and we whooped, Adrian patting my shoulder even though he had lost. I now had over $3000.

I glanced over at Anne to see if she wanted me to still keep going and she nodded yes. God, I love this woman, I thought. She's even crazier than I am. But I decided to play it a little safer and put it on black. Adrian, seeing I was having luck, followed with 2000 francs on black as well. The ball landed on 26 and now everyone at the table cheered as the croupier replaced some of my chips with a plaque. I had 48,000 francs, about $7,000, sitting on the black. It had been a phenomenal run. My God, I thought, doing 'if' as all gamblers do, if I had left it on the four-number play, I would have had nearly $30,000!

"*Faîtes vos jeux, Messieurs, Mesdames. Faîtes vos jeux,*" the croupier called again. Everyone was watching me and I didn't know what to do. If I just left the chips there and black came up one more time, I would have $15,000, enough to cover our expenses and give us a nice cushion till I finished the book and got my next check from

England. On the other hand, what were the odds of black coming up one more time?

Black – red. It's still 50-50. The wheel has no memory. It's always 50-50, except for zero. I decided to let it ride one last time. The croupier span the ball. Suddenly, I panicked. This was crazy. I started to reach to pull my chips back when the croupier said, *"Les jeux sont faits. Les jeux sont faits."* Too late. We watched the ball roll and roll, then settle in, jump a number and I didn't need the croupier announcing, "*Douze, rouge,*" to know we had lost. There was a groan from the crowd and an attractive blonde woman with long gold earrings gave me a sad smile as Anne patted my arm. The three of us walked over to a *serveuse* with a tray of drinks, clinked glasses and drank.

"*Dommage,*" Adrian said. "That was a hell of a run, Andy."

"Well, I was almost James Bond," I said. "I think that's as close as I'll ever get."

"Do you want to play some more?" Adrian asked.

"No," Anne said. "I think we've had enough excitement for one night."

"That was very close," Adrian said.

"I'll never forget it," I said.

That night, after we picked Justin up from Sally's and took him home. As we put him to bed, he insisted I read to him. I told him it was late, but he wanted me to read *Where The Wild Things Are* to him again, although by now he could recite the words along with me. After I read him the story and tucked him in, he looked at me.

"I really like you, Daddy," he said.

I leaned over and kissed his cheek.

"You know, Justin, I really like you too," I said and turned out the light. As I went down to shut the lights downstairs, for the first time in my life, I felt like a success.

Chapter 18

The Twelve-Hour Lunch

"Do you think we are becoming alcoholics?" Anne asked. We were on our way to Gorbio, a medieval village high in the Alpes Maritimes. Justin was in his car seat in the back. We were meeting Max and Sally and assorted friends for lunch.

In France, Sunday lunch is a tradition quite unlike the American-style Sunday brunch. For the French, it is a family affair, where children, grandchildren, in-laws, cousins, and friends assemble at the grandparents' or parents' house. A French Sunday lunch is not merely a few hours of eating, but a serious social occasion with an etiquette all its own, that often lasts much of the day. It can be the impetus for marriages, divorces, family feuds lasting generations, sexual liaisons, and other goings-on are not uncommon. For expatriates like us and our friends, Sunday lunch involved an excursion to a country restaurant or some new place someone had discovered. So far our record was ten straight hours of non-stop eating, drinking, talking and gossiping.

"I don't know. Are we?" I said.

"Well, we drink about a bottle of wine a day apiece."

"Yes, but that's with lunch and dinner combined. Everyone in France does that."

"Plus cocktails, *pastis*, whatever, during the *cinq à sept* hours. It all adds up."

"Well, what makes someone an alcoholic? What's the definition in France, where even kids drink wine?"

"That you can't stop, I suppose," she said.

"I thought it was that you drank alone. Sneaky, solitary drinking."

"No, it's whether you can stop or not. That's how you can tell."

"I think we could stop if we wanted to," I said.

"Do you want to?"

"God, no. Do you?"

"No."

Neither of us said anything. We drove up the winding mountain road, the slopes and valleys falling away below us.

"Maybe we are becoming alcoholics. I guess we'd better watch it," I said.

"I guess we better," Anne said. The road led up into the mountains, where there were no towns or villas. The mountains were gray rock and green from all the rain. They looked primeval in the shafts of sunlight breaking through the clouds. Sally's directions were simple enough. Go to Gorbio and park. We'd find everyone at the inn although there were no directions to the inn.

We had spent the previous day with Colette at her apartment in St. Laurent du Var. It was only the second time we had seen her since moving to Eze. Her cousin, Georges, and his wife Marie were also there, down from Troyes. Colette served a simple lunch that featured her special *raclette*, a cheese dish melted fondue-style with chunks of ham and potato, all of it washed down with a white Bordeaux and finished off with a homemade *tarte aux myrtilles* (blueberry tart). Afterwards, we went for a walk in a nearby park where Justin could run and tumble on the grass. Colette had brought an old soccer ball and Justin was trying to kick it, though he spent as much time throwing and running after it as kicking.

"So you like it better in Eze?" Georges asked me as we walked in the park. Anne, Colette, and Marie followed, Marie talking French and Colette translating for Anne.

"Our villa is smaller, more *intime*. Less expensive, too," I said.

"*Ah oui*, money must always be considered," he sighed.

"Not to many of the people we know. Some are *très riche*."

"That can be an even worse problem."

"One I'd like to have."

"Don't be so sure. When are you coming up to Troyes? There are bottles and bottles of champagne waiting for you."

"Maybe when I get the book done. My publisher is anxious to see it."

"And it goes?"

"Yes, but I'm not sure where."

"You'll find your way," he said.

"How do you know?"

"All writers feel that way. '*Ah! que n'ai-je mis bas tout un noeud de vipères, plutôt que de nourrir cette derision?*'[1]" he quoted.

"Who's that? Baudelaire?"

"*Formidable!* You know him?" he clapped me on the shoulder.

"No, but it sounds like him."

"In what way?"

"Depressing."

"I believe that is *la condition littéraire*."

"*La condition littéraire* or *la condition humaine*?" I said.

"Now you talk like a Frenchman," he laughed as Anne and the others caught up.

"What's so funny?" Anne asked.

"The human condition," I said, kicking the ball back to Justin who had rolled it to me.

"You see," Colette said. "Men never talk of anything of consequence. What they talk about only sounds important."

"*Pouf!* And women talk just to talk. What do women say that is of such consequence?" Georges said.

"Anne was telling us that the old woman in Eze village, the one who made the incredible bread for the village, has died," Colette said.

"The bread was good?" Georges asked me.

"The best *baguettes* I've ever eaten in my life. Even in Paris," I said.

"*Oh-là-là!* That is a serious matter. For a small village, a *tragédie*," Georges said.

"The whole village is in mourning. People refuse to speak to one another. I don't know where I'm going to buy bread. I used to drive forty-five minutes every day just to buy *baguettes* at her *boulangerie*."

"*Oui, c'est grave, très grave*," Marie nodded.

"What will happen to the *boulangerie*?" Georges asked.

"No one knows. Some in the village say someone new is planning to take it over," Anne said.

"Perhaps he will succeed," Colette said. "One never knows."

"No," Georges said. "People are not replaceable. Not like the football, where one goes out, you put another in play. It will not be the same."

Justin kicked the ball to Georges, who stopped it expertly, bounced it up to his knee and back to his foot and then kicked it back gently to Justin, who managed to kick it away.

"*Vous le voyez, Monsieur?*" Justin asked him.

"*Oui, mon petit. Je l'ai vu*," Georges said, then quietly to me. "Finish the book, André. You are also not replaceable."

We drove into the parking lot next to Gorbio's medieval gate. As was common with most medieval villages, you parked outside because the village streets, built narrow and winding and with sharp turns for defense in another age, were impassable for cars. We walked the cobblestone path to the inn, its wooden sign looking like it had been there for centuries, and went inside.

Bobby G. and Gaby were already there. Max and Sally came and soon everyone arrived: Chuck, Emma, and their kids, Yasper and Betje, Mark and Rachel, Nigel and Monika. We sat at a long wooden table that took up nearly the entire restaurant. Chuck ordered a number of bottles of wine, Evian water, plates of olives, *tapenades*, *pâtés*, *amuse bouches*, and sliced *baguettes* for the table.

"Well, for my money, she was murdered," Emma said.

"Who was?" Anne asked.

"The French actress, Monique something. She died in a helicopter crash near Nice," Sally explained.

"What makes you so sure?" Bobby G. asked.

"She was the Prince's mistress."

"So who would want to kill her?" Yasper asked.

"Who knows? Maybe the Prince himself," Rachel whispered.

"Why would Prince Rainier want to kill his own mistress? Makes no sense," Sally said.

"I heard he was trying to drop her. Maybe she wouldn't go. Or wanted money," Monika said.

"Maybe she was trying to blackmail him," Emma said.

"The authorities called it a mechanical failure, '*un accident machinal*,'" Chuck said.

"Then why were there reports that witnesses saw the helicopter explode in mid-air?" Monika demanded. "Also, there were rumors that the Prince had told her to leave Monaco and they had fought."

"You don't really think Prince Rainier would...?" Anne said.

"He keeps a pretty tight rein on everything in Monaco," Max said.

"That's business. Monaco sells itself as a secure tax haven for the rich. TV cameras on every street, policemen stationed everywhere, total bank secrecy. You don't see them, but there are agents watching everyone who comes in and out of Monte Carlo. He has to control things," Chuck said.

"Yes, but murder? Seems a bit *outré*," Sally said.

"Still, they fought just before she got on the flight. I know someone who said he demanded she return the jewels he had given her," Emma said.

"Jewels. That's serious," Monika said.

"They say he had a row with Princess Grace the day she died," Betje said.

"It was horrible. The car crash. The funeral. I'll never forget it," Sally said.

"The Prince was devastated," Max said.

"Everyone was," Emma said.

"I hate that road," Anne said.

"So do I," Sally said.

"Princess Stephanie was driving the car when it happened," Max said.

"The police said Grace was driving," Betje said and everyone laughed.

"Yeah, right. Grace who hated to drive, especially that car, and who was too upset and furious to drive. That's why Stephanie ran after her, to at least prevent her from driving," Max said.

"Stephanie said Grace was driving, but we heard the witnesses who saw them taken out of the car say no," Nigel said.

"Afterwards, Stephanie didn't want to talk," Sally said.

"They kept her away from the reporters. They wanted to protect her. Afraid of what she might say," Monika said.

"When they took Grace to the hospital, it was a total screw-up," Max said. "The elevator was too small, so they had to carry her up the stairs on a stretcher. The stairwell was too narrow, so they had to bang and tilt the stretcher, making the blood rush to her head. For all we know, she might have survived if not for they way they carried her up. When the Prince found out, he was furious. He fired the lot of them. It was awful."

"Why were they fighting?" Anne asked.

"Over his mistress, of course," Monika said.

"Which one?" Rachel said.

"The one that died in the crash?" Anne asked.

"Or was bumped off," Emma said ominously.

"You sound like a dame in a Hollywood movie," Nigel said.

"I like Hollywood movies," Emma said. "Speaking of which, has anyone see *Out of Africa* yet?"

"We have," Anne said. We had seen it in Nice with Colette babysitting Justin.

"How is it?"

"We liked it. It really recreates that time and place."

"I heard it was slow as hell," Chuck said.

"A woman's film," Max agreed. "People walk around with guns, but they don't shoot anything, just talk about having affairs."

"I like that Robert Redford, all right," Emma said.

"Don't we all," Sally said.

"He's so handsome," Gaby said.

"Absolutely," Anne said.

"All right. We'll take it as a bloody given that all the women at this table want to shag Robert Redford. Makes me wonder what the rest of us are doing here," Nigel said.

"Substitutes for the fantasy, that's us, the 'B Team.' *Santé*, ladies," Bobby G. said, raising his glass and drinking.

"That's what makes Frenchwomen so sexy. They think the fantasy, but they're practical when it comes to husbands and lovers," Max said.

"What's practical?" Sally said.

"Practical is thinking Robert Redford while *Mademoiselle tire une pipe* (performs fellatio) with guys like us," Chuck said.

"That's so *élégant*, Chuck. Thank you for the image. Thank God, the food is here," Sally said, as the waiter brought course after course, starting with a salad with a white Ste-Croix Bordeaux wine, artichoke hearts with poached eggs, fish soup, of course, a Côte d'Azur prerequisite, followed by a good red St. Julien wine.

An old Frenchman and a woman, he with a mandolin, she with an accordion, sat in a corner and started to play Edith Piaf songs as we ate. Emma's boys ran outside to play and Justin wanted to join them. Anne and I looked at each other. I told him he could as the waiter served portions of *pigeon au pot* topped with *foie gras* with

Parisien-style *petits pois*, presented with an amazing St. Emilion wine. The food was fantastic, but I was worried about Justin, unsupervised on the streets of a medieval village he had never been in before. Emma was talking about *au pairs* and how hard it was to find one who wasn't trying to seduce any male on the *plage*, as I signaled to Anne that I was going outside to watch Justin. As I got up, Emma said, "Let him on his own. You're too overprotective."

"Maybe," I said and went outside, where her two boys, both older than Justin, were chasing each other and Justin with sticks and cursing in French.

"*Venez, salaud!*" the older boy called.

"*Qui parle? Oiseau de merde!*" the other said, hitting his brother in the shoulder with the stick. I grabbed the stick away from him and told him to stop, then ran after Justin, who had climbed onto a notch on the parapet of the old town wall. I grabbed Justin and looked down from the parapet, It was a sheer drop of hundreds of feet and nothing to keep him from falling. I had gotten there just in time.

"Are you okay, Justin?" I said.

"They hit me and used bad words, Daddy. I ran away."

"I know, I heard. Do you want to play with them?"

"No, I don't like them."

"I don't either. Do you want me to stay out here with you?"

He nodded and took my hand. We began to explore the cobblestoned streets of the village. I stopped by a little café and bought him a vanilla *glace*. I went back to the car and got a Frisbee and we played catch in the parking lot. When we came back, Emma's sons were fighting and grappling on the ground. I pulled them apart and told them to stop.

"Who asked you, *tête de veau?*" the older one said.

"I asked me, you little shit," I said, lifting him off the ground by his shirt. "Now you stop fighting now and watch your mouth, or I'm marching you in and letting your father deal with you."

I got the three boys to play Frisbee and watched for a while. Eventually, Justin and I went back in and I handed him over to Anne.

"How are the boys? I told you they'd be fine," Emma said.

"Actually, they were fighting with sticks and there are precipices with hundreds of foot drops on this street," I said.

"Well, they do fight," she said and went back to talking about some woman whose husband owned the new Jaguar car dealership in Monte Carlo as if I hadn't said a word. By this time, it was getting late. The lights came on as the shadows lengthened over the street outside the restaurant. The old man and woman with the mandolin and the accordion left and a giant cheese tray with dozens of cheeses was sitting on the table. Things were slowing down, so Sally invited everyone to continue the lunch at her villa.

We left the restaurant and a caravan of cars followed Max and Sally's car back to their villa in Cap Martin. The villa and garden were lit with lights strung on overhead lines. Sally broke out dessert *tartes* and bottles of Max's homemade wine. We sat outside under the lights on the garden *terrasse*, while Justin played with some of the toys that Sally now kept in a lower drawer for him that he went to on his own.

"Where's Maia?" Chuck asked.

"In Switzerland with Adam."

"I thought they had broken up," Anne said.

"Not as far as she is concerned," Sally said.

"You've got to give her credit, she goes after what she wants," Emma said.

Carl came by on his motorcycle. Apparently, the Count and Contessa di Portanova were in Monaco for some party or other. He had just flown them back from their house in Acapulco.

"You've got to see this place," Carl told me. "It's on a cliff overlooking the bay and it's incredible. They let us stay there sometimes when they are not using it. You wouldn't believe it. It's the most amazing house I've ever seen," Carl told me.

"What's amazing about it?" I asked.

"I don't know how to describe it. It's got a kind of sea theme and there are all sorts of sculptures and mosaics and things. Even the silverware is different. It's shaped like seashells or something and made of solid gold. The whole house is like that. I don't know how to describe it. But if you're interested, come to Acapulco, I'll arrange it," he said.

"We'd love to," Anne said.[2]

"Has anyone been to Mougins since Papa Doc arrived?" Bobby G. asked.

"The Frogs got rid of his Tonton Macoute goons. So far, things are quiet," Max said.

"Thank god the Marcoses didn't come here too," Sally said. A popular revolt had overthrown Philippine president Ferdinand Marcos and his wife, the notorious Imelda Marcos.

"They went to Hawaii," Chuck said.

"Is there enough room in Hawaii for all her shoes?" Rachel said. Imelda Marcos was rumored to own more than 3,000 pairs of shoes.

"Well, at least she's not here."

"They say, Prince Andrew and his fiancée, Fergie, are coming here," Sally said.

"Yeah, but the British Royal family won't let them meet with the Monaco Royal family. They regard them as *parvenus*," Nigel said.

"That's ridiculous," Max said. 'The Grimaldi's have ruled here for seven hundred years. It's the British Royals who are the real *nouveau riche*, barely on the throne two centuries. And they're not even English! They're Krauts!"

"Of course they're British," Rachel said.

"Not true. The current family came from Hanover in the eighteenth century. They couldn't even speak English. And Prince Albert, Queen Victoria's husband was from Saxe-something or other. They're all Germans. They named the family after Windsor Castle because of anti-German feeling during World War I. They got their name from a castle!"

"Still, we like having the monarchy," Nigel said.

"Why?" Max asked.

"Someone needs to open shopping malls in hideously frumpy British clothing. It sets a standard," Nigel said.

"What standard?" Gaby asked.

"It allows us to be simultaneously unfashionable and superior. And, of course, it brings in the tourists. They line up in droves around Buckingham Palace. Sort of like beggars in Calcutta, but with money," Nigel said.

"So this whole British royalty thing is just the British version of Disneyland. Then why bother going to Ascot and Wimbledon like you guys do?" Anne asked.

"First, because it's fun. One sees more ridiculous hats than at the Mad Hatter's Tea Party. And second, they're the only royals we've got, poor things," Nigel said.

"Prince Charles and Princess Diana came here for their honeymoon, but not to Monaco," Sally said.

"That marriage is a sham," Monika said.

"Why? Do you believe the tabloids?" Anne asked.

"Those two don't even appear together in public any more. Charles's got a mistress for sure," Max said.

"Only one?" Gaby asked.

"Of course only one. He's British, poor bugger," Nigel said and everyone laughed.

It was past midnight by the time we picked up Justin, fast asleep on the sofa, and carried him to the car and drove back to Eze.

"Twelve hours for lunch. A new record," I said, as we drove the dark coast road back to Eze, passing the lights of a freighter anchored in the water off Cap d'Ail.

"That was fun. I'm glad you went out and watched Justin, though. You're a good Daddy," Anne said.

"Emma thinks we're overprotective."

"That's what people say till something happens."

"Why? Do you think something will happen?"

"It usually does," she said.

Chapter 19

Le Bal de la Rose or The Princess Wants To Dance

I had gotten back into a rhythm on the book. In the mornings I would get up early, before Anne and Justin, and go down and make *café américain* and bring it up to the balcony outside our bedroom, the wooden chairs outside cool and wet with dew. I would wipe off the chairs with a rag and drink the coffee and look out over the villas and the trees and the washed-out blue of the sky over the sea. The mornings were still cold and I would shiver in my sweater as I drank the coffee and go over what was happening in the book.

Sawyer and Suong had been captured by the warlord, Bhun Sa. The threads were coming together: Bhun Sa and Sawyer's mission, intrigue in Bangkok and Phnom Penh, Toonsang still trying to kill Sawyer, and Sawyer beginning to wonder which side the girl, Suong was on.

The next part of the book was action. I was still plotting it out over breakfast when Anne mentioned the *Bal de la Rose*, the highlight of the social season on the French Riviera.

"We have to go. Everyone will be there," Anne said.

"Who's everyone?" I asked. "Will Max and Sally be there?"

"I don't think so. They've been in the past, though. I guess it's old hat to them."

"So who will be there?"

"The Royal Family of Monaco. Everyone. You know, it was Princess Grace that started it. Apparently, it's decorated with thousands and thousands of roses," she said.

"Hence the name."

"Don't be cute. It's *the* event of the year. Can't we go? I've never been to a society ball."

"How do we get invited?"

"You can buy a ticket. It's five thousand francs."

"Five thousand per couple!" I said. "That's over $800!"

"Per person."

"Oh well, that's so much better!"

"But it's the event of the year! And it's for a good cause. The money goes to charity."

"What charity?"

"I'm not sure. The Monaco Red Cross, I think."

"Well, that's good. I'm sure they'll help us the next time a tornado hits Eze," I said.

"You know you're being ridiculous. Lots of people are going. Chuck and Emma, Stuart and Glenda, Mark and Rachel, Maia and Adam. It'll be fun."

"And expensive," I said.

"Can we afford it?"

"Maybe, if we don't send Justin to college."

"I hate it when you carry on this way over money," she said.

"At these prices, get used to it."

Over the next three days, over lunch by the marina in St. Jean Cap Ferrat, helping Anne at the Algerian laundry, at the *supermarché* in Nice, while washing the car, visiting the *Jardin-Exotique* for a project for Justin's *crèche*, buying *baguettes* in Roquebrune now that the old woman in Eze Village was gone, over dinner or wine by the fire while Justin watched France's hottest new hit for kids, the old

Fess Parker *Davy Crockett* black and white TV series, the *Bal de la Rose* was *the* topic of conversation.

"It's $1600," I told Anne.

"It's only once in a lifetime. Besides, you'll meet billionaires there. Maybe one will buy your book or want to hire you for a writing contract. Think of it as a business investment."

"OK, suppose we decide to go. That's $1600 and that's it, right?"

"Well, you can't wear your suit. You'll need a tux. I think there's a place in Nice where you can rent," she said.

"What about you? The black dress?"

"That thing! You must be joking!"

"I didn't think so, but I guess I was."

"It's the high society event of the year! Every woman there will be wearing the latest *couturier* original and her best jewelry. I can't go wearing that old *shmatte!*"

"Can we rent a gown?" The look she gave me was the kind of condescending look women bestow on the male moron they are stuck with when matters of importance to women are discussed. "So you have to buy a designer gown? How much is that?"

"At least five thousand for anything decent," she said.

"Francs?" I said hopefully.

"Dollars."

"Great. So far we're up to $6600, not counting the tux or babysitting. Say $7,000. What about jewels?"

"That's a problem," she admitted.

"What about fakes. You know, zirconia or something?"

"I–don't–wear–fakes," she said through gritted teeth. "Besides, you can always tell and it's worse than wearing no jewelry at all."

"You can't tell," I said.

"Trust me. These women can tell the difference."

"So if we add in getting your hair done, makeup, going out afterwards, drinks, odds and ends, not counting jewelry, we could do it for about $7500. Is that it?"

"Basically."

"$7500 to go out one night? Babe," I sighed, "you're married to the wrong guy." "It is a lot," she said softly.

The next day, we talked about it over drinks with Nigel and Monika at the American bar in the Hotel de Paris, Justin sending toy trucks racing across the empty table next to us. Anne asked them if they were going.

"Actually, we hadn't decided. I'd need a new dress," Monika said. "Nothing last year is acceptable. The latest original is absolutely *de rigueur*."

"It's a lot of money," Anne said.

"Actually, we went the last couple of years and except for what happened before and after, it was a bore," Nigel said. "Besides, all those bloody roses make me sneeze. Truth be told, it's not the same without Princess Grace."

"Nigel's right. Besides I've got a better idea," Monika said.

"What?" Anne said.

"The *Bal* itself is nothing. All right, it is something, but it's not *really* something."

"What exactly does that mean, in English?" Nigel said.

"It means, everyone comes here for drinks before the *Bal*."

"Here, meaning right here, the American Bar?" I asked.

"Everyone will be here. Everyone who matters, except the royals, although sometimes even them," Monika said. "Then afterwards, everyone who's anyone goes out clubbing either to Jimmy'z or nowadays to Noroc's. Actually, Noroc's is the 'In' *club privée* now that Regine's is closed."

"Why did Regine's close? I heard she's huge in Paris," Anne said.

Monika motioned us closer. "She and Princess Stephanie got into a fight," she whispered. "They say Regine slapped her. The Prince ordered Regine out of Monaco and closed the place down. Stephanie's pretty wild, but he has to back his daughter."

"Quite right. Can't have just anyone slap a royal. They have people to do that for them," Nigel mumbled.

"So what are you suggesting?" Anne said.

"On the night of the *Bal*, we all meet here for drinks. Nigel's table is always reserved. Then when everyone else toddles off to the *Bal*, we go out for a nice dinner. After dinner, when everyone leaves the *Bal*, we'll be at Noroc's. We'll have a ringside seat. Truth be told, we won't miss a thing except the speeches and boring stuff," Monika said.

"Can we get into Noroc's?" I asked.

"I'm a member," Nigel said. "We've got several bottles of Glenlivet in the lockup."

"Why do we need our own bottle?" I asked.

"You'll see," he said.

The night of the *Bal de la Rose*, we got dressed to the nines, I in my rented tux, Anne in her black dress and pearls. We dropped Justin off at Max and Sally's.

"You're sure he's no bother?" Anne asked Sally, curled up on the sofa with a glass of wine and a book. She had stocked one drawer with all sorts of toys, including a set of building blocks that Justin was busy piling up.

"Actually, we enjoy him." Sally thought for a moment. "I never thought I'd say that about having a kid around so much, Max's are all grown you know, but it's true."

"We really appreciate this," I said.

"You guys look fantastic. Let me know how it goes," she said.

We drove to the parking structure on the Avenue de la Costa in Monte Carlo and walked down to the Hôtel de Paris. The American Bar was unbelievably crowded and noisy and we had to squeeze through the crush to Nigel and Monika's table.

"Glad you're here. Had to beat off two countesses and the Monagasque Finance Minister to keep your chairs," Nigel said.

"How'd you hold them off?" I asked.

"Told them you were President Reagan's illegitimate son. Odd thing is, they believed me."

"What are we drinking?" Anne asked.

"Champagne cocktails, of course. It's the *Bal de la Rose*," Monika said, signaling the white-jacketed waiter. "Oh my god, look at that!"

"Who's that?" Anne asked about an attractive dark-haired woman in a low-cut red gown wearing the most incredible diamond and ruby necklace, with at least half a dozen rubies the size of walnuts.

"That's Francesca. Don't know her last name. It keeps changing," Monika said.

"How'd she get such a fabulous necklace?"

"She used to be a hooker. Married one of her wealthier customers. Apparently he died leaving her a lot of money, but she likes to gamble, so if anyone's interested, for the right price . . ."

Madame Bacardi was at the next table wearing a yellow gown and a diamond necklace not to be imagined outside a Harry Winston showcase. Mark and Rachel waved to us from across the room, Rachel was in a see-through blue chiffon wearing a large sapphire on a platinum necklace. With them was Madame Piaget, dripping with diamonds and wearing a pearl and yellow diamond necklace on her forehead *à la* Princess Diana. But the prize for diamonds, Anne and Monika agreed, had to go to a woman in her sixties, her hair dyed a violent black, wearing a square-cut diamond ring that had to be at least two inches long, trailed by a blonde man in a satin dinner jacket who was at most half her age.

"Who's that?" Anne asked.

"Don't know," Monika said. "Might be Princess Isabelle. Someone said she was coming."

"What's she princess of?" I asked.

"Orleans. Related to the Count de Paris," Nigel said.

"And he is -- ?"

"Heir to the French throne if there were such a thing. Odd these titles without property, a bit like a jockey without a horse, if you know what I mean."

"How do you keep track of all this?"

"You have to remember, on the Côte d'Azur, gossip, not francs, is the local currency," Nigel said as the waiter brought our champagne and dropped sugar cubes into the glasses.

Niarchos, the Greek billionaire came in a group with three women, the film star, Yves Montand, the designer Yves St. Laurent wearing his Legion of Honor pin, and Prince Albert, who was with a blonde even more spectacular than the redhead he had brought to Mark and Rachel's yacht were at the bar. A number of the Monagasques bowed and young women curtsied to him, which he waved off and gestured to the barmen to give them all drinks.

"Incredible if you think about it," Monika mused. "There's probably more wealth in this one room than in most countries."

"And half of them are sleeping with someone they shouldn't," Nigel said, eying a French actress on the arm of an Italian film producer famously married to an Italian movie star who was nowhere to be seen.

"Who's the blonde with Prince Albert? She's spectacular," Anne said.

"Some supermodel. Swedish, I think," Nigel said.

"Why is he always with a different girl?" Anne asked.

"Camouflage," Monika said, darkly. "There've been rumors..."

"Shhh! Change the topic!" Nigel whispered. "Here comes Henri," he said, nodding to a burly man in a suit who had just come from speaking to the Prince. "*Bon soir, Henri.* What are you up to?" he called out.

"*Bon soir, Nigel. C'est le Bal.* Have to keep one's eye out. All the *gros légumes* are here tonight. The jewels alone, *mon Dieu*," he said, rolling his eyes to indicate the value of the jewels and moving on.

"Who's that?" Anne asked.

"Monaco's Chief of Police. Tough old bugger. Lives in the apartment below ours." Nigel checked his watch. "Well, cheerio, chaps. *Bal*'s about to start. Watch! In twenty minutes, this place'll be a morgue."

Sure enough, a few minutes later, someone called out, "*Le Bal, le Bal*," and people began to leave. We left too and went to Pulcinella, a *fin de siècle* Italian restaurant that was Nigel's favorite in Monte Carlo.

As we were eating, Anne sighed. "I just realized I'll never in my life have the kind of jewelry and clothes we've seen tonight."

"Did you see the size of that Princess' diamonds?" Monika said.

"Unbelievable!"

"They're just rocks. Chemically no different from coal," I said.

Anne looked at me. "Is that supposed to make me feel better? Less jealous?"

"Just trying to keep things in perspective."

"Whose perspective? Mr. Boring Scientist. Explain to me again why I keep you around?"

"Because I think even without diamonds you're more beautiful than any of those women."

"How do you do that?" Anne demanded.

"Do what?"

"Say the right thing just when I'm about to get pissed at you. He gets away with murder," she said to Nigel and Monika.

"Well done, chap!" Nigel said. "Thought you'd bought it that time," he muttered in my ear.

"So did I."

After dinner, we went to Noroc's, with uniformed doormen outside only letting in members they knew by sight. Inside, the club was jammed with people packed tighter than a New York subway car at rush hour, everyone talking, shouting, the darkened room lit with revolving lights sliding across bodies gyrating to the music, the floor shaking with the sound. A friend of Nigel's, a bodyguard of a wealthy duchess whose name Nigel told me, but I couldn't hear over the noise, forced a path through for us to a table next to the dance floor.

A sexy *serveuse* in a mini-skirt came over and Nigel gave her the number of his bottle of Scotch and ordered Perrier water to go with it.

"Why the numbered bottle?" I asked Nigel.

"Check the drink menu," he said, handing it to me. I looked at the list and nearly choked. Cocktails were 400 francs apiece, nearly $70 per drink! Wine was from 200 to 3000 francs per glass! Champagne was really expensive! A bottle of Dom Perignon was listed at 120,000 francs (about $20,000)! Anne ordered a champagne cocktail, like the one we'd had at the Hôtel de Paris!

"Wait! She'll have Scotch with the rest of us!" I shouted over the noise.

"No, I want a champagne cocktail," Anne said.

"No, she doesn't," I said, showing Anne the drink menu and sighed with relief when Anne, giving me a look, said, "I'll have the Scotch."

We drank our Scotch and I pulled Anne onto the crowded dance floor, knocking into someone as I did so.

"*Faîtes attention!*" I said.

"*Pardon, Monsieur,*" Prince Albert said, as he led the spectacular blonde from the dance floor. Anne and I squeezed onto the floor and began dancing.

"Do you know who you almost knocked over?" she asked.

"Prince Albert. That's some blonde!" I said.

"Maybe if you pulled your eyes back into your head, you wouldn't be knocking royalty over."

"I only have eyes for you, dear," I sang into Anne's ear.

"And the blonde," she said.

"Well, if Monika's right, she's no good to him," I said and gasped as she jabbed me with her elbow. The DJ started a slower song and we danced again.

"Is this what you hoped it would be?" I whispered.

"It's almost as good as going to the *Bal*. After all, how often do you get to almost knock over a prince?" she said.

"Ah, but I did it the French way, with style," I said, swirling her around.

The club filled with more and more people coming from the *Bal* and letting their hair down. A young couple at the next table were kissing passionately. People were tossing paper streamers and confetti over the dancers. Stuart and Glenda stopped by to say hi. Mark showed up with a Scandinavian twenty-something woman.

"Where's Rachel?" Anne asked.

"Haven't the foggiest? Probably off shagging somewhere. My God, doesn't she look bloody delicious," Mark said to Nigel and me, indicating Anne.

"First rate. Absolutely," Nigel said thickly, the whiskey starting to show.

"What about me?" Monika said.

"Love of my life. That's the bloody truth," Nigel said.

By three in the morning, we had nearly emptied Nigel's bottle and ordered cocktails on our own and Anne signaled me that she was getting tired. I tried to give Nigel money to pay for our share of the drinks and he pushed my hand away.

"You're a bloody writer. Bloody writers never have any bloody money. But we are the true aristocrats," he slurred. "The only true aristocrats."

I went to the cloakroom to get our coats. Princess Stephanie, looking beautiful in a sleek black gown and jewels, was standing by herself in the vestibule. I recognized her at once from her pictures in the media. She was swaying to the music, her eyes half-open. She looked like she was on something. Booze, drugs, something.

"I want to dance! Dance with me!" she demanded, throwing her arms around my neck and stepping on my toe. She smelled of champagne and Guerlain. A heavy-set plainclothes security guard, at least that's what I took him for, pleaded with her to come home.

"*Je vous en prie, Altesse. Il faut partir immediatement, rapidement,*" he said.

"I want to dance!" she announced. "Don't you want to dance with me?" she whispered, pulling me close, her cheek on mine. I didn't know what to say. It was the strangest feeling I'd ever had. Embarrassment for her and myself mixed with the not unpleasant sensation of a beautiful young woman's body, a Princess no less, pressed against mine, combined with the suspicion that she was probably stoned and the thought that my wife and friends were about to walk in any second and see me with another woman's arms around me.

"*S'il vous plaît, Princesse. Ce n'est pas correct. Je vous en prie,*" the security man pleaded.

"I want to have fun. They never let me have any fun!" she pouted, holding me tight. "Don't you like me?" she said, her dark eyes looking into mine as if seeing me for the first time.

"You're very beautiful, your Highness, but my wife and I were just leaving," I said, disengaging her arms from around my neck and stepping back.

"You're no fun! You missed your chance," she snapped and turned and walked into the club, passing Anne, Nigel, and Monika just as they were coming out. The security man looked at me, shrugged as though we were both somehow complicit in something, then followed her into the club.

"Wasn't that Princess Stephanie?" Anne asked, wide-eyed.

"It *was* Stephanie," Monika said.

"Did you talk to her?" Anne asked.

"What did she say?" Monika said.

"She wanted to dance," I said.

"What did you say?" Anne said.

"I told her I was married."

"Damn right. She better keep her paws off my man," Anne said.

Later, after we picked up Justin from Max and Sally's and were driving home, Anne said, "Interesting night, *le Bal de la Rose.*"

"You know, international high society and royalty isn't much different than any other kind of society," I said.

"I guess not."

We drove in silence, the outlines of the hills slowly becoming visible against the pre-dawn sky.

"Well, I almost danced with a princess. Not bad for a kid from the streets of Brooklyn," I said.

"That's true, Babe. You almost did," Anne said.

Chapter 20

A Cold Spring In Paris

We had come to Paris to do our income taxes and to settle a bet I had made with Max. Our taxes were complicated because I had earned money both in the U.S. and from my publisher in England, plus there was supposed to be a tax exemption for Americans living abroad, and I wasn't sure how it was all supposed to be handled. We couldn't find anyone on the Côte d'Azur who could answer our questions.[1] Max and Sally recommended an expatriate American accountant in Paris, Richard, who did their taxes. The problem was that we couldn't handle it all by phone or mail and Richard would not leave Paris. So we would have to get on a plane... not that anyone ever needs an excuse to go to Paris.

It had been several years since either Anne or I had been in Paris and living on the Riviera, for all the sophisticated company, there was always a sense that we were still in the provinces, that the real action was in Paris. Also, Max and I had gotten into a debate one night at Stuart's pub over where the true center of France was.

On every road in France, one sees signposts with a kilometer number, for example *"Kilomètre 519," "Kilomètre 302,"* etc. These signs advise motorists how far they are from a specific point in Paris, which is considered the center or locus of the French road system. Max maintained that the point from which all these *Kilomètre* signs were measured was the *Etoile*, as the French refer to the traffic hub where the *Arc de Triomphe* is. I seemed to recall that there was a marker in the pavement in front of Notre Dame cathedral. Egged on by Bobby G. and Stuart, we wound up betting $100 on it. If a marker showing that the center for roads in France was in front of Notre Dame, I would win; if it were anyplace else, Max would win.

With tax day, April 15th fast approaching, we made an appointment with Richard and booked a flight to Paris. The night before we left, Anne woke me in the middle of the night.

"There's someone in the yard. I think they'll trying to break in," she whispered.

"What?" I said, fumbling for my glasses.

"They're in the front yard. Hurry!" she said, holding an iron, the cord dangling, as a weapon. The only window upstairs from which we could see the front yard was in Justin's room. We crept into his room so as not to wake him and peered down from the open window. Sure enough, we could just make out two figures in the front yard, shadowy in the light from the streetlight and hear the murmur of them talking in French.

"Can I help you? What do you want?" Anne called down in English. The shadows froze and they stopped talking.

"What are you talking to them in English for? You think there's a guild of English-speaking French crooks?" I whispered.

"It doesn't hurt to be polite," she whispered back.

"To thieves?! In the middle of the night?!"

I leaned out the window.

"*Attention! Qu'est-ce que vous faîtes ici? Allez-vous en! Je vais téléphoner au police!*" I shouted down.

"*Attention, vous-même, salaud!*" one of them shouted back as if there might be a confrontation. But instead, they walked calmly out of the yard and got into a van parked near the streetlight. I tried to make out the license plate but couldn't see it as they started to drive up the hill. They made a U-turn and I spotted the license number as they drove under the streetlight on their way down to the *Corniche*.

"Quick, I need a piece of paper," I said.

"Why?"

"Never mind," I said, trying to remember the number as I raced down the stairs to my office, stubbing my toe as I banged into the desk and wrote down the license number of the *camionnette*. I got my flashlight and went around the house, making sure all the doors and shutters were locked, then went back up to Justin's room, where Anne was still peering out the window.

"Anything?" I asked.

"They're gone," she said, looking down at Justin. "He slept through the whole thing."

"That's good," I whispered, motioning her back to our room.

"Should we call the police?" she asked.

"It's a small town. There's nobody there. We'll call in the morning. Did anybody know we were leaving?"

"Just Max and Sally. Oh, and the real estate agent. We were supposed to notify her."

"You don't suppose she's in cahoots with the thieves?" It was not uncommon on the Côte d'Azur for thieves to break into villas closed for the *fermeture annuelle*. If someone thought there was no one home in our villa, it would be an ideal time to rob us – only maybe they got there one night early.

"I don't think so, but who knows?" she said.

The next morning, we left for the airport in Nice. I called the local *gendarmerie* from the airport and gave them the license plate number, then called the *propriété immobilière* to let them know about the attempted break-in and asked them to follow up while we were out of town.

"I'm a little nervous about leaving," Anne said, as we boarded the flight to Paris.

"We'll be OK," I said. We had taken everything important,

including my manuscript, with us. The worst we could lose would be some clothes and books and things.

After the Côte d'Azur, Paris was cold and gray and we were glad we had brought our winter clothes. In the past, Anne and I had always stayed on the Right Bank, but this time, with me in the middle of the book, we were feeling literary and decided to stay on the Left Bank at the Hotel Saint Simon, near the Boulevard St Germain.

The hotel, with its old-fashioned French courtyard with outdoor tables, rooms filled with antiques, the vaulted catacomb-like dining room in the basement, a bed in our room in which, according to the *directrice* at the front desk, Humphrey Bogart and Lauren Bacall had slept, and a really good inexpensive bistro on the corner, would have been perfect, except that Jerry Hulse, Travel Editor of the L.A. Times had apparently written an article about the Saint Simon and the place was packed with American tourists.

It felt strange, hearing American English all around us after all this time and except for breakfasts in the dining room, we spent little time there. Most important for Justin, there was a small toy store on the way to the nearest Metro station, and it became a habit for us to stop in each time we passed.

Richard had an office on the Right Bank, near the Boulevard Haussman. After a morning spent going over numbers, we went to the Tuileries Garden, where Justin could run around. We had crepes at a stand with tables under the trees. The day was cold and we decided to play tourist, although Anne was still worried about the villa.

"Do you think she'll call?" she asked, meaning the real estate agent. We had left her our hotel phone number and asked her to call if she found out anything.

"I don't know, but we don't want it to ruin our time here."

"So where do we go first?"

"Notre Dame. I want to win that bet," I said.

We took the Metro to the Ile de la Cité station and after a bit of searching, Anne found the circular marker with the star in the center labeled "*Kilomètre Zero*"embedded in the cobblestones in front of the entrance to Notre Dame cathedral. We took snapshots of the marker and of Anne pointing down at it, with Notre Dame in the background.

Afterwards, we went inside Notre Dame and while tourist groups followed guides around to peer at the stained-glass windows, I picked up Justin and told him about the Hunchback who had lived among the gargoyles in the tower and had fallen in love with the beautiful girl and when we got outside, I showed him the gargoyles sticking out of the side of the cathedral. Afterwards, we crossed the footbridge to the Ile St. Louis and went to Berthillon's for their wonderful ice cream.

The next day, we had our second encounter with thieves. We were on our way to the Jeu de Paume, where the Impressionist paintings were still kept back then. Things had changed in Paris. All along the Rue de Rivoli and in the Tuileries, black African street peddlers were hawking rugs, bracelets, and toy birds, all of them the same and obviously from the same source. Some of the immigrants were aggressive, shoving them at passers-by and when I went ahead up the stairs with Justin and the stroller, Anne was surrounded by a swarm of Gypsy children.

A teenage Gypsy girl shoved a newspaper at Anne, as if to get her to buy it. Anne fended her off, but as the girl suddenly backed away, Anne realized that her purse had been opened and that her alligator notebook, that looked like a change-purse, was missing.

Anne ran after the Gypsy girl. She ripped the notebook out of the girl's hand, all the while yelling in English that this girl was a thief and for someone to call the *gendarmes*. As she did so, the Gypsy children scattered, disappearing into the crowd.

"A lot of help you were," Anne said when she caught up to Justin and me.

"I didn't even know it was happening. Besides, I had my hands full," I said, indicating Justin and the stroller.

"My hero. Some protector you are."

"Sorry, but if I have to choose between losing some money and hanging onto Justin, I'll pick Justin any time."

"I know. What's come over this city?" she said, as we got in line for the Jeu de Paume. "All these Africans and Arabs and Gypsies hustling everyone."

"They're displaced – and desperate. We've been living in a cocoon on the Côte d'Azur. There's another France."

"Someone tried to rob us down there too."

"I know. Something's happening," I said as our part of the line entered the Jeu de Paume.

Basically, there are two ways to do a museum: You can run around and try to see everything, especially everything famous, just so you can say you've done it. This can be exhausting and if you do it that way, in memory, the whole experience is often a blur. The other way is to take your time and select just a few things and instead of just glancing at them – with the appropriate amount of reverence due some cultural icon that supposed to be great art, even though 99 out of 100 people haven't a clue what makes it greater than something you can buy for a dozen francs on the Rue de Rivoli – you can really look at something that a master may have spent a lifetime working up to and see something that will give you joy.

Anne's first time in Paris had been with her grandmother, who took her to Europe as a high school graduation present. Her grandmother had marched her through every museum and tourist attraction in Paris. Anne's memory of it was as a kind of cultural forced-march and she was more than ready to try the second method with me.

While we enjoyed the Cézannes, the Van Goghs, the Gaughins, the Sisleys and such, what really caught us were the Monet haystacks, four of them in the same room. We spent nearly an hour just looking at them, because in them, each of them a picture of the same haystacks, you could see Monet literally inventing and extending Impressionism as he was painting them. Each was the same, but different, and what was different was the light, or rather the artist's perception of the light on the same thing at different times and in doing so, he makes you the viewer, a witness to the change, something you could never understand if you saw just one of the paintings, but only if you saw them all together, next to each other in the same room, as we were doing.

"So where are we going for lunch?" Anne asked.

"How about the Closerie? We can't come to Paris and not go to the Closerie," I said. I wanted to go there because it had been Hemingway's favorite hangout in Paris, and also mine when I was a young freelance reporter for the *International Herald Tribune* and could scrape together the money. Also, the oysters. We took the Metro to the Boulevard du Montparnasse and walked to La Closerie des Lilas.

The Closerie was no longer the café of Hemingway's day. It was now a combination restaurant and American bar, with its famous *terrasse* separated from the street by hedges. We avoided the restaurant and went into the American Bar, where each of the tables had an embedded brass plaque with the name of one of the many famous people who used to eat there: Hemingway, Sartre, Becket, Camus, Lenin, Man Ray.

We sat at André Gide's table and ordered the platter of fresh oysters with a white Sancerre wine. The waiter brought a dozen oysters on a bed of ice and pointed the different types out to us: flat Belons from Brittany, Gravettes from Arcachon, Marennes that were *Fines de Claire* (oysters that have spent at least three weeks in special clay ponds after removal from the oyster bed to acquire additional taste and tint), and *Speciales* from Normandy. Anne and I devoured the oysters, while Justin had his favorite *moules marinières*.

"God, these are the best oysters I've ever had," Anne said, as the waiter poured the last of the Sancerre. "They're so fresh."

"Less than three hours ago, they were either in the sea or *les claires, Madame*," the waiter said. "More than that and we would not serve them."

"We need another dozen," I said.

"Which?"

"*Les Speciales de Normandie,* I think," I said, looking at Anne. They were just the right size, number 3's, and so fresh it was as if they had come just dripping from the sea.

"I love the *Speciales,*" she said, starting to feel the wine and turning to me. "You do know how to talk sexy."

"And the wine, Monsieur?" the waiter asked.

"*Pour les Speciales, que croyez-vous, une Pouilly Fuisse?*" I asked.

"*D'accord, Monsieur. Parfait,*" the waiter said.

I looked around the mahogany bar, feeling that this was the Paris I wanted, the Paris of Hemingway and Gide and Sartre, not the tourists and Gypsies and poor exploited Africans selling toy parrots. Only I wasn't sure anymore which was the real Paris and which the illusion. I thought about Gide, whose table, according to the little brass plaque, we were sitting at. Was I, by running away from responsibilities and the States, so different from Michel in *The Immoralist?* Gide had written about how things get away from you. Michel begins with a little rebellion and soon things start to move in a way he never imagined.

Certainly, the book I was writing was becoming something more than a thriller though I hadn't intended that. The story was getting stronger and more about the war and the writing better as I went along and I certainly hadn't intended that, especially nowadays when you want your best stuff up front to hook the reader right away. A book that starts with a bang-up beginning and then declines will likely outsell a book that starts OK and then gets better. Still, sitting there with Anne and Justin, eating the best oysters I'd ever had, I wondered, was I as much of a hedonist as Michel? Take it easy, I told myself. It's Paris. Like the cop in Polanski's movie, *Chinatown,* says, "It's Chinatown, Jake," meaning that's how certain things are. You can't change them. And if Paris is anything, it's meant to be enjoyed.

We had intended to get together with Colette's son-in-law and daughter, Jean-Claude and Freddie, but when we called Jean-Claude told us they couldn't make it. France had just gone through another general election. In Paris, the kiosks and walls around the city were still plastered with election *affiches*. Jean-Claude's party, the Gaullists, had won a majority in the Assembly. Mitterand, who was still the President, had been forced to appoint his opponent, Jacques Chirac, Prime Minister, and Jean-Claude was up to his neck trying to make the new government made up of opposing parties, dubbed a government of *"cohabitation"* by the media, work.

"If you can't make it, what about Freddie?" Anne prompted me to ask.

"For these functions, socially, Freddie is *un avantage*, how do you say in English, 'an asset,'" Jean-Claude said.

"Freddie is definitely an asset," I said. Jean-Claude expressed his regrets and invited us to visit them in Picardy as soon as things settled down in Paris.

The rest of the time in Paris, Anne and I revisited our old haunts, the places we had been on our honeymoon: drinks at the piano bar at the Ritz, the Brasserie Stella on the Avenue Victor Hugo for the best *choucroute* in Paris, at night, a visit to the Crazy Horse show, something Anne had always wanted to see, "They're not human, these women. Not a stretch mark or imperfect breast in sight. It's not possible, not even with plastic surgery," she said, ice cream for Justin at the Café Flore on the Boulevard St. Germain, where Sartre and Camus used to hang out, dinner at La Coupole, still filled with eccentric and obnoxious waiters, where a woman suddenly stood on a table and started singing an aria from *La Bohème* making Justin laugh, and on our last night, a hotel babysitter watching Justin, something we couldn't have afforded when we first got married and had always promised ourselves, dinner at Tour d'Argent, seated at a table by a window overlooking the Seine and Notre Dame lit up at night, watching the waiters literally snap to attention when Claude Terrail himself came over to our table and asked us if everything was perfect and Anne said, "Has it ever been otherwise?" and Terrail responded, "Not while I am here, Madame."

When we flew back to Nice, we still hadn't heard from either the police or the *propriété immobilière*. I called them from the villa in Eze.

"It was all *un grand malentendu*, a big misunderstanding, Monsieur," the real estate agent assured me. The *camionnette* was from the electric company. The men were *employés* responding to an emergency, *un état d'urgence*."

"You expect me to believe that?! French utility workers never show up when they're supposed to during the day, much less in the middle of the night!" I said.

"*Quand même, Monsieur*. You can speak with the *sergent* at the *gendarmerie*. He will tell you the same."

"That's what I'm afraid of. I must tell you, Madame, I do not believe any of this," I said and hung up. I then called the *sergent* at the *gendarmerie*, who told me the same story. The men we had taken for thieves were only workmen on a job, who, according to them, had entered our yard by mistake.

"No one enters a *cour de villa* by mistake at three in the morning, *Monsieur le Sergent*," I said. He hung up.

"What's going to happen?" Anne asked.

"Nothing. It's all *un grand malentendu*, if you believe it," I said.

"Do you believe them?" Anne asked.

"No. Do you?"

"No. I guess we better watch ourselves," she said.

"I guess we better."

That night we went back to Maria and the Chef's in Villefranche for dinner. After we ate, Maria and *Monsieur le Chef* sat at our table and told us they were selling the restaurant. They were retiring.

"*C'est difficile, Monsieur*, running a restaurant. Long hours, little time off, and there are only the two of us," *Monsieur le Chef* sighed. "It is time to retire."

"We want to spend more time with our grandchildren. And travel. And the new owner offered us a good price. For us, it's time, Monsieur. We are tired," Maria said.

"But what will we do?" Anne said. "Justin loves your *moules marinières*."

"And no one makes *soupe de poisson* like you, Monsieur."

"*Merci*, Monsieur. That gives us great pleasure. I am glad we part as friends," he said, shaking my hand.

Afterward, we walked down to the harbor, Justin's hand in mine, the lights along the *quai* shining on the dark water.

"Is it France that's changing, or is it our perception of France that's changing?" Anne said.

"I don't know," I said. It had been a sunny day, the air mild with just a hint of Spring in it, the sea a sparkling blue, and the wildflowers around our villa coming into bloom. It was stunningly beautiful, the Riviera we had sought all along, and yet, we were uneasy. "We have to remember, we chose France. She didn't choose us. And I love it. It's like Eden here."

"But even in Eden there's always a snake," Anne said.

The next day, our feelings about France got more complicated because of an explosion in Berlin.

Chapter 21

War, Riviera-Style

A discotheque known to be frequented by U.S. servicemen in Berlin had been terror bombed. According to the French TV news, which talked of nothing else, two American soldiers had been killed and two hundred and thirty people wounded, seventy-nine of them American GIs. Evidence at the scene and from the CIA indicated that it had been the work of Libyan terrorists. Everyone waited to see what the Americans would do. For a week nothing happened. Then I woke up early to the BBC news on the radio: American war planes had bombed Libya. I drove down to the *tabac* in Eze, bought a copy of the *International Herald Tribune* and brought it, along with some *croissants* from the *boulangerie*, back to the villa.

According to the *Tribune*, President Reagan had ordered U.S. military jets to bomb targets in and around Tripoli and Benghazi. The French government had ordered troops to the Côte d'Azur and the French navy to protect the southern coast of France from a possible Libyan attack. I woke Anne and when it came time for the TV news, the *commentateur* reported that President Mitterand had not allowed American F-111 jets from Britain to pass through French air space in order to attack Libya. For American jets, this meant detouring around France, requiring thousands of miles of additional flying involving mid-air refueling that further complicated their mission.

"They're so obnoxious, the French. Why are they doing that?" Anne asked.

"You mean apart from their normal insistence on doing their own thing?" I said.

"What is it with them?"

"You're the psychologist. You tell me. It gets them noticed."

"That's it? They side with terrorists against their allies just to get noticed? That's perverse, even for the French."

"It's also money," I said. "And fear. They do a lot of business with the Arabs. It's where they get all their oil. Also, they have a big internal Muslim population that worries them. Remember Paris?"

"So you're saying, they like to screw the United States because it's in their self-interest."

"Every country acts in its own interest. Reagan is bombing Libya because he thinks it's in America's interest. For the French, the pleasure of thumbing their nose at the Americans is an added bonus."

"This is scary," Anne said, tapping the newspaper photo of bodies being taken from the bombed nightclub. "Are we safe here?"

"Is anybody really safe anywhere?" I said. "Let's see how it plays out."

Anne was nervous, but decided to take Justin to the *crèche* anyway. Meanwhile, I got back to the book. I was writing a series of action sequences. Sawyer and the Eurasian woman, Suong, were being hunted by Bhun Sa's men as they tried to escape from the Golden Triangle. Sawyer had discovered that the morphine base was hidden in one of the ruins near Angkor Thom in Cambodia. At the time I was writing, Cambodia was the most dangerous place on earth. The Vietnamese Communists, the Thais, the Khmer Rouge, and other Cambodian factions were all fighting each other and if any of them captured Sawyer, the best he could hope for was to be tortured to death.

Every so often, I would stop writing and turn on the radio for the news. The claims about the American attacks on Tripoli and Benghazi were confused, but there was a report that the Libyan leader, Colonel Khaddafi's house had been bombed and his daughter was among those killed.

Anne called and said she had Justin. She and Sally and Gaby were all going shopping to stock up on supplies for the house, just in case. She said French military forces had been put on full alert and Prince Rainier had announced he would be closing the borders of Monaco, in which case she might not be able to get back. I told her that was fine, to stay with Sally and Gaby and just take care of Justin. I felt a hollowness in my gut. The war had separated us.

I went down to the seaside restaurant by the pebbly beach in Eze-sur-Mer and had a *Croque-Monsieur* sandwich and a beer on the *terrasse*. As I was eating, a gray French navy destroyer sailed by. It sailed parallel to the shore headed towards Monte Carlo. The *propriétaire*, in a food-splattered white apron, stood beside me as we watched the ship pass.

"*Vous êtes américain, Monsieur? De la Villa Olivia en haut, je crois,*" he said.

"*C'est moi,*" I said.

"*Vous permettez?*" he said and sat down with two beers, one for himself and a fresh one for me. We watched the destroyer sail past the point at Cap Ferrat and out of sight.

"You think there will be a war?" he asked in French.

"With Libya? No," I said.

"Why not?"

"Too one-sided. Even Khaddafi is not that crazy."

"They could attack *la* Côte. They are crazy enough for that."

I shook my head. "The American Sixth Fleet is in the Mediterranean. They'd have to get past both the American and the French navies. I don't think so."

"Don't be so sure. These Muslim *fanatiques*, they are crazy. One never knows what they will do. I know, I was in *Algérie*," he said.

"So was I," I said. I'd covered the final months of the war as a stringer for the *International Herald Tribune* in Paris.

"So you know," he nodded. "It's the sun. It's so hot all the time there, it makes them all crazy. You want world peace? Buy everyone in the Middle East air conditioners. If their brains were not boiling all the time, they might be able to think rationally for a minute."

"You could be right."

"You were there, *n'est-ce pas?* The heat made everyone crazy. We did things as bad as them after a while. *Regardez, Monsieur,*" he gestured at the beach and the green hills and the sea. "Beautiful, no? And now they want to ruin it because their brains are *friré tout* (completely fried) by the sun," tapping his head.

"Why won't the French government let the American planes fly through French air space?" I said. He motioned me closer.

"Remember the *terrorisme* in *Algérie?* They fear the same again. More bombings in France if they are seen as being on the side of the Americans. Let the Americans do it," he shrugged. "But if you ask me, Monsieur, better to buy them all air conditioners. In the end, it will be cheaper," he said.

I went back to the villa and the book. Anne and Justin were safe. I had to believe that. Writing about war with war so close to us made it more real. While on the run, Sawyer had managed to connect with his case officer, Harris, who told Sawyer he would have to escape into Cambodia.

That evening, waiting to hear from Anne. I watched a clip of President Reagan's speech on TV, followed by Mitterand declaring France's neutrality and that the French Navy was now patrolling the coast off the Côte d'Azur. All at once, Anne and Justin came into the villa, Justin ran jumping into my arms and hugged me tight. Anne behind him, lugged two arms-full of plastic shopping bags.

"We snubbed him!" she announced triumphantly.

"We snubbed him, Daddy," Justin repeated.

"Snubbed who?" I asked.

"The Libyan ambassador. We snubbed him!"

"Who snubbed him?"

"Monika and me. We were having drinks in the Hôtel de Paris and who walks in but the Libyan ambassador to Monaco."

"What happened?"

"Well, he knows Monika and Nigel. Probably through Arthur, Adrian's son-in-law's brother. Anyway, he came over and said *"Bonjour, Mesdames,"* to us and we snubbed him. We turned our heads and refused to answer or even look at him."

"Good for you," I said.

"Wait, it gets better. Then no one would look at him. So he goes up to the barman, Jacques, and asks for a drink and Jacques refused to serve him. Told him he was not welcome in the Hôtel de Paris. The Libyan just stood there. It was dead silent and no one would look at him and finally, he just slunk out of the hotel. What do you think of that?"

"Good for Jacques. Remind me to buy him a cigar or something."

"And what about Monika and me?"

"Good for you too. I'm proud of you," I said.

"Wait till you see," she said, opening the plastic shopping bags and pulling out tins of *foie gras*, *pâtés*, caviar, champagne, wine, *baguettes*, cheeses, and bottles of Evian. "We decided to stock up, in case of attack. I'm ready for anything."

"Caviar and champagne are staples?" I asked.

"This is war Riviera-style. We need to show the enemy not only that we're not afraid, but that we have class," Anne said.

"I'm sure that'll impress them in Tripoli."

She came over and kissed me. "I know it's silly," she said. "When Rainier closed the border, I was worried we wouldn't be able to get back to you."

"It's not silly. You've done more for the war effort than I have," I said.

That night, after we put Justin to bed, we sat in front of the fire and drank Calvados and talked.

"Do you think we should stay? Is it safe? Maybe it's time to go home," she said.

"For now, I think we're okay. They'd have to get past the Sixth Fleet. I don't see any way the U.S. Navy will let that happen."

"I hate this," she said, snuggling against me.

"I didn't like being separated from you two. It sucks."

That night, I couldn't sleep. I went back down to my office and finished the chapter I had been working on. The morphine base Sawyer had to find was in a part of Cambodia controlled by the Khmer Rouge, they of the Killing Fields. I had finally come to the part of the book that had made me want to write it in the first place, the ancient temple ruins overgrown by the jungle. In order for it to work, I needed to let the reader know that like Anne and me and everyone else, Sawyer was afraid, in his case, of going into Cambodia.

Or maybe, thinking about Libya, Cambodia was coming to us.

And then I realized how wise Anne was with her caviar and her Riviera style. The antidote to death is life, preferably as Anne pointed out, with a touch of class.

Chapter 22

Visitors, Part Two: The Hollywood Scene

After the U.S. attack on Libya, everyone braced for more terrorism in Europe, but it didn't happen. In Lebanon, three hostages, one of them American, were executed in reprisal by Arab gunmen. A U.S. diplomat was assassinated in the Sudan, and the Russians called off talks with the U.S., but within a week, the French Navy no longer patrolled the coast and life on the Côte d'Azur returned to normal. Libya no longer challenged U.S. planes flying over the Gulf of Sidra and except for those killed or wounded and their families, it was as if the crisis had never happened.

At the Hôtel de Paris however, Jacques the bartender was the man of the hour. People came by to shake his hand and buy him drinks. Nigel, Max and I chipped in and bought him a box of Cuban cigars. Colette came to visit us in Eze and we took her for lunch to the Voile d'Or in the port in St. Jean-Cap-Ferrat. Maurice, the owner, whom I had gotten to know working out together at the California Terrace fitness center, made a fuss over us and insisted that instead of us ordering that he would take care of lunch. He had the chef make us the best *brandade de morue* (puréed salt cod) I'd ever eaten, but that didn't matter, because Colette was pouring her heart out to Anne. The problem was her other daughter, Michelle, also in Paris and married to a manager in an Engineering company. The marriage was in trouble.

"He's having an affair?" Anne asked.

"Of course. *C'est normal*. If only that were all, but *il est bizarre*, her husband," Colette said. "He wants her to move in with them."

"Who? The mistress?"

"A matter of economics. He does not wish to pay for two apartments. He wants a *ménage à trois*. Michelle is furious."

"I can understand her problem," Anne said.

"That is not the problem. She is a grown woman. She can handle these things. Besides, she says she likes the woman."

"You mean she's actually considering it? The two women in the same house?"

"*Impossible*. That would be, how do you say, *être la fin des haricots* in English?" she said to me.

"That would take the cake," I said.

"Then what is the problem?" Anne asked.

"She wants to leave Paris and come back to the Côte d'Azur. She wants to move in with me. I can't have that. In my little apartment? *Impossible! Alors*, one has one's own life, *après tout*," Colette said.

"I see the problem," Anne said. "Perhaps Michelle could have her own affair and kick the husband out of the apartment. Or you say she likes the woman, perhaps the two of them could share the apartment and throw the husband out."

"*Voilà*, you see. I said your wife was a sensible woman," Colette said to me.

"She's becoming very French. Don't give her too many ideas," I said, getting up. I could tell Justin was restless.

I left Anne and Colette plotting strategies to annoy the husband and keep Michelle in Paris and took Justin back to the villa, where I had intended to work, but instead wound up playing Zorro with Justin, fencing with plastic swords. I was pretending to jump on top of the stone fence when I heard the phone ringing and just made it into the villa to pick it up.

"*Chez Kaplan, bonjour,*" I answered.

"Andy?" said the voice on the line. "It's Sid." Sid was S.L. Stebel, a writer friend from L.A., whose work included the screenplay for the film, *Picnic at Hanging Rock*, the play *Fathers Against Sons* starring Henry Fonda, and a number of novels, including one about the Arctic I particularly liked called *Spring Thaw*.

"Where are you?"

"Jan and I are in a little hotel in Nice. We were in Paris with Ray and Maggie and decided to come down to visit. Everyone's wondering what the hell's been happening with you."

"Did Ray and Maggie come with you?" I asked. Ray was the famous sci-fi writer, Ray Bradbury, author of *Farenheit 451* and *The Martian Chronicles*. Maggie was Ray's wife. They had all talked about coming to see us, but I hadn't really thought they would do it.

"Ray's got a presentation in Paris. Besides, he wouldn't get on another plane," Sid said. Everyone knew Ray hated to fly.

"How on earth did you get him on a plane to Paris?" I asked.

"How do you think? We got him so loaded he didn't know where he was. He snored the whole flight over. So how are you doing?"

"Pretty good. Do you have a car?"

"I've got a rental."

"Come on over," I said and gave him directions to the villa.

I first met Sid through Mann Rubin, a veteran screen and TV writer, who at the time was a lead writer on a prime-time TV drama called *Dynasty*. Mann, Ib Melchior, a well-known writer-director-author, who practically created sci fi on television, and I had been judges together on a PEN awards committee and in our arguments with the other judges, had become close friends. That year, we gave the PEN award to *Stones for Ibarra*, which was, incredibly, a first novel about a Mexican village written literally by a little old lady from Pasadena, who made it easy for us by writing something so superior to anything else done that year that the three of us were able to prevail over the other judges to give her the award.

One of the things I enjoyed most about Mann was that he had been around since the so-called "Golden Age of Television" and he had a story about almost everyone in Hollywood from Harry Cohn, the legendary head of Columbia Pictures who had first brought him out to Hollywood to John Huston. Mann was one of Huston's poker-playing buddies. So much so, that Huston used to fly Mann and some of the others, such as actor Eliot Gould, down in a private plane to his place in Puerto Vallarta for a poker game.

By the time Sid arrived, it was late afternoon. Colette had dropped Anne back home and we sat on our *terrasse* over wine and olives.

"Where's Jan?" I asked. Sid had come alone and that hadn't surprised me. His wife, Jan, a noted painter and sculptor in her own right, had a heart condition and I was surprised she had been well enough to even make the trip.

"She's tired now, but we're hoping to spend time with you tomorrow. This is pretty nice," he said, looking around. "Not as fancy as I expected. I thought you'd be in a beret, lounging by a pool with Catherine Deneuve."

"No such luck. We did see Brigitte Bardot once."

"Where?"

"In Saint Tropez."

"Yeah, we want to go there. How'd she look?"

"All covered up. You wouldn't have known her."

"That's depressing. So how's the book coming?"

"So far so good. What's happening in Hollywood?"

"The usual crap. The Guild is talking about a new contract. Of course, they don't have the balls to do anything about it. There's this Oliver Stone movie about Vietnam that's getting buzz. You're doing something on Vietnam too, aren't you?"

"Not exactly. Mine is contemporary, but there are resonances."

"So far, it's the best thing he's ever done," Anne said.

"That's encouraging. Maybe it's a trend. Maybe I should do something on it," Sid said.

"Can you believe it's been eleven years since we got out?" I said.

"That's your generation's war. Mine's the Big One. You're the baby of the group. Did you guys get all the news about the Challenger?"

"That was awful," Anne said.

"We didn't get the coverage like you guys did. In a way, I think it's better," I said.

"It was a big story."

"Yeah, but seeing it over and over. It's like an obsession. The whole country walks around with a case of depression. Here, after a few days, it was gone."

"So what does the French news show?"

"Important stuff, like the Assembly debating whether Canal Plus will be allowed to add a new TV channel. The way the French see it, why does a country need more than three TV channels?"

"After all," Anne said. "How many strip shows and ads with naked women can you put on?"

"Strippers on TV?"

"*Vive la France*," I said.

"Do you miss it?" Sid asked.

"What, L.A.? I'll tell you what I don't miss. The Hollywood crap, the agents who don't return your calls, 'taking meetings,' people who tell you you've written the greatest thing since *Casablanca* and then never get back to you. Sometimes it's piled up so high, you need a snorkel just to breathe."

"I'll tell you what I miss, besides the fact that no one takes women seriously here, unless they're trying to seduce you," Anne said.

"That sounds very French," Sid said.

"I miss not understanding everything everyone says or being able to just turn on the TV and understand every word," Anne said.

"Everyone speaks English," Sid said.

"Yeah, but they don't treat you the same as they do when you speak French. Like this one," she said, jabbing me with her elbow.

"How is your French?" Sid asked.

"I get by," I said.

"You want to know how good his is? He laughs at the jokes on TV."

"Only when they're funny," I said.

That night, we joined Sid and Jan for dinner at the Aux Gourmets on the rue Dante in Nice and in the morning, after dropping Justin off at the *crèche* and arranging for Gaby, who volunteered to pick him up, we took them on what we had begun to think of as 'the Riviera tour.'

We showed them Polanski's villa in Cap d'Antibes and the King of Arabia's yacht, which happened to be anchored nearby.

"Unbelievable! It's like an ocean liner," Jan said.

"We have a friend who's got a boat almost as big," Anne said.

"Onassis's is even bigger," I said.

"Niarchos's is bigger than Onassis's," Anne said.

"Sounds like we're talking about something other than boats," Sid said.

We went to Gatsby's Beach at the Plage de la Garoupe, the Heineken estate, where the guards still knew us and waved hello, the bar at the Hôtel du Cap and then up into the hills to Saint Paul de Vence.

"This is pretty nice," Sid said over lunch in the garden at the Colombe d'Or, where the barman, Auguste, waved hello to Anne and me. "Are you going to stay?"

"I'm not sure. It gets expensive in summer. I don't think we can afford the summer rental," I said.

"What are you going to do?" Jan asked.

"First finish the book. Then we'll figure it out," Anne said.

We drove back to Nice the long way, down the Esteral coast toward Cannes.

"God, this is exquisite," Jan said, taking in the red rock hills and trees and white villas with red-tile roofs perched on cliffs above the sea.

"Yeah, this is where they should've shot Brian's *Old Man And The Sea*," Sid said, meaning Brian Garfield, a good mutual friend and author of *Deathwish*, *The Stepfather*, *Hopscotch*, and a boatload of other books and movies and I started laughing so hard I almost drove off the road.

"What are you talking about? Hemingway wrote *The Old Man And The Sea*," Anne said.

"Yeah, but they wanted Brian to write the remake of the Spencer Tracy movie," I said. "You know how he got the offer?"

"No, how?"

"The same producer had done the TV movie *Relentless*. When they asked Brian on that one whether they had to shoot it in real snow, Brian told 'em if they could figure out how to shoot *Moby Dick* without the ocean, why not *Relentless* without snow? So they figured he was the perfect writer to figure out how to deal with this one teensy 'minor' problem with the star, Anthony Quinn."

"What was the minor problem?" Anne said, smiling.

"Seems the Mighty Quinn had a tendency to get seasick. They wanted Brian to write *The Old Man and the Sea* so they could shoot it on a soundstage. Can't imagine why he turned it down," I said as we all whooped with laughter.

"Speaking of Brian Garfield stories, did he ever tell you about the one-word pitch?" Sid asked.

"He sold something with one word?" I said.

"It was a TV movie," Sid said. "Brian and the producer go in and the producer tells the exec at ABC it's about the Rockettes at the New York Radio City Music Hall. The producer says to Brian, 'You tell him.' So Brian spreads his hands and says one word: 'Legs.'"

Anne laughed. "That's funny," she said.

"That's not the funny part," Sid said. "The ABC exec starts pacing up and back, up and back and suddenly turns to them and says, 'Do you realize this could be the greatest thing since James Joyce's *Ulysses*?' LEGS!"

"That's like Mann's Sinatra story," I said, when we stopped laughing.

"What's Mann's Sinatra story?" Jan asked.

"Mann was writing for a TV detective show, *Quincy*, with Jack Klugman and Frank Sinatra wanted to do an episode," I said.

"That wasn't Mann in that story, that was Joe Gores," Sid said. Joe was another screenwriter friend. "And it wasn't *Quincy*, it was *Kojak*. But it's a great story."

"OK, you better tell it," I told Sid as I drove towards the Croisette in Cannes.

"Joe was one of the writers on the show. Sinatra and Telly Savalas were buddies. Sinatra wanted to do the show, so they start thinking about how to include him in an episode," Sid said. "Then Joe gets a call from the producer that 'Mr. Sinatra wants to see him.' Joe asks when he should go over and the producer tells him, 'Sinatra's in Vegas. There'll be a limo and a private plane to take you to him.' 'When?' Joe asks and the producer tells him the limo's already on its way over.

"When Joe gets in, there's a Network Guy, a couple of producers, and one of Sinatra's people waiting for him in the limo. All the way to LAX, they're giving Joe instructions. 'You just answer Mr. Sinatra's questions,' they tell him. 'And whatever you do, I mean whatever you do, *do not*, I repeat, *not* ask Mr. Sinatra any questions. Do you understand?' 'I understand,' Joe says. 'No, I don't think you do,' the Network Guy says. 'I mean whatever happens, no matter what, YOU DO NOT ASK MR. SINATRA ANY QUESTIONS.'"

"Oh wow," Anne said. "What happened?"

"They land in Vegas," Sid said, "and drive in another limo to Sinatra's penthouse suite at the Sands. 'Remember,' the producer and the Network Guy tell Joe before they go into Sinatra's suite, 'No matter what, no questions to Mr. Sinatra.'

"So they go into the suite and there's a couple of guys and half a dozen broads in the living room and they take Joe into the bedroom. Sinatra is in a dressing gown, talking on the phone. When he gets off, he says to Joe, 'You the writer?' and Joe says 'Yes.' 'OK,' Sinatra says, 'The show starts with me alone in a nightclub men's room. Washing my hands or something. Two big goons come in and start beating the shit out of me. Then they take me and hold me upside down with my head in the toilet.' That's all Sinatra says. For a long minute there's complete silence. Finally, Joe can't stand it anymore. 'So what happens?' he asks, suddenly realizing everyone is staring at him horror-stricken. He broke the rule. Sinatra looks at Joe and snaps, 'How the hell should I know? You're the goddamn writer!'

"They leave the suite in dead silence. No one says a word, Joe thinking his career is over. They're standing by the elevator and the Network Guy rubs his hands together and says, 'I think we're talking Emmy here!'" Sid finished and we all laughed.

As we drove down the Croisette in Cannes, I pointed out the Carlton, the Grand, and the Majestic hotels, that were the headquarters of anybody who was anybody at the Cannes Film Festival. I also pointed out the topless *au pairs* and women with kids on the beach near the Carlton. It was getting time to pick up Justin and we dropped Sid and Jan off at their hotel.

"Listen, we want to check out Saint Tropez tomorrow. Are you coming with us?" Sid asked.

"It's too far for a day trip. Justin goes to his *crèche* every day. But try Le Café on the Place des Lices. What about the day after?" I said.

"Back to Paris," Sid said.

"Say hi to Ray and Maggie for us."

"I will. Are you coming back to L.A.?" he asked.

"I don't know," I said and meant it. "Ask Anne."

"I don't know either," she said, as we let them out of the car.

"Give my love to all the guys," I said.

"I'll tell them you're living with millionaires and topless *au pairs*," he said.

"Tell them *au revoir*," Anne said, as we drove away.

"All those Hollywood stories. Does it make you want to go back?" she asked. We drove past the harbor area in Nice with its World War One monument and along the *Corniche* back to Eze-sur-Mer.

"I feel more like a writer here than I ever did in L.A.," I said. "I mean we live in a country where they name the streets after writers."

"I know, Babe," she said. "I know."

Chapter 23

A Dangerous Cloud

"What are we going to do for the summer?" Anne asked. We were sitting under an umbrella on the pebbly beach in Eze-sur-Mer, drinking *pastis* and watching Justin chasing and retreating from the gentle waves breaking on the shore. The water was too cold for swimming, but the sun was high and the day had a feel of approaching summer.

"What do you want to do?"

"Stay here."

"We can't afford it," I said.

"I like it here. I don't want to move. What's the sense in moving when everyone wants to come where we already are?"

"The rate for June is 30,000 francs. July and August are 50,000. That's over $8,000 a month! We can't do it."

"We should've taken a year's lease."

"The landlord wouldn't give us one, remember. I can't blame him. Summer's when he makes his money. And don't forget, in summer, this place is a zoo. Half the people in Europe will be here. Crowds everywhere. You won't be able to go anywhere or find a place to park or anything."

"Well, I don't want to move."

"There's lots of other places. We can use it as a time to travel and then, when summer madness is over, we can come back."

"Like where?" she said, adding more ice and water to her *pastis*, turning it a milky yellow.

"I don't know. Other parts of France. How about Brittany, or the Dordogne? Let's go up to Picardy to see Jean-Claude and Freddie. Or we'll go to Champagne and visit Colette's cousin Georges. Max and Sally and Bobby G. and Gaby like Corsica. Didn't they do a motorcycle trip there? There's Tuscany, Spain, Portugal. I've heard Portugal's not expensive and I've always wanted to see the Algarve."

"Spain and Portugal are too hot and crowded in summer," she said. "I'll bet Brittany and the Dordogne get inundated in August too, just like the Côte d'Azur."

"We could go in the opposite direction from everyone else. Everyone comes south in summer; let's go north."

"You mean like Denmark or Sweden?"

"Scandinavia is expensive. How about someplace in the mountains, where it'll be cool, like Austria?"

"What makes you think there won't be a million tourists in Vienna too?"

"Who says Vienna? Let's go someplace pretty, like Carinthia, or Salzburg, or the Tyrol. Maybe find a pension or something that's not too expensive. Drink beer and yodel all day."

"You'll have me milking cows next. What do I get out of this exactly?" she said.

"Hopefully, a roof over our heads and escape from the madness of a European summer. We need more information though."

"I'll talk to Sally," Anne said.

That afternoon, Anne went with Justin to see Sally and I went back to the book. I was writing well, perhaps as well as I ever had. I was in a groove and wanted to keep it going. I was approaching a climactic moment, when Sawyer would confront the woman, Suong, and try to uncover her real purpose. I was conscious of living this strange hybrid existence: part of me was living on the Riviera and part of me was with Sawyer in the Cambodian jungle ruins, a region ruled by the ruthless Khmer Rouge.

I was coming to the part of the book I had looked forward to and dreaded from the beginning: where Sawyer confronts Suong and she finally tells her story. I looked out the window at Nietzsche's path, green as the Cambodian jungle with rays of sunlight filtering through the trees, anxious, yet concerned about how to tell Suong's story. I had to do it not in my voice, the third-person omniscient narrator I had written the book as, but something I had never done before, writing as a woman character telling her story in her own voice.

"You're not going to believe it!" Anne declared when she and Justin came home. "For a while, I thought we were going to be imprisoned. It was like something out of a movie."

"What movie? What are you talking about? I thought you went to see Sally."

"I did," Anne said, as she started preparing a dinner of *pot au feu*. Justin had turned on the TV and was watching "*Les Botes*," a French cartoon about robots, one of which was female and despite being a metal contraption, probably a little too sexy for kids if they were old enough to understand it, which thank God, Justin wasn't. "She couldn't help much. She and Max usually lie low or go back to the States during the summer. She says you're right. It's an absolute zoo here. August is the worst when the whole country of France is off and practically all of them come down here."

"So where does the imprisoned part come in?" I asked, opening a bottle of wine and pouring her a glass.

"I decided to follow up on what you were saying and get some information. So I went to the Austrian Consulate in Monte Carlo."

"Sounds like a good idea. So what happened?"

"Well, it's in this building in Monte Carlo and we went in. I mean all I wanted was some brochures or something. There was a little reception desk and I rang the bell and some man in a suit came out and I told him, 'We'd like to go to Austria.' He gets very nervous and says, 'Vait here, Madame,' in a German accent. So Justin and I are standing there waiting and finally, he comes out with another man, who says, 'Zis vay, pleeze' and leads us down some stairs to this tiny bare room with just a cheap office table and a couple of chairs in it. He told us to sit down and leaves, locking the door.

"At this point, Justin is starting to get anxious, and to tell you the truth, so was I. A few minutes later, another man opens the door, locks it behind him, sits at the table and says, 'Vat is your nationality, pleeze?' I told him American. He says, 'You vant to go to Austria?' I said we were considering it, but not if this is the way we were going to be treated. "Vy do you vant to come to Austria?' he asked. 'We just want a change. And also because we want to get away from the crowds and high prices on the Côte d'Azur in the summer,' I told him. 'So vy are you requesting political asylum?' he asked."

"He thought you wanted asylum?!"

"I guess," she laughed. "I told him, we don't want asylum. We just wanted brochures and tourist information."

"So where are they?"

"He said they didn't have any. He just seemed very relieved we didn't want asylum. I guess he could see this turning into some kind of international incident."

"Doesn't sound very hospitable," I said.

"I'm not sure Austria is right for us this summer," she said. "Personally, I'd still rather stay right here in Eze." She stopped cooking for a second. "I guess this won't be our last conversation about it."

"Doesn't look like it," I said.

The next morning something extraordinary happened. I began writing as the female character, Suong. "I was married before," she says and begins to tell the story of what it was like to be a wife and mother in Cambodia at the time when Cambodia was the worst place on earth. Her story was pouring out of me. It was the story of Cambodia and Vietnam, only it wasn't the American story, the grunts in the jungle and the generals in Saigon, it was the Asian side of the story, how they experienced it and why so many of the people we thought were ours went over to the Communist side and why we lost the war. Telling it not from our perspective, but from theirs, people forced to live in a culture with a dilemma we couldn't have imagined. The words kept coming. I had never experienced anything like it in all the years I had been writing. I was riding an obsession now and I had to stay with it and go with it as far as it would take me.

I didn't want to stop for food or sleep or anything. Anne came to meet me for lunch and I told her I was in the middle of something and she just had to take care of Justin and let me be. I couldn't stop and I couldn't get off the horse. She looked at me worried, but also, she had seen where the book was going. I just told her I was writing the Eurasian woman and I hoped she'd understand. Justin wanted to play and I told him I couldn't and Anne kept him away and busy, taking him to the zoo in St. Jean-Cap-Ferrat or whatever, anything to keep away from me. I didn't want to leave the room. I told her I'd be sleeping in my office and I could see she was worried. "I'll be OK," I told her. "I just have to do this till it's done." And that's when I knew I had married the right woman, because she didn't carry on. She just kissed me and said, "I trust you. Do what you have to."

I had never worked like that in my life. For three days and nights, I didn't leave the villa. Except to go to the bathroom, I didn't leave the room. For me, there was only Suong and her Cambodian officer husband and her child and 'the Angkar' as the Khmer Rouge called themselves and the view of the woods and Nietzsche's path from my office window that for me, was now Cambodia and the Killing Fields.

All this time I had been living in two worlds, the world of the book and the real world of the Côte d'Azur, but now there was only one world, the world of the book. All I did was write. At the end, after three days, that sequence was done.

I stumbled out of the room in a daze. I knew that I had written in a voice that was not my own, but Suong's, and that it was by far the best thing I had ever written, maybe one of the best things anyone had ever written about Vietnam and Southeast Asia and the war.

Anne and Justin weren't home. I went out to the *terrasse* overlooking the garden and opened a bottle of wine, not giving a damn how much I drank. I looked at the villas and the trees and just breathed and drank until Anne and Justin came home.

"Are you back?" she said, looking at me. I nodded, barely able to talk. "Daddy's back," she told Justin, who yelled "Daddy!" and leaped into my arms.

"You want to play Zorro?" Justin asked. "I can get my mask and sword."

"I'd love to play Zorro," I told him. Anne and I kissed and hugged.

"I want to read it," she whispered.

"Be prepared," I said, as Justin pulled me away to play.

That night after we put Justin to bed, Anne went down to my office and read what I had written. I sat in the *salon* by the fire, drinking Calvados and waiting, nervous as a cat at what she would say. Finally she came and sat beside me.

"It's not a thriller," she said.

"No. Not that part."

"It's incredible. It's the best thing you've ever done. The best thing anyone's ever done on the war."

"Thanks, Babe," I said and held her close.

"I never really understood why we lost in Vietnam. For the first time, I think I finally understand. We were clueless, weren't we?"

"Pretty much."

"Are you going to drink all the Calvados yourself?" she said. I poured her a glass. "You're almost done, aren't you? With the book, I mean. I can't believe it."

"Getting there. Maybe another four or five chapters. Maybe I'm crazy, but I don't think there's a thriller like it," I said.

"I don't either. We need to celebrate. Go somewhere, do something."

"Like where?"

"Anyplace but Austria," she said.

"As soon as I finish the first draft, we'll do it. Where should we go?"

"What about... Italy? We had a great time in Florence."

"You want to go back to Florence? Tuscany is beautiful."

"No, let's do something different. Where haven't you been?"

"Everywhere. Rome, Venice, Naples. I never really spent time there. What about Rome?"

She shook her head. "Venice," she said. "Definitely Venice."

"You've been there, right?"

"With my grandmother. But that doesn't matter. You can never go to Venice only once in life. It isn't allowed."

"To Venice," I said, clinking glasses and drinking.

So we had a plan. And the book was nearly done. For the first time since London, I could see the finish line. And once I turned the manuscript in, I would be getting more money from my publisher. Maybe we could even stay in Eze for the summer. But I had forgotten a Yiddish saying of my grandmother's, *"Der mensh trakht und Gott lakht"* (Man makes plans and God laughs). Because an accident in another country a thousand miles away, like a distant cloud on the horizon, was about to threaten our very lives.

Chapter 24

Why The French Are Different

For some time I had been experiencing upper abdominal pain. At first, I thought it was something I had eaten, but the pain had persisted. It seemed to be getting worse, not better. We were having lunch with Max and Sally in the garden of their villa, Justin running around playing with the garden hose, when I got another attack.

"You might have a peptic ulcer, like I did," Max said, getting me some antacids, which I swallowed with water.

"Can you recommend a doctor?" Anne asked.

"Don't waste your time with regular French doctors," Max said. "All they're taught in medical school is a single sentence: '*C'est un mal de foie, Monsieur.*' Everything is a liver problem. If you have a migraine, it's a *mal de foie*. If you break your toe, it's your liver. If you get shot in the head, it's your liver. For the French, everything is your liver."

"And the prescription is always the same. No matter what," Sally said. "Diuretics, antibiotics, and always, an enema."

"Why an enema?" Anne asked. "What has that got to do with it?"

"They say it cleans the system. You have to be French to even begin to understand it," Sally said.

"Personally, I think they do it just because they like to imagine their patients in humiliating postures," Max said.

"Well, I've still got this pain in my stomach. What do I do?" I said.

"Don't waste time," Max said. "Go straight to the *Clinique Gastro-enterologique* in Menton. It's where you'll wind up anyway. They're the only ones who know what they're doing. Wait, I'll make you an appointment."

Two days later, we drove to the clinic in Menton, a medium-sized town on the Italian border, with nineteenth century architecture and a nice harbor and beach. Anchored beside the Promendade du Soleil was a black pirate ship that Roman Polanski had used for his movie, *Pirates*, starring Walther Matthau of all people as a pirate, and which had recently been converted into a floating restaurant. I parked outside the clinic, Anne and Justin still in the car.

"What are you guys going to do?" I asked.

"We'll wait," she said.

"It's going to be hours. I don't want you just sitting here."

"We'll wait. We're concerned about you. Maybe Justin and I will grab a bite, look around the town."

"Sure. Check out the pirate ship. Justin'd like that, wouldn't you Justin?"

"Do they have swords, Daddy?"

"I don't know. Why don't you go and tell me," I said, kissing them and going inside.

The staff at the *Clinique* was very professional. They put me in a white hospital gown. I saw the doctor for a minute, who told me they would be doing a full GI series, and I spent the next several hours doing the tests and X-rays and when it came to the Barium enema, if it weren't for the discomfort, I would've laughed thinking of Max and Sally and their theories on French enemas. Afterwards, as I wiped myself with the coarse paper the French use for all functions *personnel*, the doctor came in.

"*Monsieur le Medicin, qu'est-ce que c'est la cause de la problème?*" I asked.

"There is something, but we are not *certain*. We will need more tests, Monsieur," the doctor said in French, scaring me.

"What tests?"

"An *endoscopie*. Do you wish to do it now, or schedule for tomorrow?"

"Please, let's just get it over," I said, unaware that I was about to experience the equivalent of Nazi torture, because the French way then to do an *endoscopie* was to insert a tube half the thickness of a garden hose down your throat into your esophagus while you are lying naked on your side and gagging, without the benefit of anesthesia. Those twenty minutes seemed like a lifetime and if they had asked me, I would have confessed to murder just to get it over with. Finally, they withdrew the tube and I staggered naked to the dressing cubicle, clutching the ragged remnants of my humanity as I got dressed. I waited in the reception area for the doctor, who finally came out. I was about to learn the real difference between French and American medicine.

"I regret to tell you that you have a peptic ulcer, here, Monsieur," the doctor said, poking me in the abdomen, causing me to gasp with pain. He wrote a prescription and handed it to me. "You will need to take this medication. Also, you will have to change your diet. This is an absolute requirement. There can be no *déviation, comprenez-vous?*"

"*Oui, je comprends,*" I said.

"You must avoid all fatty and spicy foods, minimize caffeine, as in café, tea, cocoa. Also no *citrus, tomates* or *chocolat*. Tell me, Monsieur, how important is alcohol in your life?"

"To be perfectly honest, alcohol does play a part in my life."

"*Hélas, Monsieur,* I regret to inform you that until your ulcer is cured, which will take at least three to six months, you may not drink any alcohol," he said.

"Nothing! Not even a drop?!" I cried. This was worse than the Nazi torture.

"I regret, Monsieur," he said, sympathetically patting my shoulder. "For you, *il est défendu*. Alcohol of any kind is absolutely forbidden. Not even a drop."

"My God! Not even wine with dinner?"

"Oh no. Of course I didn't mean that," he snapped, annoyed. "A meal without wine. Ridiculous!"

That night, Anne made pasta with pesto sauce for me (no tomatoes) and *sauce* Bolognese for her and Justin and we had it with red wine.

"You see, it's not so bad," she said. "You'll survive."

"Yeah, but will I want to?" I said.

Over the next few weeks, I watched my diet and drinking, worked out at the California Terrace and managed to lose about ten pounds. During the day, I worked on the book, while Anne made plans for our Venice trip.

"Sally recommended a little hotel not too far from the Piazza San Marco called the Hotel Do Pozzi. I've made reservations for the beginning of May," she said.

"Suppose the book isn't finished by then?" I said.

"Then you better hurry," she said.

The next day, Anne said she wasn't feeling well either.

"Well, I know a place in Menton they've got Nazi medical techniques," I said.

"I'll be fine," she said.

That morning, I finished the book.

One minute I was writing and then it was done. I didn't know what to do with myself. I took a long walk up to the top of Nietzsche's path, then down the path into the woods. I thought about the journey I had taken and how it had changed me.

I was a better writer than I was when I started. Living in France had changed the book too. The woods were quiet, shafts of sunlight coming through the canopy of trees. What had Nietzsche thought when he had finished Zarathustra here? I wondered. He must have known what he had done, a work of philosophy unlike anything anyone had done since the Christian Gospels, much as that thought would have irritated him – and them.

Nor could he have foreseen what happened with it. Its early failure, selling only seven copies and the printer stopping the run to print an anti-Semitic pamphlet instead, and only long after his madness was it recognized for the masterpiece it was. You'd better stop thinking like that, I told myself, walking back up the path and back down toward the villa. Neitzsche knew what he had done was good and you know what you've done and that's it. You'd better just think about doing the final edit and cleaning it up and getting it off to London and hope to Hell they like it so you can get paid.

I walked down Avenue Lamaro past the villa to the *Corniche*, picked up a copy of *Nice-Matin*, and sat down at the café on the corner to wait for Anne and Justin. I felt a bit lightheaded and without direction, like a kid getting out of school for the summer. We'll have to celebrate, I thought, but suddenly felt a icy shiver slide down my spine as I read the headline. When I was a kid, people used to say that meant "someone had stepped on your grave."

Nuclear scientists in Sweden had reported extremely high radiation levels throughout the country. Reports from Finland, Norway, and Denmark confirmed radiation levels four to five times normal, despite seasonal snow and rain. Meteorologists studying weather patterns stated that the radiation was being spread by wind currents coming from the Black Sea, whipping across the Ukraine, over the Baltic and into Scandinavia. Some mysterious force somewhere in the Ukraine or Russia was spewing highly dangerous radiation. It was everywhere: in the atmosphere, the ground and the buildings and the air that people were breathing. The Scandinavian governments had angrily demanded an explanation from the Kremlin, but so far, Moscow had refused to comment. It was a mystery. *Nice-Matin* speculated that perhaps the Russians had resumed nuclear bomb testing, but the U.S. government stated that their monitors and satellites had picked up no evidence of nuclear explosions in Russia.

That evening, on the French TV news, the announcer reported that Moscow TV had announced that an accident had occurred at the Chernobyl nuclear power station north of Kiev. One of the reactors had been damaged and "measures were being taken" to deal with the accident. Meanwhile, in addition to *exceptionnel* levels of radiation in Scandinavia, significant increases in radiation were now being reported in Poland, Germany and Czechoslovakia. The danger, whatever it was, was spreading fast. The *commentateur* reported that the French Cabinet was meeting in emergency session to deal with the situation.

That night, we met Max, Sally, Bobby G., Gaby, Nigel and Monika for dinner at Les Lucioles in Roquebrune on the *terrasse* overlooking the lights of the port.

"What the hell is going on?" Gaby wanted to know.

"Maybe it's the 'China Syndrome,'" Anne said, referring to the Jane Fonda movie about a nuclear reactor meltdown.

"Could that really happen?" Sally said.

"Yeah, it could. Especially with all the old equipment and incompetence among the Russkies," Max said.

"What does it mean? Could a reactor literally melt its way through the earth?" Gaby asked.

"No, but it could do plenty of damage," I said.

"How much damage?" Bobby G. asked.

"Depends," Max said.

"On what?"

"On a lot of things," he said impatiently. "On how big the reactor core is, how big the meltdown, if it is a meltdown, how much of the reactor is burning, how much radiation has escaped, not to mention other poisonous stuff, like lithium and cesium, that might've been released into the atmosphere, the wind patterns, the levels of contamination. There are a million factors."

"What could be contaminated?" Anne asked, looking at Justin playing with his food in the restaurant high chair.

"Everything," Max said. "The air, the water, the ground, plants, animals, food, the milk the kids drink, our bodies, our fingers, everything."

"What can we do?" Gaby asked.

"Get drunk," Nigel said.

"I mean it. What can we do?"

"Nothing. Pray the winds shift. Goddamn Russkies," Max said.

"With the jet streams and the ocean currents, eventually it'll go all over the world," I said.

"Yeah, but it'll be diluted. The closer to ground zero, the worse it'll be, those poor bastards," Max said.

"How bad could it get?" Monika said. "I mean, it couldn't kill us, could it?"

Max didn't say anything.

"Well, could it?"

"Probably not," he said. "We've got a chance. The Alps'll stop some of it and maybe we'll get lucky with the wind patterns."

"But the radioactivity and whatever could kill people?" Monika demanded.

"Probably already has," Max said.

"Or give them cancer twenty years from now?"

"No one knows," Max shrugged.

"So all we can do is just sit here and wait?" Anne asked.

"And see which way the wind blows," Max said.

"The French government says they're meeting about it," Bobby G. said.

"That'll generate a load of hot air right there," Nigel said.

"We were planning to leave for Venice. Now I don't know whether to go or not. Whether it'll be worse there or if we stay here," Anne said.

"Well, if one is to die, Venice is a good place for it. I always thought it had a sort of 'funereal' atmosphere, black gondolas and all," Nigel said.

"You know, that's not funny," Monika said.

"Sorry. Gallows humor seemed rather *à-propós*. Anyone read *Death in Venice* lately?"

"Nigel!!"

"Sorry, chaps," Nigel said.

"So what do we do?" Anne said.

"We wait," I said.

"And meanwhile, while we wait, we enjoy the *bouillabaisse*," Max declared as the waiter brought the food. "If we're going to all glow green, at least we're going to have a great last supper."

The next few days were spent scouring the newspapers and TV for every scrap of news. Radiation levels were climbing in the Netherlands, Belgium, and Scotland. Elsewhere, increases in radiation were reported in Baden, Bavaria, Austria, and Hungary, and had reached the borders of France and Italy. There were protests against the Russians in cities all over Europe.

In Germany, the Green Party staged a massive demonstration carrying banners that read "Chernobyl is Everywhere." According to the *International Herald Tribune* that we picked up in Nice, American spy satellite photos suggested that a large nuclear reactor fire at Chernobyl was burning out of control. Long plumes of smoke releasing more and more radiation into the air could be seen in the photos. A Dutch ham radio operator claimed to have picked up a broadcast from someone near Chernobyl who said that two reactor units were on fire and hundreds, perhaps thousands of people were dead. The Russian operator begged the world to come and help them.

While Moscow maintained an official silence, the French Canal Plus TV news reported that Soviet officials in Bonn and Stockholm had approached those countries' nuclear authorities for advice on how to put out a nuclear graphite fire. The only good news was that the increase in radioactive levels in most of Europe was lower; Scandinavia appeared to have borne the brunt of it.

Anne was growing increasingly nervous. She pulled a suitcase out of the closet and stared at it.

"I'm ready to get on a plane," she said.

"To where?"

"As far away as I can get. Australia, South America, I don't care."

"Meanwhile we stay inside the house as much as possible. Dust in the air could be dangerous."

"What about Justin? Does anyone know how this stuff affects children?"

"No one knows anything, but I'm going to," I said, grabbing the car keys.

"Where are you going?" she said.

"Back to college. But just to be on the safe side, keep yourself and Justin indoors with the windows closed."

She put her hand on my arm to stop me.

"What are you talking about? Where are you going?"

"There's a university in Nice. It's supposed to have a good library, *La Bibliothèque de l'Université de Nice-Sophia Antipolis*. I'll be back in a few hours."

I drove to the University in Nice, found the library building and went in. A short-haired woman of *un certain âge* was at the front desk.

"*Pardon, Madame, je cherche l'information...*" I began, but she waved me to stop.

"The information you want is already out on the table *là-bas*," she said, pointing at a long table packed with French people of all ages pouring over large physics textbooks. Obviously, others had had the same idea. I found a seat next to an old Frenchman in a beret. He smelled of garlic and tobacco smoke.

"*Pardon, Monsieur,*" I whispered. "*Avez-vous trouvé quelque chose?*"

"This is interesting. One learns a lot, if one bothers to look," he said, pointing to a table in a thick textbook. I learned that radiation was measured in *curies*, absorbed radiation was measured in *rads*, while its impact on the body was measured in *roentgens*. The table showed equivalences of Alpha wave radiation, the most dangerous kind of radiation, as compared to things we could understand, such as the number of *roentgens* associated with normal background radiation that's always there, to wrist watches with Radium dials, to chest X-rays, to nuclear containment units. "*Regardez, Monsieur,*" the Frenchman said, tapping one of the numbers. "That is the amount being reported in Denmark and northern Germany." It was equivalent to about two chest X-rays and I suddenly began to breathe a lot easier. "*Venez,*" he said, jerking his head, meaning outside.

We went outside and both ordered *pastis* at a nearby café.

"*Santé,*" we said, clinking glasses.

"I'm Pierre. I have a *commerce de nettoyage à sec* (dry cleaners) near the Place Garibaldi."

"One of my favorite parts of Nice. I'm André," I said.

"It pays to get real information, *non?*" he said. "Otherwise people go crazy."

"My wife was nervous. We have a three-year-old boy."

"She's a mother. *C'est normal,*" he shrugged. "So what do you think? We have more nuclear facilities in France than any other country on earth. We are probably getting more radiation now, you and I sitting here, than when the radiation comes from *la Russie.*"

"So if the Northern Europeans are getting the equivalent of two X-rays, by the time it gets to us, what with the Alps and the Alpes Maritimes to block some of it and the wind dispersal we'll get what? Maybe the equivalent of one chest X-ray?" I said.

"Perhaps not even. Although you will see, the French government will say zero," he smiled.

"Why would they lie like that?"

"Because it is France, Monsieur. Foreign radioactivity would not dare touch sacred French soil," he laughed. "*D'ailleurs,* we French have to be different."

"Why with the French does everything always have to be different, whether it's medicine, marriage, even radioactivity? Why?"

"It's our nature," he shrugged. *"Ecoutez, Monsieur.* You are American, *non?"*

"Oui."

"You must understand, Monsieur. France is the country of the Enlightenment, of Voltaire, Rousseau, Montaigne, and Diderot. For us French, reason and logic are... I don't know... what the American flag and Coca-Cola is for you Americans. When French parents want to scold their children, the worst thing they can say to them is *'Tu n'es pas raisonnable.'* You are not being reasonable. That is our dilemma, our paradox. We believe in reason in an obviously irrational world. How else explain that in the country with more nuclear reactors than any other, we are threatened by radioactivity from Russia, a country with which, unlike the Americans, we are friends? You see, it is *absurde.* We French are different because we see ourselves as the only rational humans in a world that is completely mad."

"De vous à moi, Pierre, I think you do it just to be perverse, for the sheer pleasure of *faire offense à quelqu'un,"* (offending others)," I said.

"That too. Everyone is capable of being petty, after all," he laughed. "But it's not just the French that make the problems. What about *les américains?"*

"What's wrong with us Americans?"

"You are all so sure you are *les bons gens.* To think you are always, how you say, *le* 'good guy' is not so good. It makes a people self-righteous. Self-important too. That is the problem we Europeans have with you *américains."*

"You are a wise man, Pierre," I admitted. "I guess we're not so easy either."

"Ecoutez, André, tell your wife the radioactivity would not dare to touch French soil. Tell her she has more to fear from French doctors than from Russian reactors."

I went back to Eze and told Anne it wasn't as bad as Max and the newspapers had made out. The worst we could get would be the equivalent of a chest X-ray.

"What makes you think that's so great? If there was no problem with X-rays, why do the technicians always wear lead aprons and get behind lead barriers when they give you one?" Anne said.

"Because they do twenty, thirty a day. That's a hundred, a hundred and fifty a week. For them it adds up, that's why they take precautions."

"Well, what about the effect on Justin? He's just a baby."

"Babies get X-rays too. He'll survive."

"I never expected anything like this," she said. "It's like something Biblical."

"No one did. But the Alps will help protect us from even that little bit of radiation."

"What about the winds?"

"The winds will eventually take it all over the world. There'll be Aboriginals in Australia who'll be absorbing some of this. America too."

"But where is it safer? Here or if we go to Venice?"

"Italy has Alps too. And the wind is probably more southwest than southeast."

"But I just heard the BBC. The French government is saying that there is no increase of radioactivity in France."

"That's what Pierre said they'd say. Like there's a glass wall in the sky around France keeping out the wind," I laughed.

"Who's Pierre?"

"A dry-cleaner from Nice. He helped me in the University library. An interesting fellow."

"So to hell with everything? We go to Venice?" she said.

"We go to Venice," I said.

"But we watch the news and the reports about the wind, right?"

"My Dad used to say, it's always a good idea to keep an eye out for which way the wind blows."

Chapter 25

You Can Never Go To Venice Only Once

Venice was a dream. We couldn't have come at a better time. The tourists were down to a trickle because it was still off-season and many had been scared away by Chernobyl. The weather was perfect, sunny during the day, cool enough for a jacket at night. The drive across northern Italy on the *autostrada* took hours and by the time we parked the car in the municipal structure near the train station and took the *vaporetto* on the Grand Canal, it was late afternoon. A porter in the Piazza San Marco carried our luggage to the hotel, located in a narrow courtyard, the Corte Dei Do Pozzi, filled with palm trees in stone urns and a stone ivy-covered well, a few blocks from the *piazza*.

We checked in to a small antique-filled room, then headed back to the Piazza San Marco to an outdoor table at Florian's, the famous café. Justin, looking like an Italian child with his long curly hair, was in his element. More than anything, he loved to chase pigeons and since there are more pigeons per square foot in the Piazza San Marco than anywhere else on earth, he was having a field day, running and scattering them all over the *piazza*.

The sun was setting, casting the shadow of the Campanile far across the nearly empty *piazza*, A quartet of musicians were playing something by Mozart as the white-jacketed *cameriere* brought a Compari and soda for me and a champagne cocktail for Anne, looking unbelievably beautiful in a blue dress with a twisted gold necklace.

After six years of marriage, I sometimes took her beauty for granted, only once in a while really taking in her long dark hair, flawless face and those incredible multi-color eyes, blue, green and gold like a lion's. At that moment, I realized again just how breathtaking she was and once again, fell in love. Anne sighed and said, "I'm in heaven."

"So's Justin," I said, as he charged into a group of pigeons that a tourist had been trying to line up for a snapshot, sending them flying,. "*Chin chin*, Babe."

We clinked glasses.

"You did it. You finished the book," she said and kissed me. "This is so nice. I love this café," she sighed.

"Everybody loves Florian's. It was Casanova's favorite café," I said.

"How do you know that?"

"I read it in a guidebook. But he mentioned it in his memoirs."

Justin came running up.

"Did you see me, Mommy?" he asked. "I chased all the birds."

"I saw, Sweetie."

"They have lions too," he said, pointing at the statues of the two lions beside the cathedral. "They're not real, are they Dad?"

"They're just statues, Justin. We can play with them tomorrow if you like."

"I like Venice," Justin said, running off to chase more pigeons.

"So do I," Anne said.

"So do I," I said.

"So what are we doing next?" Anne asked.

"As little as possible," I said, thinking about the phone conversation I'd had with my agent, June, just before we had left. I had called her to tell her I'd finished the first draft of the book. "That's wonderful news," she said. "When can I see it?"

"I'll need two or three more weeks to get it on a good computer, edit, reformat it," I told her.

"I'll alert your publisher. There's, um, lots of interest," she said.

"I thought there was before," I said, a little nervously.

"Well, of course. I'll explain after I've had a chance to read it," she had said, making me more nervous than ever.

"No, I mean *next*, right now," Anne said.

"Are you hungry?"

"I'm still full from lunch," she said. We had stopped off for lunch in Brescia on the drive from the Riviera. While driving, we had been following developments from Chernobyl on the car radio. The BBC said there had been slight, but measurable increases in radiation in Italy, Spain, and Britain. The Soviet news agency, TASS, claimed the reactor was under control, but offered no specifics. In Poland, authorities fearing radioactive contamination, had banned the sale of milk. The Romanian government urged people to stay indoors and to avoid drinking rainwater. In Austria, outdoor fruit and vegetable stands were instructed to wash and cover their produce. French Prime Minister Jacques Chirac, however, had gone on television to declare that there had been no increase whatsoever in France. When I heard that, I thought about Pierre in Nice and laughed.

"How about something light?" Anne said. "Drinks and a snack? Maybe spaghetti for Justin if he's hungry? Where should we go?"

"The Gritti Palace."

"Why the Gritti?"

"An *homage* to Hemingway. It was his favorite. He used to stay there."

"Isn't it expensive?"

"For a meal, too expensive. But for snacks, we should be OK," I said.

It was growing dark as we walked through the streets and across the little arched bridges over the smaller canals, that the Venetians call "*rii* canals" to the Gritti Palace Hotel. We went inside and got a table on the balcony overlooking the Grand Canal.

"So this was Hemingway's favorite spot?" Anne asked the *cameriere*, as he served us *misto fritti* and *chianti* and Justin, a plate of *spaghetti Bolognese*.

"Actually, I am told he liked that table, *signora*," the *cameriere* said, pointing to a table in the corner.

"So Hemingway actually lived in the hotel?" Anne asked.

"So they say. He wrote *Across The River And Into The Trees* here. It was the worst thing he ever wrote," I said.

"Is it really that bad?"

"You know, about once every five or ten years, I tell myself it couldn't possibly be as bad as I remembered. And then I start to reread it, and each time it's even worse. It's so bad it's got to be the worst book ever written by a good writer. I mean maybe they should make that a new category for the Guinness Book of Records: 'Worst Book Written By A Writer Who Should Have Known Better' or something."

"I wonder why?"

"I think he was writing just to write. Maybe because he was 'The Big War Writer' and everybody expected him to write the great World War Two novel. He was there, he was a correspondent in it, but in a way, it wasn't his war the way the Spanish Civil War and World War One had been. It's like Sid and me talking about Vietnam. He's of the wrong generation. We lived it. Personally, I think for Hemingway, the gas tank was just empty."

"You don't suppose Venice had anything to do with it?" Anne asked.

"I hope not," I said, looking at the lights of the boats and the palaces reflected on the Grand Canal. "Although, there's that line in the *Alexandria Quartet* where Pursewarden tells the story of his fellow poet, Negroponte, who falls in love with a female vampire during Carnival, everyone disguised in *dominos* and masks and rampant sex, and Pursewarden says of Venice, 'I felt as if I was living in a Gothic novel. Never have I written worse poetry.' So maybe there is something about Venice, the unbelievable romanticism of it, that's too much for writers."

"Maybe it's a good thing you finished the book before we came."

We sat quietly, listening to the sounds of a piano coming from the dining room. In the distance, the Santa Maria della Salute, was lit up ghostly white in the darkness. "God, I love this place," Anne said.

The next day, we played tourist. We went inside the Basilica di San Marco and dutifully saw the gold Pala d'Oro altar and all the rest, though the best part was when Justin and I sat on the two stone lions of St. Mark, growling at each other like lions.

Lunch was a *trattoria* near the Rialto. After that, we saw the Bridge of Sighs and the clock on the Torre dell'Orologio with its automated figures of the Magi and the two bronze Moors striking the bell on the hour, that I couldn't look at without thinking about the fight behind that clock between James Bond and a bad guy in one of the Bond films.

We went back to the hotel to dress for dinner, Justin in his little navy blazer, me in mine – we had decided to splurge on Ristorante Ivo, recommended by the concierge – and I thought we were going to Florian's for drinks, when we passed a gondola station and Anne insisted we take a gondola ride.

"*Quanto?*" I asked the gondolier, an older man in the traditional striped shirt costume.

"*Ottanta mille, signore.*"

"*Quanto tempo?* For how long?"

"You see everything, *signore*. The Grand Canal, the side canals, Marco Polo house, *tutti*."

"*Quanto tempo por ottanta mille?*"

"*Venti minutos*, maybe more *signore*."

"How much?" Anne asked.

"Eighty thousand lire," I said. "That's like fifty bucks for twenty minutes."

"We'll take it."

"Anne! Fifty bucks for twenty minutes in a rowboat?"

"We can't come to Venice and not go in a gondola. If you do that, you can't say you've been to Venice."

"Fifty bucks!" I said. "Just to say I've done it."

She came close. "Trust me. You'll be glad you did it."

I reluctantly handed the gondolier the money.

"You won't be sorry," she said, as we got into the gondola.

"My wallet is already sorry," I said, as we settled into the comfortable seat made for two, the gondolier behind us, Justin in front of us in the prow of the gondola.

The gondola made its way through the boat traffic on the Grand Canal and into a side canal, bordered by houses hundreds of years old. Justin was being very good, sitting quietly and looking ahead, fascinated by the novelty of being on the water in such a different way.

It was nearing dusk. The sun turned the windows in the buildings and the water to gold and suddenly, it was very still, the only sound the quiet splash of the oar as we glided through the side canals. It was as if the constant noise in my head, what I understood was stress and consciousness of the modern world, suddenly stopped. Everything was silent, as if we had stepped back centuries in time, and I thought, this is the way the world is supposed to be.

"*La casa di Marco Polo*," the gondolier said, gesturing at an old multi-story house he said dated to the thirteenth century. There had been another gondola behind us, but we turned a corner and were alone. The sides of the houses were reddish-gold in the sunset.

As we turned a corner we heard music. Someone in one of the apartments had left a window open. On her stereo was a woman singer with a wonderful operatic voice, singing, of all things, "*Tea For Two*," in English. Anne took my hand and we smiled at each other and I thought, this is perfect. The book finished and it was very good, Anne and Justin, both so beautiful and healthy and all of us loving each other, the canal and the sunset and "Tea For Two" and I thought, I can die now, because I know what a perfect moment is and

Once Upon A Villa

no matter what happens, I've had the best life has to offer and I loved it. The sound of the music followed us as we glided on the canal:

"We will raise a family,
A boy for you, a girl for me,
Can't you see how happy we could be."

After the gondola ride, we went to the restaurant, where the waiter made toy animals for Justin out of wine corks and toothpicks: a toy horse, a camel, and a hippopotamus. The food and wine were very good and the waiters opened the restaurant windows that were set at floor level so we could see the gondolas glide by in the darkness, their prows lit with lanterns, the gondoliers singing *"O Sole Mio."* I gave Justin a few thousand lire for tips and our waiter, who had made him the toys, took Justin by the hand so he could stand by the window and be serenaded by the gondoliers. We watched as Justin stuck his hand out and handed them the tips and as he did so, people in the restaurant applauded.

The night was magical. Anne asked me if the fifty dollars for the gondola ride was worth it. Her face was shining. I had never seen her so happy.

"It was worth every penny," I said.

After dinner, we walked through the dark streets to Harry's Bar near the Piazza San Marco for a nightcap. At first we couldn't find it and when we did, we realized we were standing right next to it and I started laughing, remembering how the same thing had happened to my friend, Ib Melchior. Successful in his own right as a longtime writer-producer-director-author known for science fiction, Ib was also the son of the famous Wagnerian tenor, Lauritz Melchior, about whom there was a famous incident when Bugsy Siegel, the Mafioso who was to create Las Vegas as a gambling and tourist destination, tried to buy his Beverly Hills house; a scene shown in the Warren Beatty movie, *Bugsy*, although in real life, Melchior didn't actually sell Bugsy the house.

In appearance, Ib was a dead ringer for Ernest Hemingway, down to his white beard and the way he wore his hair. On Ib's and his wife, Cleo's first trip to Venice, when he couldn't find Harry's Bar and asked someone, the man said in astonishment, "*Scusa,*' Signore Hemingway, *you* don't know where Harry's is?!!" Later, when Ib and Cleo went to the bar, the barman, deciding to play along, said loudly to Ib, "Well, Papa, you've written about war, Africa, and bulls. What the hell are you going to write about next?!" startling all the tourists in the place to silence, while he and Ib roared with laughter.

Anne and I went into Harry's and ordered *bellinis* at the bar. I sat holding Justin fast asleep, his head on my shoulder.

"With your ulcer, should you be drinking *bellinis?*" Anne said.

"No, but this is where they were invented. When you're at the source, how can you say no?"

"So this was also Hemingway's hangout. He did a lot of drinking," Anne said.

"Occupational hazard for writers," I said.

"Why?"

"I don't know. It just is," I said, thinking of all the writers I knew who had a problem with booze. There were a lot of them.

"The *bellini's* good. If you have to have a vice, drinking is an attractive one."

"Most vices are, I guess. Otherwise people wouldn't do them," I said, squeezing over to make room for a newcomer at the bar, who turned out to be an American who worked at the Jet Propulsion Lab in Pasadena. I had once consulted there on a secret U.S. Army contract and we tried to see if we knew someone in common. I asked what he was working on and he mentioned the Mariner space mission I had read about in the newspaper.

"If you like, I'll send you some really good photos we took of Uranus," he said.

"I'd love it," I told him, giving him our address in Eze-sur-Mer, not really expecting him to do it, but sure enough, two weeks later, we received the photos in the mail from JPL. I remember staring at the pictures of Uranus thinking here was a planet maybe fifteen, twenty times bigger than the earth and until a few weeks ago, no one had ever seen what it looked like, except as a speck of reflected light. I felt almost as if I was the first person to ever see this new world and I thought, no matter what awful things people do – and there is no species so savage or capable of more horror – but so long as we were capable of doing something like this, sending a machine to take a picture of a world billions of miles away, that we were worth saving, that there was something extraordinary in us.

The next few days followed the same pattern, doing tourist things like going to the glass factories and shops in Murano, the Doge's Palace and the Bridge of Sighs, seeing the Titian paintings in the Santa Maria della Salute and the intricate wooden model of 15th century Venice in the Museo Correr, having drinks at Florian's listening to the musicians play as Justin chased pigeons in the *piazza*, wonderful *risottos*, and nightcaps at Harry's. It was with regret that we packed up and took the *vaporetto* back and picked up the car from the parking structure.

We stopped in Verona for lunch. I picked up a copy of the *International Herald Tribune* from a *tabaccheria* next to the restaurant. The Soviet Union had announced that it was closing all of its nuclear reactors with the same design as the one at Chernobyl. However, another article noted that the Chernobyl crisis and the way the Russians had handled it had clearly dealt a setback to Gorbachev's efforts to improve relations with the West. Only the French were unmoved, a spokesman for the French atomic ministry announcing in Paris that "French opinion overwhelmingly favors nuclear power." Score one again for Pierre, I thought.

"Something famous happened in Verona, what was it?" Anne said.

"Romeo and Juliet. '*In fair Verona, where we lay our scene, where civil blood makes civil hands unclean,*'" I recited. "Sounds like the Democrats and the Republicans, doesn't it?"

"Sometimes you're such a smartass. How can you stand yourself?" Anne said.

"Well, politics is a blood sport, isn't it? This place sure had its share," I said, glancing around the small *piazza*.

"Was there a swordfight, Daddy?" Justin asked.

"You know, as a matter of fact, there was," I said.

After lunch, we drove to Lake Como to look at the villas along the lake as a possibility for the summer, then back on the *autostrada*. We had almost reached Genoa, when I asked Anne to get our passports ready for the border crossing back to France.

"You have them," Anne said. "You were supposed to get them from the hotel safe."

"No you were," I said, pulling the car over to a center strip on the *autostrada* with a gas station, *restaurante* and parking area. We both searched our bags and pockets and came up empty. We had left our passports, travelers checks, and the keys to the villa in the hotel safe in Venice.

"We could have the hotel send it to us," Anne said.

"Where? Here? How do we cross the border now? And even if we got across, the villa's locked up tight, how do we get in? Plus we left the money there."

We called the hotel from a public phone in the gas station. They opened the safe and confirmed that we had left everything there.

"What do we do?" Anne whispered.

"We go back. We hadn't wanted to leave Venice in the first place," I said, reserving a room for another night at the hotel.

We turned the car around and headed back on the *autostrada* to Venice. Night was falling. I had been driving most of the day and I was tired. Worse, the drive back to Venice at night on the *autostrada* was the scariest driving I had ever experienced. There are no speed limits on the *autostrada*. I drove through the darkness at 100 miles per hour, which made me the slowest car on the road and the scary parts were the Italian drivers coming up behind me within a few feet before flicking their lights indicating they wanted to pass.

One guy in a Ferrari didn't even bother. He came up within inches of my back bumper, then whipped around me to the right and back in front of me in a second, moving away from me as if I was standing still. It was the longest hardest drive of my life and I was thrilled to arrive back at the parking structure and take the *vaporetto* past Santa Maria della Salute to the Piazza San Marco again, the piazza empty so late at night as we trudged like refugees back to the hotel with our suitcases.

As we entered the Do Pozzi courtyard, Anne reached over and kissed me.

"That was some drive, Babe. You did good," she said.

"Scared the hell out of me."

"I know, me too."

We checked in and went back up to the same room we had left that morning.

"After all that driving, we're right back where we started," I said, falling into bed.

"I told you, didn't I? You can never go to Venice only once," Anne said.

Chapter 26

The Monte Carlo Grand Prix

We were having lunch at the Cap Roux restaurant across from the beach in Eze-sur-Mer and feeling sorry for ourselves when Justin acquired an admirer, a blonde little girl, perhaps two years old, from another table, who began to follow Justin around like a puppy as he wandered around the restaurant with one of his toy trucks. She obviously belonged to a young couple at a nearby table, who watched her closely, but let her follow Justin. As for Justin, he was doing his best to ignore her. Anne and I nodded to the other couple, but otherwise left the children alone.

We were feeling sorry for ourselves because Stuart and Glenda had come by with Max to invite us to come with them to the Film Festival in Cannes. Stuart had rented a suite in the Carleton, "I'd buy the hotel, if it was for sale," he told me, just to give his daughters some excitement meeting the movie stars and such. Also, he wanted my opinion on buying distribution rights for some of the films. My protestations to the contrary, that I knew nothing whatever about that business, didn't dissuade him. He and Glenda had decided that the fact that I was a writer and came from Los Angeles automatically qualified me as an expert on the movie business. Anne wanted to go, but I told them we couldn't take the time.

With Max and Sally acting as go-betweens, Chuck had agreed to let me use a workspace and one of the computers in his office to do a rewrite and edit of my book in exchange for me paying part of the electric bill and giving his people an occasional hand on a brochure or technical document. As a result, I was tied up full time on getting the book into shape to send to my agent and publisher in England. Also, although we liked Stuart and Glenda, we didn't want to feel obligated to them. One of the problems in dealing with rich friends is that no matter how nice they are, they tend to regard your not having lots of money as a type of character defect. Their *noblesse oblige* creates an uneasy sense of obligation we were trying to avoid.

That year in Cannes, besides the usual topless starlets, directors, and stars coming to plug their films for foreign distribution and a tribute to Cary Grant, who had recently died, the leading contenders for the Palme d'Or according to *Nice-Matin*, were three films: *The Mission*, a film directed by Roland Jaffe, starring Robert de Niro and Jeremy Irons about faith and the Spanish conquest of the Amazon, *Thérèse*, a French film starring Catherine Mouchet as a 19th century nun who becomes a saint, and a Swedish film, *The Sacrifice*, about World War III and a man on a Swedish island who offers to sacrifice his little son to God to save the world, that with its Biblical echoes of the Abraham and Isaac story was getting a lot of buzz. The big American movies of the year, like *Ferris Bueller's Day Off*, *The Three Amigos*, and the upcoming *Top Gun* starring Tom Cruise, while represented by stars and producers at the Festival, were not to be screened.

Max, who got a gig covering the Festival for a German magazine, had a different take. "The Frogs try to pretend the Festival is about cinema as 'art,' with the topless babes as a little *divertissement* for the *paparazzi*. That's why they ignore all the Hollywood movies, while gushing over the Hollywood stars. It has as much to do with art as my ass."

"Now that's an image to contemplate," Glenda said.

"Then what is it?" Anne asked.

"Cannes is just a glorified trade show. Besides bringing in some needed tourist bucks, it's where distributors of independent – which is basically synonymous with crappy – movies; we're talking great epics, like moody Slavic semi-porno pieces, Hong Kong kung fu crap, Bollywood romances, and the like, find distributors for countries that otherwise could care less about them, in hopes of making a quick – often desperate – buck. You've got to remember, half the films being traded here were made on someone's credit card. That's the glamorous Cannes Film Festival!"

"What about the serious films?" Anne asked.

"Camouflage. It's the fig leaf to give a phony French respectability to what's really going on: deal-making in third-rate goods."

"So why do the stars come?" Glenda asked.

"To plug the real movies, the Hollywood ones the Frogs won't show at the screenings, but that'll make all the dough."

"You see," I told Stuart, "you don't need me. Max's got it figured out."

"Well, the offer stands, if you are interested," Stuart said and tapping me on the shoulder, whispered, "I know you are looking for a new villa. Once my place in the country is finished, I've got an offer for you, if you're interested."

"Thanks," I said. "I've got to finish the book at Chuck's office. And besides, Chuck's charging me for the electricity."

"Sounds like Chuck," Stuart grinned. "We'll talk after Cannes."

Justin climbed into my lap to get away from the little girl, who followed by sitting next to me. The couple who had been watching, came over.

"I think you've got our kid," the young woman said in English.

"I think I do," I said, gesturing for them to join us.

They introduced themselves as Ron and Roxanna Patterson. It turned out they also lived in a villa on our street, Avenue Lamaro, but near the top of the road. Ron was the Concertmaster and First Violin of the Monte Carlo Philharmonic orchestra; Roxanna was First Viola. They had come to Eze from Arcadia in Southern California.

"Near Santa Anita?" I asked. The race track.

"And the Arboretum. Though we love the track," Roxanna said.

"I've dropped a few bucks there myself," I said.

"How did you wind up in Monte Carlo?" Anne asked.

"Princess Grace. She brought us here," Roxanna said.

"We met her skiing in Vail. Right on the slopes," Ron said. "We were pausing during a run and she skied to a stop next to us. We started chatting and the next thing we knew, she said, 'We're trying to make the Monte Carlo a world-class orchestra. We could really use you.' She got Prince Rainier to make us an offer and here we are."

"What was she like? We've heard so many different stories," Anne said.

"She was really nice. Smart. Knew what she wanted, very persuasive. She sure persuaded us," Ron said.

"Did you know her well?"

"We did. She was very interested in the orchestra. She thought it would be a real attraction for Monaco and she worked closely with us. We used to spend lots of time with her and the kids – of course they're not kids any more – at the Palace," Ron said.

"Less now. Everything changed when Grace... well, everything changed," Roxanna said.

"So you know Prince Albert and Caroline and Stephanie well?" Anne asked.

"Oh sure. Though not so much any more, now that they have their own lives. Have you met them?"

"Sort of. Andy almost danced with Stephanie," Anne said.

"She was pretty out of it," I said.

"She's had a tough time since the accident," Roxanna said.

"Well, Stephanie was always Stephanie," Ron said. "This is great, you guys living here. You'll have to see our villa. We built it around a tree. That's if I can tear my daughter away from your son."

"We'll set up a play date for lunch or something," Anne said.

"And you'll have to come hear us play," Roxanna said. "It's great having another American woman with a little one to talk to on the same street."

Afterwards, I asked Madame Finot, who was scolding me on the state of my *tomates*, which were small misshapen things compared to hers, why she hadn't told me about the other Americans, *les* Pattersons, also living on the Avenue Lamaro. She was watering and trimming her tomato vines one at a time, each one just so.

"They are *les artistes, les musiciens*. One does not disturb such people. One must allow the creativity to happen."

"I'm an *artiste* too, a writer," I said.

"The other Americans, they make music. That is art. What you do, it is not *serieux*, like Hugo, *n'est-ce pas?*"

"No, not like Victor Hugo."

"*Alors*, you see," she shrugged. "It is *artifice*, not *art*. *Ce n'est pas la même chose.*"

"How do you know?"

"Because if you were a true *artiste*, you would take better care of your *tomates*," she said, raising her finger. "The true *artiste* seeks *perfection*. You just like to write."

"But I'm working all day in Monte Carlo. I have no time," I protested.

"Now you are making excuses, which we both know has nothing to do with art or anything else and which is unworthy of us both, Monsieur. Also, you need to take better care of your wife," she said.

"What's wrong with my wife?"

"You'll see. Men are *imbéciles*," she said, shoo-ing me away.

I went back to our villa. Anne was on the *terrasse*, writing invitations to Justin's birthday party – he was about to turn three – while Justin played Davy Crocket in the front yard, stalking squirrels using a bent branch as a musket.

"Are you OK? Madame Finot seems to think you're not," I asked.

Once Upon A Villa

"My stomach's been bothering me a bit lately," Anne said. "I'm OK."

"Maybe you should get it checked out?" I said.

"What? Go to a French doctor and have them tell me it's my liver?" she said and we both smiled, thinking of Max. "Besides, I have to do Justin's party and we've got the Monte Carlo Grand Prix coming. We'll see after that."

"Why? What are we doing for the Monte Carlo Grand Prix?"

"Apparently, the balcony of Chuck's office has a perfect view of a key part of the course. Chuck's putting on a Grand Prix party. We're all going to watch the race from his office. You should be pretty familiar with it by now."

I was getting used to going in to Chuck's office complex every day and working on editing the book. It was oddly reassuring, after working in solitude for so long, to be working in an office among people again. I was going at it full-time, trying to get it ready to send off to London and for much of those weeks, instead of meeting Anne for lunch, I would either have lunch with some of Chuck's employees, or meet Bobby G. at a little Moroccan place for *couscous* on Wednesdays, since Max was tied up at Cannes, or at Rosie's Bar nearby. The advantage of Rosie's was that it was headquarters *central*, for drivers, crews, and wannabe's for the Monte Carlo Grand Prix.

When I came to Rosie's at lunchtime, Bobby G., sitting with an Englishman and two gorgeous Scandinavian blondes, made the introductions.

"Jack's on the pit crew for the Lotus team. This is Inga and Greta. They say they've come for the sport. Personally, I think it's to seduce Alain Prost," Bobby G. explained as I sat down. The waiter came over and I ordered a *croque monsieur* and a glass of *vin blanc*.

"Is he this year's heartthrob?" I asked.

"Well, 'e's French and 'e's the favorite. 'e's got the pole position," Jack said in Yorkshire-ese.

"Isn't it exciting? The best drivers in the world," Inga said.

"How much of an advantage is the pole position in this race?" I asked.

"In this race, it's bloody everything, mate. See, this 'ere's the tightest, narrowest circuit in all of Formula One," Jack said. "You know the streets 'ere in Monte. It's so bloody narrow, with high curbs, close crash barriers, all 'airpins with almost no straight-aways 'cept the Tunnel after the Virage du Portier (Portier curve), it's damn near impossible to overtake. Blokes've died trying. It's a bloody nightmare."

"So it's truly dangerous," the other blonde said. "The drivers could die."

"Too bloody right," Jack said.

"What's the most dangerous part?" Bobby G. asked, signaling the waiter for a vodka.

"The start. No question."

"How come?"

"See, the Monte Carlo is the one Formula One race that you don't start from a dead standstill. There's a straight-away before the starting line. Most blokes'll hit it at around 170."

"Miles per hour or kilometers?" Inga asked.

"Miles, luv. And the bloody second you cross the line, you've got to take the Virage de Sainte Devote. 'at's a bloody 90 degree right turn at 170 as soon as you cross the line, braking and gearing down to second at near 4 G's, your rear end fishtailin' like it's on ice, then gearing right back up to sixth to head up the Beau Rivage, so you'll be doing 165 coming right past Rosie's 'ere," Jack said, inclining his head.

"Prost is driving for McLaren, isn't he?" Bobby G. asked.

"Yeah. It's their MP4-2C. Bloody killer car, mate."

"Might have a mechanical breakdown. There's always that chance," Bobby G. said.

"Not likely. See the Monte's not that tough on the cars. 'Cause of all the 'airpins, the cars aren't going that fast, so your engines are never operating at full throttle. Cuts down on the wear and tear, see.

Tough on the drivers, though. You'll do 36, 37 gear changes in a single lap. Over a 78 lap course 'at's like 2,800 gear changes."

"I hear Formula One cars don't have a speedometer," Inga said.

"What you need a bloody speedometer for?" Jack said, draining his beer.

"To see how fast you are going, yes?"

"Listen, luv. If a driver doesn't know within a tenth of an MPH how fast 'e's goin', he bloody well better not drive. 'Sides, if you took 'alf a sec' to look at your dash, you're pie and mash all over the bloody road."

"Does anyone else have a chance?" I asked.

Jack motioned us closer. "We do," he winked.

"The Brazilian!" Greta said excitedly.

"Who's the Brazilian?" I asked.

"Ayrton Senna. 'e's driving for us. Prost is the superstar. 'e's like a bloody god in France. On all the billboards and telly sellin' Froggie bubble water, but Senna's a driver, mate. Best I ever seen."

"I like to, how you say, take him in the bed," Greta said, tossing her blonde hair.

"That's how we say it," I said.

"I too," Inga said.

"We'll let him know. He might skip the race altogether," Bobby G. said.

"So if it's so narrow, where could he overtake Prost?" I asked.

"Only one place. See, you can't do it by the Casino, even though there's a little downhill, 'cause 'fore you can say 'Bob's your uncle' you're at the Mirabeau in 4th at 130 MPH, gearing down like a bloody maniac into a 'airpin right to the Virage Loews, followed by a 'ard left 'airpin crawlin' at maybe 20 MPH, then 'ard right at the Portier and into the Tunnel. 'At's the only spot, inside the Tunnel in 5th at say, 150, if you've got the balls, 'cause coming out is a sharp left and right at the Nouvelle Chicane and back down to 30, if you're lucky, or if not, total disaster and you're a splash of red on the bloody front page."

"So where are you watching the race from?" Inga asked Bobby G. and me.

"We've got a party at an office with a balcony view," Bobby G. said.

"With our wives," I added.

"We be in the Lotus pit, yes?" Greta asked Jack.

"That Brazilian going to have a tough time keeping his mind on the race," Bobby G. said.

"Too bloody right. You ladies better stick with me," Jack said, putting his arms around both of them.

Bobby G. and I left the bar and walked back to work.

"What do you think?" Bobby G. asked.

"I think it's going to be harder to concentrate on the book this afternoon," I said.

"I know what you mean, pard," he said, putting his hand on my shoulder. "We're running twenty-fours hours a day knocking out the caps and pennants and all in time for the Grand Prix."

On the day of the Grand Prix, Anne, Justin, and I took the coast train into Monte Carlo, on the advice of everyone, who assured us there would be no parking and most of the streets in the principality would be blocked off anyway. From the train station in Monte Carlo, we took the public elevator up and walked to Chuck's office building, overlooking the downhill Tabac section of the course beside the harbor, with the big AGIP oil company banner stretched over the course. In the distance, near the Casino, a giant crane had been set up to remove cars from the road in case of a crash.

By the time we arrived, almost everyone was there: Chuck, Emma, Mark, Rachel in from London, Nigel, Monika, Gaby, Max, Sally, Maia, Adam, Yasper, Betje, Annette, who had helped us with Princess Caroline and who we waved to, all of Chuck's employees, some others I didn't recognize, including a number of attractive young women, possibly from other parties, who just seemed to have showed up.

Chuck's assistant, the Finnish girl, Eva, had set out a buffet with food trays and tubs of ice filled with bottles of white Bordeaux wine on one table, reds on another. And of course, Gaby brought Bobby G.'s Monte Carlo Grand Prix souvenir tee-shirts that she handed out to everyone. Bobby G. was still busy making sure he got all his supplies of souvenirs to his retailers. He would be by later, she said.

"So who's going to win?" Chuck said. He was running a pool.

"Who are we betting?" Anne asked.

"Prost," I said.

"But he's the favorite. He's only paying 2 to 1," Anne said, studying the list Chuck had handed out.

"Prost," I said. "With Senna for second place."

"How do you know this?" Gaby asked.

"I got it from a Brit with two Swedish girls. If Senna survives the Swedes, he's definitely good for second," I said.

"When did you become such an expert?" Anne asked.

"At lunch at Rosie's Bar the other day with Bobby G.," I said.

"What all this about Swedish girls?"

"They're in love with the Brazilian, Senna, if love's the right word," I said.

"I worry about you," Anne said.

"Likewise." I could tell that Anne was not one hundred percent. She handed Justin to me. I took him out on the balcony, holding him so he could see over the rail, and told him about the Grand Prix and how the cars would come very fast down the street and make the turn right below us."

"When will they start, Daddy?"

"You'll know, Justin. You'll hear them," I said, and almost on cue, there was the piercing scream of Formula One engines racing down the hill and gearing down for the turn. Everyone rushed to the balcony to see. There were spectators in stands behind barriers along the course and the balconies and windows of every building were filled like ours with people watching and cheering.

"It's started!" someone shouted over the roar of the crowd, as the first car, a white, red, and blue McLaren streaked down the course and turned toward the harbor and the *Piscine* (municipal swimming pool) complex by the port, followed by a white Lotus, that had to be Senna, and a red Ferrari, others further back positioning behind them.

"Is that Prost?" Sally asked, pointing at the lead car.

"I believe it is," Max said.

"They say it's the ultimate sport," Mark said, squeezing in beside us. "One man cars, each costing millions and capable of 200 plus miles per hour on real world streets, not some oval track. The ultimate challenge."

"It's nothing like driving at a hundred plus on the *autobahn*," said Max, who was writing an article on the race for *Der Spiegel*.

"Then what is it like?" Emma said.

"It's like driving at a hundred and fifty miles per hour on the worst twisting mountain road in the world, if the road was ice, slick as hell," Max said.

"It's dangerous, all right. Look at all the ones who have died. Look at Fangio," Mark said.

"They say Fangio won his first Grand Prix here," Chuck said, raising his voice to be heard over the cars racing below us.

"So, Justin," I said, "what do you think of the Monte Carlo Grand Prix?"

"Zoom, Zoom!" he said loudly and everyone laughed.

We watched the cars race by, their tires squealing as they slowed to take the corner to the *Piscine*. The noise of the engines and the crowds was deafening. Justin began to play with a toy Formula One car Chuck had on display and the rest of us sampled the buffet, where I ran into Mark's wife, Rachel.

"I hear the book's finished," she said.

"Almost. I'm doing the final edit before sending it off. I thought you were in London."

"I always come for the Grand Prix, darling. There's something about race car drivers, the daring to put your life on the line, that sets a woman's heart pounding."

"The last real men?"

"Exactly. God, I love it when a man talks like that," she said.

"So how did the new set," I said, indicating her chest, "do in London?"

"Smashing. I've got a lovely new friend and he loves them. Everyone's positively jealous."

"You're lucky Mark is so open-minded."

"Mark's a dear. Most understanding man on earth," she said, letting Mark, who had wandered over, kiss her cheek.

"Quite right. Can't let these go to waste," he said, cupping one of her breasts.

"So how's the yacht? Find any buyers?" I asked.

"Oh that thing? Got rid of it. Not a bad price either. Got a new one. 175 feet on the waterline and polished like a baby's arse. Might want to sell it once we've got it cleaned up. Keep trading up. That's my motto," Mark said.

"That's right, darling. Now go see if you can find someone to play with," Rachel said, dismissing him. "So what do you think?"

"What do I think about what?" I said, reddening.

"You know what," she said, looking straight at me.

"My wife's right there."

"American women are awfully provincial about these things, aren't they?" she said, glancing at Anne talking with Sally, Annette and Gaby.

"American men too. For the record, I'm just watching the race. I'm not in it," I said, heading away. I scooped up Justin and almost bumped into Adam Shaw and Maia.

"Heard the book's done," Adam said.

"Almost," I said.

"What happens next?"

"Send it off to my agent. Hope the publisher likes it. Hope they pay me."

"That's it?"

"Well, we've done it kind of backwards. Usually, you sell it in the

U.S., then sell it in England. With this one, once the Brits accept it, we try to sell it in New York, where the real money is."

"I'm jealous," Adam said.

"You'll get there. I suspect your father had hard times too. His career had plenty of ups and downs."

"He told me. I don't know if it's worth it."

"A lot of the time, neither do I," I said, heading out to the balcony with Justin. As the cars screamed by, Anne came over with Nigel and Monika.

"Nigel and Monika have a suggestion for us," Anne said. "They're leaving for England in June. They'll be gone for eight weeks. They've offered to let us stay in their flat in Monte Carlo, while you get the book done and we sort things out. What do you think?"

"*Gratis*, of course, old chap," Nigel said. "Can't charge a fellow scrivener."

"Why are you going to England?"

"The season, Ascot, Wimbledon," Monika said. "Gives Nigel a chance to go back to Oxford and renew the 'Old Boy' connection. Gives me a chance to dress up for Ascot in something utterly outrageous that only the British upper class would be seen dead in. So are you interested? In the flat, I mean?"

"That's incredibly generous. I don't know what to say," I said.

"You'd be doing us a favor. Even though the *commissaire de police* lives right underneath, we always worry, especially about raids from Nigel's ex or his children from hell. They're capable of anything. It'd make us feel better, knowing there was someone there," Monika said.

"It would solve things for the immediate present. We've got to tell our landlord something soon," Anne said.

"Let us talk it over," I said. "We'll get back to you."

After the race was over, with Prost the winner, as expected, the party started to wind down. I could see Anne was tired and we left. I carried Justin, asleep with his head on my shoulder, to the station and we caught the train back to Eze.

"I spoke with Sally and Annette about seeing a doctor. Annette's going to talk to Princess Caroline again."

"Good. It's probably nothing, but it's best to make sure," I said.

"I know. I want to be good for Justin's birthday party," she said.

That weekend, Justin turned three and we celebrated his birthday with a party at our villa. We kept it to just our closest friends, Max and Sally, Bobby G. and Gaby, Nigel and Monika, and Colette. Anne had asked Justin if he wanted any friends from his *crèche* in Monte Carlo and he said no. It gave me a pang, because of the friends he had made at the *Ecole du Cap* we had pulled him out of, remembering the children all calling "*Au revoir, Justin*" after him and the little girl who kept waving as we drove out of sight.

The day was sunny and we set up tables on the *terrasse*. Everyone brought toys and wore little birthday party hats and sang "Happy Birthday" and Justin opened his presents. Sally had brought action figures from the TV cartoon, *Les Mondes Engloutis*, which Justin was very excited about. As we were cleaning up after the party, Annette called. Princess Caroline had arranged for Anne to see her own personal doctor, Dr. Fleurier. I asked her to thank the Princess. Annette said Princess Caroline had wanted to come to Justin's party with her son, Andrea, but didn't want to impose. I told Annette to thank her again and that as soon as we were settled in Monte Carlo, perhaps we could arrange a play date for Justin and the Princess's children.

Keeping in mind the nine-hour time difference to California, that night we called Anne's parents and my mother in Los Angeles. After Justin told Grandma he loved her, I got back on the line.

"He sounds so big. I miss him terribly," she said.

"He misses you too," I said.

"So when are you coming back?"

"I'm not sure. There's a lot going on. Why don't you come here? We'd love to see you."

"I can't travel. It's a lot of money. There's my health..."

"What's the matter with your health?"

"It's nothing," she said.

"Mom, is there something wrong?"

"Why? If there were, would you bother to come?" she said. You had to hand it to Jewish mothers. When it came to guilt, they were in a league all their own.

"Of course we would come. Is there something wrong?"

"Wrong? What could be wrong? You go have a good time, darling." See what I mean?

"Mom, we love you. Please come see us."

"This call is costing a fortune. You take care of what you have to. Give Anne and Justin a kiss for me. At least, he still speaks English," she said and hung up, leaving me somewhere between concerned and wanting to wrap the telephone cord around her neck.

That night, Justin in bed, Anne and I sat on the balcony outside our bedroom, watching the sun setting over the sea. Things were happening fast and all I could think about was Anne and finishing the book and getting it off.

"I hate leaving this place. It's really become home," she said.

"I know. So do I."

"You don't want to talk about it?" she said.

"I don't want to jinx it," I said. Anne had had endometriosis and it had required surgery in order for her to be able to have Justin. Even so, the odds weren't great. It had been difficult and we thought about him as our Miracle Baby. We had been trying for years to have another child, knew it might require more surgery, and didn't quite believe we could have another naturally. And the timing, with the book, the potential move to Monte Carlo, our money running low, couldn't have been worse. I didn't want to think about the other possibility, that it might be something worse.

The next day, I finished the book at Chuck's office and printed up a complete manuscript copy. We went into Nice and spent hours at a copy shop, making a Xerox copy that cost over a hundred dollars, then spent the rest of the day in Nice, walking around the Place Masséna, window shopping on Jean-Médicin Avenue, having pizza and ice cream on the Rue Masséna, till the main *Les Postes et Télécommunications* office was open. After standing in a long line, I shipped the manuscript off to June in London. I asked Anne if she wanted to go have a drink to celebrate and she hesitated and said no and we went back to Eze.

The next morning, I literally had nothing to do. I wandered aimlessly around the villa, pulling all my papers, notes, research material for the book together and putting them into cardboard boxes I'd picked up from behind the *supermarché*. I sat at my desk and stared out the window at the woods and Nietzsche's path and wondered what I might do next. I had been so preoccupied with the book, I hadn't even thought about what I might do next or write next. It all seemed so remote, as if I were still in the Cambodian jungle. It's like a soldier coming back to civilian life. You look like you're back, you pretend you're back, but you really aren't, I thought. What did they call it for the soldiers back from Nam? "Post-Traumatic Stress Syndrome." Well, you've got a family, I told myself. You can't afford a Syndrome.

I picked up Justin from the *crèche* and bought him an ice cream while we waited at an outside table on the *terrasse* of the Café de Paris in Monte Carlo for Anne to come back from the doctor. No matter what she says, it's going to change everything, I thought.

"Justin, how do you like Monte Carlo?" I asked.

"Zoom, Zoom, Daddy," he said and we were laughing as Anne came over. I stood, unable to stay seated.

"Well?" I said

She nodded, taking my hand and holding it tightly, her eyes sparkling.

"He's sure," she said. "We're going to have a baby."

PART 3

Monte Carlo

Chapter 27

You Are Either Pregnant Or You Aren't

We moved from the villa in Eze-sur-Mer to Nigel and Monika's apartment at 7, Boulevard de Suisse in Monte Carlo. As to which floor we lived on led to lengthy discussions between Anne and me that only ended in confusion.

"We live on the second floor, right?" Anne would start.

"Please, do we have to do this again?" I said.

"Humor me. We climb up one flight of stairs and our apartment is on the second floor."

"Absolutely. Are we done now?" I said. I was trying to read the *Nice-Matin* on the apartment balcony that overlooked the port area, La Condamine, and the boats in the Monte Carlo harbor across to 'the Rock,' topped by the Royal Palace.

"So why when I said to our neighbor, Madame D'Alessio, that I liked living on the second floor, she corrected me and said we lived on the '*premier étage*,' not to mention she looked at me funny?"

"Because we don't live on the '*deuxième étage*' which is what you said, we live on the *premier étage*, which is what the French call the 'second floor,'" I said.

"Why do they call the second floor 'the first floor'?"

"Because in French, the first or ground floor is the '*rez-de-chaussée.*' So the second floor is actually the first floor *after* the ground floor. The '*deuxième étage*' which is what you said to Madame D'Alessio, is actually what Americans would call 'the third floor.'"

"So we're actually living on the second floor that we pretend to call the first floor, because the French can't make up their mind what floor they're on," Anne said.

"Something like that," I said, trying to bury myself in the paper.

"So why did she look at me funny?"

"Because you said '*de deuxième étage*' when you should have said '*au deuxième étage.*' Jeez, now you've got me doing it. When you should have said, '*au premier étage.*'"

"What's the difference?"

"'*Au premier étage*' means 'on the second floor'; '*de premier étage*' means in the first stage, like of a project, or first place, like a prize. By saying said '*de deuxième étage,*' you actually said to her that we lived 'in third place.'"

"Why do they deliberately make things confusing?" Anne said.

"To give American women a chance to torture their husbands," I muttered.

"What?!"

"When are we going to lunch at Ron and Roxanna's?" I said, changing the subject.

"After we pick up Justin. You know, I think I liked it better when you were working on the book in the mornings."

"So did I."

"It seems weird to be going back to Eze to see someone."

"I know," I said, getting up. "Let's go get Justin."

"All right," she said. "And don't think you got away with something. I heard that crack about American women torturing their husbands."

"*Quel coup de chance pour moi,*" (lucky me) I said.

"Was that nasty?"

"No, but I'll make it nasty if you like."

I took her arm going down the stairs to the street.

"I'm pregnant. You should be nice to me," she said.

"I'm just playing. Trying to figure out what we do next."

"God, I try so hard in French and I just can't get it," she said.

"It's a harder language than it seems. I make mistakes in it all the time."

"They don't laugh at you, though."

"I think they appreciate an American even trying to communicate to them in French. For them, I'm a novelty. Believe me, I get it wrong all the time," I said as we got into the Renault, picked up Justin, and drove out of town and back to our old street, Avenue Lamaro in Eze.

Ron and Roxanna's villa was at the top of Avenue Lamaro, where the road ended because of the steepness of the mountain. When we arrived they were out on the *terrasse*, where a dining table was set under the trees. From their *terrasse*, you could see all of Eze-sur-Mer and the Mediterranean through the trees. As soon as we drove up, their daughter, Joanna, came running up to be with Justin.

Ron showed us around the villa. He had built most of it himself, structuring it around a large tree that they'd incorporated inside the house. He had cut steps into an upward inclining branch and added a rail and we climbed up the tree branch from the *salon* to the upper part of the villa, which had the feel of a tree house, but with bedrooms and a large glass-enclosed music room and instruments and music stands that looked out through the trees to the sea. On the wall were framed pictures and letters from Shapiro, Compinsky, Heifetz, and Piatigorsky. "My teachers. I played chamber with Piatigorsky," he said off-handedly.

"You studied with Jascha Heifetz?"

"Sure."

"What was he like?"

"For me, less unapproachable than his reputation. He wanted you to spend a lot of your practice time doing scales, but with all the bowings, rhythms, double-stops, which can get tedious, but really helped my technique. Wait, there's something I want you to hear." He called Joanna and handed her a little child's violin and she immediately began to play.

"Not yet two and she has perfect pitch," he said.

"Incredible," Anne said and listening to the little girl, it was. This toddler, only just beginning to talk, was making real music!

"She'll be a great musician," I said.

"If that's what she wants. Who knows?" Roxanna said, coming in and we went down outside for wine and lunch, while the kids climbed on a play set Ron had built.

"We think it's ridiculous, you guys leaving Eze and living in Monte Carlo now that we've just met," Roxanna said.

"So do we," Anne said. "This being a writing family requires a lot more moving around than I counted on."

"It's the same with music," Ron said. "Either you can scratch out a living touring and living in hotels, or if you want a family, you've got to find an orchestra so you can stay put. If you stay put, you'll never be a marquee name, but at least you'll have a life."

"So what does the doctor say?" Roxanna said. She was also pregnant and had intuited that Anne was too.

"What is it with women? How they know this stuff? You know Madame Finot down the street?" I said.

"The one with the tomatoes? She always scolds us about our garden," Roxanna said.

"Good, I'm glad I'm not the only one. Anyway, she figured it out about Anne before we did."

"These old French women. They have an eye, watching things grow," Ron said.

"You're seeing Dr. Fleurier of course?" Roxanna said.

"Princess Caroline called him," Anne said.

"He's the best. So what did he say?"

"Not much. I think he's a little concerned. He wants me to have a sonogram."

"That's pretty standard. I wouldn't worry," Roxanna said.

"I thought we were going to hear you guys play, but Ron tells me you two are going on tour next week," I said.

"The season at the Philharmonic doesn't start for two months. Meanwhile, we can pick up some money. We'll be playing duets in Zurich, Milan, Rome, Hamburg, Scandinavia, London," Roxanna said.

"I'm sorry we won't get to hear you," Anne said.

"Oh yes you will. Right now," Ron said. He and Roxanna got their instruments and played for us. Sitting under the trees of the *terrasse* listening to them play Mozart and Handel, Justin climbing the play set with Joanna trying to follow, sipping wine and looking out over the sea, the afternoon was golden and as in Venice, I was aware that such moments were the coins we needed to save for our old age, because they would never come again.

But it was combined with an elegiac feeling that in leaving Eze we had lost something. For a time I thought it was just the quiet, the silent days working, Anne and I, just the two of us, in front of the fireplace after Justin went to bed that I missed, but then I realized that what was lost was that we'd been happy there.

After Eze, living in Monte Carlo was also going from rural to urban living, the talks with Madame Finot, the silence of the woods on walks on Nietzsche's path, Justin playing in the yard, were replaced by meeting friends at *cafés*, running errands on foot, busy shops and street markets. We had our little neighborhood *épicerie, boulangerie, boucherie,* the *pâtisserie* where we picked up fresh *pains au chocolat* and *croissants* every morning, the dry cleaner's, the little *tabac* where I would get the newspapers.

The weather was Riviera weather, warm and sunny every day, and in the afternoons, we would go down to the sandy *Plage Larvotto*, the beach's shallow water perfect for Justin to swim in with floatation bands on his arms and every day, increasing numbers of attractive young men and women, all of them topless, tanning and flirting among the towels and umbrellas on the sand.

Even though while living in Eze, we had been in Monte Carlo almost every day, living there gave us a new understanding of what Monaco was all about. Monaco was a sanctuary for the very rich. It wasn't just the lavish yachts in the harbor and the exclusive shops, Cartier, Hermes, Bulgari, Chanel, and such. It was a tax haven, where income was tax-free for EU citizens with banks with secrecy laws rivaling Switzerland and where security was omnipresent, with video cameras on every street and at night, going out for a walk, you would see armed Monagasque security police every couple of hundred meters or so, ever polite and ever watchful. Implicitly, the message the principality conveyed was, in an increasingly intrusive and insecure world, if you are rich, Monaco, smaller than New York's Central Park, was a safe haven. Nowhere on earth was there such a concentration of wealth, or of life devoted to pleasure-seeking.

Still, there were compensations. Every morning, while Anne took Justin to the crèche, I would have a breakfast of French coffee and a *brioche* or *pain au chocolat* on the balcony overlooking the harbor. In the ravine below us, the penthouse rooftop of a private building had been converted into a patio, where every morning, a middle-aged man would also have his coffee and breakfast brought to him by a white-jacketed servant at the same time as I was having my breakfast. We began to notice each other and each morning we would nod and raise our coffee cups to each other, two gentlemen of the world acknowledging each other before turning back to our newspapers.

"Who is that man I see in the building in the *ravin* below us every morning?" I asked our downstairs neighbor, Henri, the police commissioner.

"Truly, you don't know who that is?"

"*Non, je ne le connais pas.*"

"That is Monsieur Cummings." I looked at him blankly. "Of the military company, Interarmco," he explained.

The next day, at Stuart's pub, I asked Max about him.

"Sam Cummings is your neighbor? Interesting, Nigel never mentioned it," Max said.

"Nigel can be pretty close-mouthed about some things. Why? What do you know him?"

"Are you kidding? Sam Cummings is the largest private arms dealer in the world. They say he's the second richest man on earth. He keeps things very private, never gives interviews," Max motioned me closer. "They say he has enough weapons just in his warehouses in England to equip forty U.S. Army divisions," he whispered.

"Forty?! Wow! Any CIA connections?"

"CIA, MI6, KGB, the French DGSE, the Israeli Mossad. Sam Cummings just might be the best-connected man in the world," he said.

"He seems quite nice for such a dangerous business."

"No one knows. He's very private. If you actually spoke to him, it would be quite a coup," Max said.

By coincidence, a day later, I nearly bumped into Sam Cummings as he was getting into his Rolls Royce limousine outside the Credit Suisse bank.

"My breakfast companion, Mr. Kaplan, I believe," he said, shaking my hand.

"How do you know my name?" I asked, a little uneasily.

"The same way I'm sure you know mine, by asking around. Call me Sam. Can I give you a lift?" I hesitated. The international arms trade could be a dangerous business. It was a little like being offered a ride by a Mafia don. He noticed my hesitation. "It's OK, we're both Americans. I don't do that sort of thing and if I did, I sure as hell wouldn't be doing it in broad daylight in front of the Credit Suisse video cameras."

I got into the back of the limousine.

"Are you going back to your apartment?" he asked.

"Yes."

He told the driver to take me to the Boulevard de Suisse and offered me a drink from the back seat bar. I poured myself a Cinzano and water, ulcer be damned.

"Go ahead. Ask me. I'm sure you're dying to," he said.

"Is this CIA business? Is that what this is about?" I said.

"That was a long time ago. I'm not involved with any of that anymore."

"With Bill Casey as CIA Director, it's hard to be sure."

"Casey's old school, but no, rumors to the contrary, we don't do that. Tell you the truth, it's not good business. And even if it were, you have to be careful. They'd sell us out in a second and that's bound to happen. You know why?" I shook my head. "You should. You write about it very well. I'm a fan. I enjoyed *Scorpion* very much." He motioned me closer. "The real secret about the CIA, the KGB, and all the other agencies is that they're just as stupid as the rest of us."

"Sounds like you know them all right," I grinned.

"It's how I got started. The CIA needed someone outside the U.S. government to supply arms for the coup in Guatemala in '54. For deniability."

"The one that overthrew Arbenz."

He smiled. "You do your homework, don't you? I supplied the arms for Armas, a complete idiot, to take over. That was the beginning of my company, Interarmco. Of course, you have to remember, that was the height of the Cold War and McCarthyism. We were fighting the Commies."

"And making a profit."

"A damned good profit," he said, as the limousine pulled up to my building. "The reason I stopped you, Andrew, is, people seemed to be intrigued by Interarmco and the arms business. I keep getting requests for interviews and books, which I never do. Bad for business, our business anyway. I thought maybe I could hire you to write a book on contract telling the story from our point of view. I'd pay well. What do you think?"

"I'll have to think about it," I said, getting out. "Meanwhile, we're still breakfast acquaintances?"

"Absolutely. Whatever you decide is fine. I'll be leaving in a few weeks on business and then I'll be at my country place in Villars in the Swiss Alps. If you want to get hold of me, just go to my building and ask for my man, Guillaume," he said.

That afternoon, I told Anne what had happened.

"What are you going to do?"

"I don't know," I said. "Let's see what happens with the book."

"You haven't heard from June. It's been more than two weeks."

"I know. Not a word. Not good, not bad. Not, it's wonderful. Not, it's so lousy they're not going to pay. I'm starting to get pretty antsy."

"Me too. About a lot of things," she said.

The next day, after Anne's sonogram, we met with Dr. Fleurier. I waited with Justin in Dr. Fleurier's waiting room for Anne to come out after the sonogram. When she came out, her face was pale.

"What's wrong?" I asked.

"He's not sure. He says there may be a problem. We need to do another blood test." We asked the nurse to watch Justin and went into the doctor's office. Dr. Fleurier, a distinguished-looking man with traces of gray in his dark wavy hair, sat behind a mahogany desk.

"So, what did the sonogram show?" Anne asked.

"Monsieur *et* Madame, according to the sonogram, Madame is not pregnant."

"But I can feel the changes in my body. What about the blood test?" Anne asked.

"The blood test indicated with one hundred percent certainty that you are pregnant, Madame."

"I don't understand. Pregnancy is not a halfway-thing. You are either pregnant or you aren't. Which is it?" I said.

"*Exactement*, Monsieur. I am ordering another sonogram, with the best technician and equipment at the *Clinique Obstétrique* in Nice. Also another blood test. It is important to verify the progress of the hormone levels."

Two days later, with Gaby watching Justin, I drove Anne to Nice for more blood tests and another sonogram. The next day, we were back in Dr. Fleurier's office.

"The latest sonogram is conclusive. You are not pregnant, Madame," Dr. Fleurier said.

"What about the hormone and the blood tests?" Anne asked.

"They are also absolutely conclusive. Your hCG level is increasing and is up where it should be for a normal pregnancy. According to the blood test, one can say with one hundred percent certainty that you are indeed pregnant, Madame."

"That's impossible! What kind of medicine is this? She either is or she isn't pregnant. Which is it?" I demanded.

"It may be an ectopic pregnancy, Monsieur. We will need to repeat the blood test again in another 48 hours."

"What's an ectopic pregnancy?" I asked.

"In a normal pregnancy, the fertilized egg passes from the fallopian tube and implants itself as an embryo in the uterus. In an ectopic pregnancy, the embryo attaches elsewhere, other than the uterus, in the majority of such cases, inside the fallopian tube."

"What if it is ectopic?" Anne asked.

"In that case, surgery may be necessary. But we will know more in 48 hours."

"What about the fetus? If it's an ectopic pregnancy, can it be saved?" Anne asked.

"*Je regrette, Madame*, if it is an ectopic pregnancy, there will be no child."

We left the doctor's office in silence.

"I need a drink. Let's go to the American Bar," Anne said. I looked at her. "I know, I'll make mine a Perrier or something, just in case."

We went into the American Bar and sat at our old table, the one we used to sit at with Nigel and Monika. We hadn't been in for a while and Jacques the bartender waved to us when we came in. Anne had a Perrier and I had a glass of red wine.

"I really wanted this baby," she said finally.

"So did I," I said.

"It makes me feel like I'm only half a woman." She started to cry. I put my arm around her.

"Believe me, you're a hell of a woman and already a mother. Justin's lucky to have you. This thing's not over."

"I wanted a girl. I mean I would've been happy with anything and I didn't want to jinx it, but I was hoping for a girl this time."

"So was I. If it were another boy, Justin would just get jealous and beat the crap out of him. Besides, little girls love their Daddies," I said. "Unless you're a complete asshole, it's a slam dunk."

"Maybe Justin wouldn't've beat him up. He's a sweetie. Maybe he'd protect his little brother."

I didn't say anything.

"It isn't fair."

"I don't know that life and fair have anything to do with each other," I said.

She looked around the bar. "I miss Nigel and Monika. This place isn't the same without them. Also Max and Sally and Bobby G. and Gaby."

"They're still around."

"We need to get together," she said.

"Yes, we do."

We picked up Justin from Gaby and she and Anne started to plan something with Sally. When we got back to our building, we could hear the phone ringing. I ran up the stairs to the *premier étage*, raced to the phone and picked it up.

"Andy, it's June," the voice on the phone said.

"Hi," I said, mouthing 'It's my agent' to Anne.

"How's it going?" she asked.

"You tell me. I've been on pins and needles since I sent the manuscript out."

"You need to come to London," she said.

"Why?"

"I can't explain, but I think you should."

"Did you like the book?"

"It's good. The publisher wants you to come. There are things we must talk about."

"June, now's not a good time for me to be traveling. And money's tight right now. Maybe later?"

"Andy, you *must* listen to me. You have to come to London now. At once. It's urgent! I'll see you tomorrow. Call me as soon as you get in, all right?"

"All right," I said, hanging up.

"What is it?" Anne said.

"I have to go to London," I said.

Chapter 28

My Meeting With God

Coming into London from the sunny Côte d'Azur was like returning to winter. I was glad I had brought my Burberry raincoat with me. To save money, I had booked a tiny single room in the Regent Hotel in Piccadilly, the cheapest I could find on such short notice. It was a long way from the accommodations we had enjoyed the last time we started out in London on our way to France and a measure of how short we were getting on funds.

On the flight from Nice, I thought about Anne and losing the baby and her having to have surgery. It was starting to hit me. I had wanted the baby too, more than I had admitted, even to myself. I looked out the plane's window at the green fields of France below and thought about what it might have been like to have a little girl in addition to Justin.

With Anne as her mother, how pretty and special she might have been. I pulled myself up short. There was no little girl. This isn't a fantasy, this is life, I told myself. Also, I had no idea what was waiting for me in London. Apart from June's call, there had been no reaction from anyone to the book. I went for too much, I thought. All they wanted was another thriller in the *Scorpion* mode and I had given them something darker, more complex and more literary. Maybe they weren't going to pay me. I was due around $10,000 upon completion of the manuscript and the money would save us, only I might never see it. Or worse, they'd want back the money they'd already paid me.

"It's not bad news," Anne had insisted before I left. "They don't do bad news face to face. They would've called or written."

"I don't know. I don't know why they need me there for a face to face, unless they want a complete rewrite or something and want to be able to go over it in person. Only I don't know how to rewrite it. Everything's interconnected. A book is organic, like a human body. You can't cut into one part without affecting all the others and you can't just rearrange it. You end up putting an ear on an elbow or something," I said.

"That's all she said?" Anne said. "'It's good.' Eight months work and that's the only feedback?! 'It's good.'"

"That's it. And even that was off-hand, like a pat on the head. You know, 'nice doggie.'"

As we kissed goodbye at Nice airport, Justin hugged me and Anne whispered, "I'll take care of Justin and things here. Don't worry about us. You wrote a hell of a book. Don't forget that."

It was evening by the time I got into London and checked in at the Regent. I called June and she gave me directions on how to get to her apartment via the Tube. I watched the stations go by and walked the streets to her building, trying not to think. It can't be total disaster, the book's better than that, I told myself and rang her bell.

June buzzed me in. I walked up the stairs, took a deep breath, and knocked on the apartment door. She let me in and we sat on a couch in her office in her apartment. She was still dressed in business clothes. A copy of my manuscript along with a pile of other manuscripts and books were on the coffee table. Through the windows, I could see the lights and electric signs from the street outside.

"Do you want tea?" she asked.

"All right, thanks," I said. "But I didn't fly all this way for tea."

"I know," she said and came back with cups and a kettle and

poured us both cups of tea. "First off, I wanted to tell you myself in person. I had hoped the book would be good and commercial, but it's much more. It's fantastic. Everyone loves it. Century believes it's your 'breakthrough book.' They're gearing up for a best-seller."

"My new editor too? I don't even know her."

"She loved it. Ann's your new biggest fan. The paperback editors have gone bananas. There's even interest from the Book of the Month Club. We're starting to get calls from publishers in New York and other countries. It's beginning to happen, Andy."

"I don't know what to say."

"Well, that's why we English drink tea. When we don't know what to say, it gives us something to do."

"This is good news," I said, exhaling, not realizing that I hadn't been breathing all this time. "I guess I'll be getting a check soon."

"Don't worry about that. Do you need the money straightaway?"

"Yes. Anne may need surgery and... yes."

"I'll see what I can do."

"There's one thing I still don't understand. You could've told me this on the phone. Why did I have to come all the way to London?"

"Three reasons. One purely selfish. It isn't often an agent gets to tell someone news like this and I wanted to see your face when I did."

"Oh," I said, taking my first sip of tea. "How did I look?"

"Stunned. Like you'd been pole-axed. You hadn't a clue?"

"Anne thought it might be good news, but I'm the original 'the glass is half-empty' type. I'm completely surprised. What else?"

"Sir Anthony, the Great Pooh-Bah himself, head of Century-Hutchinson, Random-House, Arrow, the whole bloody thing; largest book publishing conglomerate in Britain, 'God' as they call him, wants to meet with you. That's the main reason."

"Why?"

"I don't know, but it must be something important," she hesitated. "You see... he never ever meets with writers. Ever. Whatever his reason, you have to see him. Now, while the kettle's on the boil, so to speak."

"You said you had three reasons. What's the third?" I asked.

"America. News like this crosses the Atlantic faster than the Concorde. You'll need to go to New York to decide on a publisher. Someone needs to represent you and sell the book in the States. I'd like it to be me."

"I thought I needed someone in New York. Someone who shmoozes with the editors on a daily basis and is right there," I said.

"Andy, I do business with all the major publishers in New York all the time. I can do things just as well from here as in New York, maybe better. It's amusing, actually. Because you're being published in England, many of them think you're a British author. I've actually had one say they were interested because you're English and all the best spy thriller writers are English."

"All these years writing as an American about Americans and they think I'm English? That *is* funny," I said.

"I'm getting calls now. You need to decide what to do, because if you want someone in New York to represent you, I can't tell or show them anything. In that case, I need to just turn it over to whomever you want. On the other hand, if you'll let me, as I hope, I'll handle everything. Let me do it, Andy. I've been with it from the first page. I care about this book and your career more than anyone. What do you say?"

I hesitated. "I need to talk to Anne. My Anne. I trust her judgment and this isn't what I expected."

"Absolutely," June said. "You have a meeting tomorrow with the other Ann, your editor, then you'll be meeting God, and then I believe Editor Ann wants to take you out to dinner. Their tab, of course. Talk to your editor, talk to God, talk to your Anne, and then we'll get together again before you leave, all right?"

"All right," I said.

I took the Tube back to Piccadilly Circus, got out at the exit near Great Windmill Street. I walked to the nearby Duke of Argyll pub to have a drink and try to sort things out and also to put off going back to that dreary hotel room.

The pub was smoky, noisy and crowded. A group of business types in suits sat at one of the tables and men and women were packed at the bar. I squeezed in at the bar and asked for a whiskey.

"Single malt or blend?" the bartender asked.

"What singles do you have?"

"Glenlivet."

"That's good, thanks." I said. All I could think of was one word June had said, 'breakthrough." A best-seller would change our lives. I wasn't sure I was ready for all that. I certainly wasn't sure if I was ready to become known, do the book tours and TV show circuit. None of that was what writing was about. Well, aren't you something? I told myself. You haven't known about it half an hour and you're already full of yourself. If I screwed up my meeting with God, none of it would happen. And come to think of it, why didn't the head of a publishing conglomerate ever meet with writers? What the hell was that about?

Next to me, two Englishmen with working class accents were arguing about sports. As they talked, it seeped in on me that they were talking about Wimbledon. Caught up with Anne and the book, I hadn't been paying attention to any of it. Nigel and Monika were in London, I realized, only I didn't know where or how to get in touch. Also, I wasn't sure I wanted to see anyone right now.

"You, what do you think?" one of the Englishman said to me, putting down his pint and pointing at me.

"Sorry, I wasn't paying attention," I said.

"Who's going to win Wimbledon, Lendl, McEnroe, Becker, or Connors?" the other one said.

I thought about the powerfully-muscled eighteen-year-old who had sat at my table at the Café de Paris in Monte Carlo, trying to figure out things outside the lines of a tennis court. I thought about the power in those big shoulders and the intensity of his blue eyes.

"Becker," I said. "In a walk."

"Wait a minute, you're an American, hain't you? The others are

American. Even Lendl's become an American. You should be rootin' for them," the first Englishman said.

"Lendl's ranked number one in the world," the other said. "I'll put a tenner on Lendl any day."

"On hard surface, maybe," I said. "Becker was born to play on grass. He'll kill him."

"You wouldn't care to put your money where your mouth is, would you?" the first one said, pulling out a wad of five and ten pound notes.

"I won't be in England long enough to collect," I said, finishing my drink, tossing some money on the bar and leaving. As I walked back to Piccadilly, a woman in a miniskirt came up to me from outside a neon-lighted club.

"Looking for a good time, luv?" she said. Under the makeup, she was young and thin, perhaps an addict, I thought. I glanced around, suddenly realizing that Great Windmill was near Soho, the sex trade district.

"No thanks," I said. I reached into my pocket and handed her a couple of one-pound coins.

"What's that?" she asked suspiciously.

"For luck. Buy yourself a drink or something."

"American arsehole," she said. As I walked away, she called after me, "Good luck, y' bugger," and I thought, thanks, I'll need it.

When I got back to the hotel room, I called Anne and told her what was happening.

"They really liked it?" she said.

"It seems so. They said it was my 'breakthrough book.'"

"What does that mean?"

"Potentially, a lot of money. What do you think I should do? About June, I mean."

"What's the downside?"

"There may be more powerful, better connected agents in New York. They're right there, eating and breathing the market. Maybe do an auction. That's where the real money is, when you get publishers bidding against each other."

"Yes, but do you know any of them? OK, maybe there's a hotshot agent you can get. But if so, he's also handling other big writers. You're just one of many. June believes in you. She believed in you when no one else did."

"She says she can do it in New York. She says we'll have to go there."

"We'll do whatever we need to."

"So we should let her do it?"

"She believes in you. That counts for a lot. Besides, maybe having the New York publishers think you're English will work for us. I say, go for it."

"What about you? What's happening?"

"I'm seeing a surgeon in Nice tomorrow. Don't worry, it's just in case. I have more tests to do," she said.

"How's Justin?"

"He misses you. Want to talk to him?"

"Yes," I said, filled with longing for both of them.

"Hi Daddy. When you coming home?" Justin said.

"Day after tomorrow. Are you taking good care of Mommy?"

Justin laughed. "Don't be silly Daddy. Kids don't take care of Mommies. What present are you bringing me?"

"You'll see," I said. I'd have to pick up something, I thought. Anne came back on the line.

"Good luck tomorrow with God and your editor. What's her name again?"

"Ann."

"Good name," Anne said. "It's a good omen."

The next day, I met with my editor, Ann, her assistant, the copy editor, and the editor-in-chief of the Arrow paperback division. We decided on a basic theme approach to the cover art, something that would suggest Asia and a thriller, with maybe red for the main cover color. The copy editor was very excited.

It's been a long time since I've had something this interesting and complex, with the Asian bits, the spy tradecraft, and such, in a long time," he said.

The paperback guy said we would need a map and could I supply one? "It's an exotic locale. Most people aren't familiar with where the Golden Triangle is, the hill people, and the Cambodian jungles, and such. And the action moves around. People will want a map to keep track of where they are," he said.

Fortunately, I recalled a map in my research material I thought I could adapt and said I'd send them one. Ann felt that the book needed acknowledgements.

"Why?" I asked.

"It cries out for it. You've got so much authentic material and interesting facts. The authenticity is one of the things that's so good about it. An acknowledgement paragraph or two is really essential," she said.

We went over some more stuff. Everyone seemed very excited and positive about the book. I was finally getting feedback.

"What do you think?" I asked the paperback editor.

"It's the best adventure thriller I've ever read," he said.

"I agree. It's a pleasure to be working on it," Ann said.

We were still going over stuff when Ann got a call.

"It's God," she said. "You have to go up."

I took a deep breath. "This is a big deal, isn't it? I heard he never sees writers," I said.

"He doesn't. I've never heard of it before," she said, looking around. "Anyone else?"

"First, so far as I know," the paperback editor said.

Ann got up and took me to the elevator.

"I'll show you to his office," she said.

"Any idea what this is about?" I asked.

"Not a clue. Now remember, after you've finished with God, you and I are going out to dinner. I've booked us at Rules for some real English food. Meet me there at seven," she said, leading me into the elevator and up to the top floor. She signaled to the secretary outside God's office. "This is Andrew Kaplan. He's expected," she said.

The secretary led me into the office and sat me on a couch in a meeting area with armchairs and a coffee table. God, a beefy middle-aged man in a Savile Row suit and dark hair graying at the temples, was at his desk on the telephone. There was a carafe of water on the coffee table and I poured myself a glass while I waited. Fortunately, I had been through this in Hollywood, where someone always keeps you waiting in his office just to establish the pecking order, to make sure you know that he is far busier and more important than you are. Hollywood executives are the world masters at this kind of thing and I relaxed a little. Compared to Hollywood mind games, God was a piece of cake.

Finally, he got off the phone, spent just enough time looking at papers on his desk to drive home my insignificance, then came over and shook my hand.

"You're Andrew Kaplan. It's a pleasure at last. Do you have everything you need? Perhaps some tea. I could have Mrs. Jensen..." He opened a gold cigarette case and offered me a cigarette. "Smoke?"

"No thanks," I said.

"Of course not. You're American. Do you prefer Andrew or Andy?"

"Either's fine. What do I call you?"

"Tony."

"Not God?" I said.

"My God, do they still do that?" he said, not entirely displeased, I thought.

"It seems the local custom," I said. "They also say you never see writers. Is that true?"

"In general, yes. I have done once or twice. I met with Len Deighton here when he was thinking about moving to another house. Of course, we didn't want that and I was able to dissuade him. Are you a fan of his?"

"Very much, especially his early stuff."

"You mean '*Ipcress*'? The Sixties stuff?"

"Yes, but more the really good ones, like '*Funeral In Berlin,*' '*An Expensive Place To Die,*' '*Billion Dollar Brain.*'"

"You don't care for the later ones? The Samson books and the World War Two ones? We've done very well with them."

"Deighton's a classic. He's always worth reading. He's been at it a long time," I said, I hoped tactfully.

"Well, never mind. I understand the new book is smashing. I want you to know we think it's your 'breakthrough book.' We're very confident about it being a best-seller and we're going to do everything we can to make it go to the very top."

"Thank you. That's wonderful."

"I also have some additional news for you. The Book of the Month Club has just selected your book for its Main Selection. Congratulations."

"Thank you." That seemed to be all I needed to say at this meeting, but inside I was going crazy. Main Selection of the Book of the Month Club! Holy shit! I couldn't believe it!

"Let me be candid, Andrew. We want a long-term relationship with you. We need you. Deighton's been around a long time and he's getting on. Fred Forsythe is remarkable, but he only does a book once in a blue moon. Spends forever on research. We need a male thriller writer and once *Dragonfire* hits the best-seller lists, we want you to be our leading men's writer. And just so there's no mistake, I wanted you to hear it directly from me face to face, so you know that this company is committed to you and your work. You may be getting other offers for your next work, but I don't want you to go with anyone else. We want to be your partner all the way, to do for you what we've done for Len and Fred. What do you say?"

"That's what I want too. I'm very happy here."

"Then it's settled," he said, standing up and shaking my hand again. "Ann's our best and most senior editor. She's become a huge fan of yours. She'll do well by you," he said.

I left his office, my head spinning. Len and Fred? At that time, two of the biggest selling authors in the world and now me in their company on a first name basis? And Main Selection Book of the Month Club! Jeez, that was a coup!

That night I had dinner with Editor Ann at Rules, the old English restaurant in Convent Garden. With its yellow walls and Regency décor, it was like a British men's private club. Editor Ann, was already at a table when I entered.

"They say the Prince of Wales comes here quite often," Ann said.

"Then I won't expect to see Princess Di," I said.

"You *are* naughty," she laughed. We ordered drinks and the English roast beef-type food Rules was known for. "How did it go with God?"

"He says he wants a long-term relationship."

"What did you say?"

"I said it was fine with me. He told me about the Book of the Month Club Main Selection."

"Is that a done deal? That's marvelous! That nails it for you here in Britain and the Commonwealth countries. How do you feel?"

"Like Cinderella at the ball. I keep waiting for the clock to strike midnight."

"You just have to sell the Americans. Of course, we'll be talking it up here. That will help," she said. "There's one thing I've been meaning to ask."

"Oh?"

"The title, *Dragonfire*... How did you finally come up with it and that legend?"

"That was a killer. It took me forever. I was very cognizant of the parameters of a title. I wanted something that would sell."

"Like what? I know my parameters, but I'd be interested in yours," she said.

"For one thing, it shouldn't be too long. Two to four words is best. I mean, sometimes you get a long title that succeeds, like Le Carré's *The Spy Who Came In From The Cold*, but that's a fluke. For a thriller, what's best is short, punchy, and conveys both excitement and something of the context of the story. This is a story set in the East. I wanted the word 'dragon' in the title as a way to convey that and also danger. For months I've wracked my brain playing around with 'dragon' in various combinations. But they were just words, they didn't have anything to do with the story."

"That's when you thought of the legend about the dragon goddess?"

"Right. But *Legend of the Dragon* or something like that didn't seem very original or much like a spy thriller. I still needed something to spark things. I remembered that dragons breathe fire and that was it: *Dragonfire*. Then I applied the fire part back to the legend of the goddess and how she could only be harmed by her own fire, which related back to the Suong character. Simple. Only took me about eight months to figure out."

"It'll do very well indeed," she smiled. "Now the next question of the day. What are you going to work on next?"

"To tell you the truth, I've been scrambling so much on this one, I haven't had a chance to think of anything else."

"Andrew, I know you've been scrambling, but I don't believe you don't have something else in mind."

"I've been toying with a number of things. Just a grab bag, really."

"Such as?"

"I don't know. A standard spy thriller set in Japan in winter, with Russian overtones."

"I love that. It sounds fascinating."

"It's just one idea. Your paperback guy said they'd love to have another novel with the Scorpion character. I've got an idea for one about the Israelis and Palestinians. Also there's one set in Argentina, but it spans generations."

"How could you make that into a thriller?"

"Haven't a clue. These are just thought fragments. There's also something in the Philippines, set during the People's Revolution that threw out the Marcoses, but reprises the characters from *Dragonfire'*

Lately, I've been thinking that *Dragonfire* is really only the middle part of a trilogy. What do you think?"

"I think any of these would be amazing. Let's get this one launched, so you can focus on something new as soon as possible and then we'll talk," she said, as the waiter brought our food.

That night, I called Anne and gave her all the good news.

"That's wonderful about the Book of the Month Club, Babe," she said, but there was something in her voice and all I wanted to do that second was to get on the next plane back to Nice.

In the morning, I met with June, told her she could handle New York and then went straight to Heathrow.

Chapter 29

Burgess, Borges, and Blue Cross

I met Anthony Burgess at a *brasserie* in La Condamine, the port area of Monte Carlo. I had gone back to my routine at Chuck's office, making edits to *Dragonfire* in response to my editor Ann's notes. Max called and we arranged to meet for lunch.

Burgess was eating alone when we came in. When he saw Max, he waved us over and I realized Max had set this up. Burgess was a man in his late sixties, with a shock of white hair and an English street brawler's mug, which I immediately decided was where *Clockwork Orange* came from.

"Andy's also a writer. He's living in Monte Carlo now. Where's Liana?" Max said.

"Making arrangements. We're leaving tomorrow for Ticino. We usually leave sooner. This time of year, the Côte d'Azur becomes the French equivalent of Brighton midsummer holiday. One has to, as you Americans say, *'get outta town.'* I just needed to finish something off," he said, lighting a brown cigarillo. "What do you write?" he asked me. The waiter came and I ordered an *andouillette* and Max, the steak tartare.

"Spy thrillers. Nothing so literate as your stuff," I said.

"It's all genre nowadays. Most critics thought of *Clockwork Orange* as sci fi, when they weren't outright trying to get it banned. Where are you staying?"

"We're borrowing Nigel and Monika's flat on Boulevard de Suisse, till we sort out some medical things with my wife."

"Nigel Liddell-Smith?" Burgess asked.

"You know Nigel and Monika?"

"Everyone knows Nigel. Made a bloody fortune with those language books of his. Why come to Monaco now? Where were you staying before?"

"All over. Villefranche, Cap d'Antibes, then Eze-sur-Mer."

"Did you meet Graham Greene in Antibes?" he asked.

"I wanted to, but I was told he was too ill."

"Bollocks. Greene's healthier than I am. He just likes to play the great author and puts that out to keep the graduate student types away. Mind you, Liana tends to keep people away from me too, otherwise I'd never get anything done. To be fair, you have to take what I say with a grain. I don't think Greene likes me and it's fairly mutual."

"Why?"

"I've always put it down to an article I did about him once in which I suggested that there was a touch of the Jansenist in him?"

"That's not uncommon in successful people," I said. "Not many of them are honest enough to admit how much a part luck plays in their success."

Burgess made a face. "No, Greene was like that even before he was famous."

"What the hell is a Jansenist?" Max asked. Burgess gestured to me. Suddenly, I was a student being tested by a professor.

"Not sure," I said. "Belief in predestination? Only the chosen few? Something like that."

"I think of it as the Catholic version of Calvinism," Burgess said. "Personally, I suspect the real reason he doesn't like me is the moral superiority of the convert towards us cradle Catholics, although only

God knows where on the Catholic spectrum Greene finds himself these days. Why spy thrillers?"

"Because for years I would write things that everyone loved but wouldn't publish. I'd get these personal rejection letters from editors. Mind you, I got plenty of the preprinted kind too. You know, 'Best of luck elsewhere,' but also a lot of personal ones, like, 'This is the best war story I ever read, only we just published one with a similar theme and it sold three copies, but please send anything else you write directly to me personally, blah, blah.' I got sick of it. After a while, it felt like I was the most popular unpublished writer in America. I decided the only way I'd ever get published was to do genre. Ian Fleming, Eric Ambler and Len Deighton were the kinds of things I read for fun and John Le Carré had made the spy thriller respectable. It worked like a charm."

"Andy just got back from meeting with his publisher in England." Max said.

"Who's your publisher?" Burgess asked.

"Century-Hutchinson. My new book just got selected for Main Selection Book of the Month Club in Britain," I bragged, showing off in hopes of having him take me seriously.

"Good for you. My book, *Earthly Powers*, was a Main Selection Book of the Month Club in America. I believe it set the world record for remainders. One sometimes regrets the trees chopped down on these."

"What are you working on now?" I asked.

"More of my memoirs and a musical version of *Clockwork Orange*. Also I've been asked to get something out on Joyce for Bloomsday in Dublin. Of course, the only reason the Irish Tourist Office celebrates Joyce is because he's safely dead. You?"

"I'm doing final edits for the English edition of my new one, *Dragonfire*. Haven't decided what's next. I've been thinking about a World War Two thing in Argentina, though I'm not sure the publishers will like it."

"Argentina," Burgess said. "Do you know Borges?"

"I've never met him, but I love his work," I said.

"Which ones?"

"The *History of Infamy* of course. I *love* the gaucho stuff. *The Aleph*, and shit, what was it? *Labyrinths*, though I'm not sure I followed all of it. Do you know him?"

"We met a few times. There was a Shakespeare thing in Washington in '76 that for reasons known only to the organizers was somehow related to the American Bicentennial. They invited Borges, Alistaire Cooke, I suppose because both he and Shakespeare were English, and me as speakers.

"Afterwards, there was a party at the Argentine embassy. Borges was afraid of being overheard by the Argentine secret police, so we spoke in Old English. '*Nu we sculan herian heofenrices weard*, you know," Burgess said.

"Did it work?" I said.

"We thought so. Only the Argentine secret coppers thought we were talking in code and that only made them even more suspicious. The way they looked at us, I was sure they were going to lock us in an embassy cellar and get out the rubber hoses," Burgess said. "I especially liked what he said during the Falklands War, even though his comments put him in real danger."

"What was that?" Max asked.

"He said Britain and Argentina fighting over the Falklands was like two fat bald men fighting over a comb," Burgess said and we all laughed. The waiter came with our food and between bites we agreed to get together after he and his wife, Liana, came back from Switzerland.

As I walked back to the apartment, I was thrilled at meeting Burgess. It felt like I'd entered a whole new world of writing. I couldn't wait to tell Anne and I nearly ran to the Boulevard de Suisse, only stopping to pick up a copy of the *International Herald Tribune* from the *tabac* on the corner. I glanced at the front page as I walked, where a small article near the bottom stated that the noted author, Jorge Luis Borges, often mentioned as a Nobel literature candidate, though he had never been awarded the prize, had died of liver cancer in Geneva.

I stopped in the middle of the sidewalk in the bright sunshine. I thought of something I had read during a time when I was devouring everything I could find by Borges. When Borges was made Librarian of the Argentine National Library and had become completely blind, he had told an interviewer he was aware "...of God's splendid irony in granting me at one time 800,000 books and darkness." I knew that if I had been similarly stricken, I would never have had the grace or courage or the exquisite sense of irony that enabled Borges to say that. That *commissaire de police* in Antibes had been right, I thought. The Swedes were idiots. Not only had Borges earned the Nobel Prize ten times over, but giving it to him would have probably done more to bring freedom and democracy or even enlightenment to Argentina than a dozen revolutions. When I resumed walking back to the apartment, it was at a slower pace, as if I had aged a little in the space of a few blocks.

The next day, Anne and I met with the surgeon in Nice, Dr. De Villiers, that Dr. Fleurier had referred us to. Dr. De Villiers was an extremely handsome Frenchman with a passing resemblance to the movie star, Pierce Brosnan, a surgeon's arrogance, and only slightly more charisma than Jean-Paul Belmondo, if you liked that sort of thing. I was impervious to his charms, but I could sense Anne perk up beside me. She even tossed her hair a couple of times.

Dr. Handsome Frenchman told us that Anne had a tubal pregnancy and that she had to have surgery. Because he spoke little English or perhaps just didn't want to, Anne waited in the waiting room with Justin while he and I made arrangements in French. He said we should plan to have the surgery as soon as possible and recommended the *Clinique St. Georges*, a private hospital in Nice. I asked him how much it would cost and whether we could arrange for our Blue Cross insurance to cover the surgery. It became clear that I would have to pay for it in cash and then get Blue Cross to reimburse us. I told him I wasn't sure we could afford it.

"*Ecoutez, Monsieur*," he said. "You have perhaps a week. Perhaps two, at most. After that, if she does not have surgery, the consequences would be *très grave*."

"You mean she could die?"

"*Vous comprenez bien, Monsieur*," he said, his words chilling me. The prospect of Anne dying hadn't occurred to me before. The idea of Justin and me suddenly alone without her scared the hell out of me.

"I could take her back to the States. She has a doctor there who did her previous surgery that she has confidence in and our insurance will cover us," I said.

"You cannot take her on a plane, Monsieur."

"Why not? It's the only thing that makes sense. Our insurance will cover us financially and she'll be able to talk to her doctors in English."

"*Impossible, Monsieur*," he said. "You cannot get on a plane."

"Of course I can," I said, annoyed. "Who's going to stop me? I buy the tickets, show our passports, and we get on the plane."

"And what if her tube bursts while you are midway over the Atlantic? *Alors quoi?*! What do you do then, Monsieur?" he snapped, using the term '*faîte exploser*' for 'bursts' which sounds even worse in French.

"You're right," I said. "I can't take her on a plane. We'll do the surgery at the *St. Georges*."

He got on the phone and made arrangements for her to have the surgery the following week. I called June and she promised to get money to us within a few days. If there was any holdup at Century, she said she would advance the money herself. Not a lot of agents – or people – like her, I thought. As we drove back to Monte Carlo, Anne said, "Looks like we're about to go another round with French medicine."

Chapter 30

Visitors, Part Three: Beach Days and Samba Nights

That evening we ran into Chuck and Emma at *Le Sporting Club*. Harry Belafonte was the headliner. The club was crowded, the lights dimmed, and there were Calypso drums and instruments on the empty stage.

"What are you doing here?" Emma asked.

"Anne's a big fan of Belafonte's," I said.

"He's terrific," Emma said.

"Max says you might be going to New York and California," Chuck said.

"Possibly."

"We need to talk before you go," Chuck said. "We'll set something up."

"Is this about the office?" I had been using the workstation in his office informally again and I wondered if he wanted to charge me.

"No, it's important. It's business." He and Emma waved at people we didn't know who were already seated at another table.

"Chuck's business acquaintances. We won't bore you with them," Emma said as they headed to the other table. I hadn't wanted to tell them the real reason we were there, apart from the fact that we really did like Belafonte and I had always thought he had done more for civil rights than a lot of so-called 'community leaders,' was to try to have as much fun as possible in the week before Anne had to go into the hospital.

Our plans were further complicated by the arrival of another visitor, A friend of Anne's, a fellow school psychologist from Los Angeles. Margot, whom we picked up at Nice airport, was an attractive divorcée, if your taste ran to slim American blondes with the kind of classic good looks you see in Ralph Lauren ads. Her son, a few years older than Justin, was spending the summer with his father. After doing the French *bisou* cheek-kissing thing as a way of introducing her into our world, we grabbed her luggage, piled into the Renault and headed back to Monte Carlo. She would stay with us, sharing Justin's room.

"I can't believe I'm really here," Margot said, looking around at the *petits hôtels*, the *bistros*, palm trees and the blue Mediterranean as we drove along the *Basse Corniche*. "It's even more gorgeous than I imagined."

We stopped for lunch at an outside table at Le Dauphin in the port in Villefranche, steps from the harbor. She and Anne caught up on what was happening in the Los Angeles school district. As usual, the school district was reorganizing, an exercise they seemed to go through at least once a year, like a restless sleeper trying to find the one position that will work, while everyone who worked there knew that that nothing would ever change so long as the district was governed by racial politics and promotion based on seniority over merit.

I left them talking and took Justin down to the water's edge to feed breadcrumbs to the fish. The sun was shining on the water and we could see the white sails of sailboats out beyond the breakwater.

"Where's Maria and Monsieur le Chef?" Justin asked.

"They're *en vacances*, Justin," I said.

"Are they coming back?"

"I don't think so. They sold the restaurant to someone else."

"Will the new person take me down to feed the fish?"

"*Je ne le crois pas*. Probably not," I said.

"*C'est tout fini?*"

"*D'accord.*"

"I miss them," he said. "Why'd they leave? Don't they like us any more?"

"They were getting old, Justin. It was getting too hard for them."

Justin tossed the whole piece of *baguette* into the water, where it was attacked by a battalion of tiny fish. He started to head back to Le Dauphin.

"Don't you want to feed the fish anymore?" I asked.

"It's no fun anymore without Maria," he said, sitting at the outside table.

"I was just telling Margot about my surgery and going to the *Clinique St. Georges*," Anne said.

"Look Margot," I said. "We're in the middle of something. This is your vacation; the only time you get off all year. You don't need to ruin it and have to deal with hospitals, doctors, and babysitting just to prove you're a friend. Believe me, we'll understand if you want to go exploring on your own. You could be having fun and you should. There are millionaires here, handsome Frenchmen..."

"You should see my French surgeon," Anne said.

"Gorgeous?" Margot asked.

"He makes Robert Redford look like Quasimodo."

"Wow!"

"Margot, about just helping out with us..." I began again.

"Don't you understand?" Margot said to me. "You guys lead the most interesting lives of anyone I know. I'm thrilled to be part of it, even if it's only for two weeks. Plus, after what Anne just said, I'm dying to meet her doctor."

"On one condition," Anne said.

"What's that?"

"You're not seeing anybody now, are you?"

"No, and you don't have to rub it in," Margot said.

"You're too nice and too pretty to go to waste. Sally and I have talked. We're going to set you up with a millionaire," Anne said.

"And how are we going to manage that?" I asked.

"Sally," Anne said. "Has a plan."

That evening, we met Max, Sally, Bobby G., and Gaby for drinks at the American Bar in the Hôtel de Paris. In between drinks, Jacques the barman made a racetrack on the mahogany bar out of olives, limes, and bar tools for Justin to race his model cars.

"What about Dr. De Villiers for Margot?" Anne asked.

"I checked. He's married," Sally said.

"Mistress?" Gaby asked.

"*Sans doute.*"

"Still, he might be available for *une affaire de coeur*, or just a *cinq à sept*, if she's interested," Gaby said.

"Doesn't any of this make you feel like a pimp?" I asked them.

"On the contrary," Sally said. "If we left these things to chance…"

"Or men…" Gaby interjected.

"People would never get together. It's our duty to find someone for Margot," Sally continued.

"Or at least see she has a good time," Max said.

"It would be better if you said that without the leer," Anne said to Max.

"I protest. Dreyfus is innocent."

"Dreyfus maybe. You, I'm not so sure about," Anne said.

"We could set her up with Mark," Bobby G. said. "He's a millionaire how many times over? She's a dish," he smiled at Margot. "He'd jump at the chance."

"Mark will never divorce Rachel. So unless Margot wants to be his mistress… She could live on the yacht. You don't get seasick, do you?" Sally said.

"She doesn't want to be a mistress. Besides, Mark's not that sexy," Anne said.

"He's horny," Max said.

"He's a man. That's a given. I'm talking about sexy to a woman," Anne said. "What about Prince Albert?" she said, turning to Margot.

"You mean date a real prince? Don't you think that's a bit out of my league?" Margot said.

"Don't be so sure. You know him. What do you think?" Anne asked Max.

"He's too young. Not to mention he's heir to the throne and she's a commoner," Max said.

"Princess Di was a commoner," Anne said.

"We all know how well that worked out," Bobby G. drawled.

"What about Carl?" I said. "He's a pilot. He could fly her around."

"He's with the Count and Countessa at their place in Lake Como. Besides, Carl's not rich. We're not doing all this for someone who isn't a 24-carat catch," Sally said.

"What about Thierry?" Gaby said.

"Possible. Very possible," Sally said. "And he told me once he likes American women. We're a challenge."

"He's rich?" Anne asked.

"A millionaire several times over. And he's got a yacht. Yasper and Betje did some work on it," Gaby said.

"Not a very big one. Only 80-something feet," Sally turned to Margot. "What do you think?"

"I can't believe you guys are really serious about this," Margot said. "You can't just arrange things."

"This is Europe, darling. We're very practical about such matters. The question is, are you willing to try?" Sally said.

Margot hesitated. "What's he like?" she asked.

"Thierry's a good guy. He's an executive with a French water company, but they're getting into telecommunications, movies and television now," Max said.

"Handsome?"

"Dark wavy hair, gray at the temples, divorced, no children.

Keeps in shape with tennis. Trust me, he's *très présentable*," Sally said. "The two of you together would be *un couple formidable*."

"How do we set it up?" Anne asked.

"Wait a minute. Don't I get to vote about any of this?" Margot said.

"And have us miss all the fun? Not a chance. Besides, you are attractive. *Mes amis*," Sally smiled, "it's like shooting fish in a barrel."

The next day, we took Margot on our standard 'Visitors to the Riviera Tour,' stopping for lunch at the Colombe d'Or in St. Paul de Vence. As we waited for an outdoors table, Anne took Margot on a tour of the hotel and grounds, the black tile swimming pool with its Calder mobile sculpture, the indoor restaurant with its paintings by Picasso, Chagall, Matisse, Leger, Miro, and Braque, all former patrons, while Justin and I waited in the outdoor bar.

I glanced at a copy of the *International Herald Tribune* someone had left near the bar. Apparently, powerful winds and heavy rains had turned the first round of the U.S. Open at Shinnecock Hills into a high-scoring mess, with only one player, Bob Tway, making par, although others were in contention, Greg Norman just one stroke back. I ordered a glass of wine for myself and a *limonade* for Justin. Auguste, the bartender, remembered me as he brought the drinks.

"How goes the writing, Monsieur?"

"It goes. How are things with you, Auguste?"

"Not so good. Too many tourists. Now is the time of year when things become impossible," he sighed, leaning over the bar. "Who is the other woman, the pretty one with your wife, Monsieur? Your mistress, *sans aucun doute*," he said.

"You guessed," I said, playing along, realizing that no Frenchman would believe any other explanation I offered anyway.

"One a blonde, your wife a brunette, a perfect matched set, Monsieur. The two women get along?"

"They are good friends."

"Ah, the creative temperament," Auguste sighed. "Able to arrange things in such a civilized manner. Picasso had more difficulties. There was an argument right here in this bar once with his wife, Jacqueline, who accused him of *mon Dieu!* ...infidelities were nothing. Imagine, all these *jalousies* when he was eighty." Just then, Anne and Margot came back into the bar. Auguste motioned me close. "You Monsieur, are a credit to the male species," he said.

"What was that about?" Anne asked as the *maître d'* showed us to our table in the garden, the sunlight shining through the overhanging trees.

"Auguste said I was a credit to the male species," I said.

"Why did he say that?"

"Because he always sees me with beautiful women."

"So it's true," Margot said. "The French really are more romantic."

"More perverted, you mean. He probably thinks you're Andy's mistress," Anne said.

"They can't begin to imagine how banal we really are," I said.

Justin's *crèche* had closed for the summer and we spent the next day at Monte Carlo's *Plage Larvotto*, sipping drinks and having *pain bagnats* on the sand and watching Justin, water wings on his arms, splashing with other small children in the water.

The day was hot and the beach was crowded with young people, families, jet setters, *au pairs*, and students *en vacances*. *Les estivants*, the summer people, Madame Finot would have called them, had arrived. Except for Anne and Margot, every woman on the beach was topless.

"Are you two going to be the only ones all covered up?" I teased.

"If you think I'm going to compete with all these pert young breasts, you're crazy," Anne said.

"They're not all perfect," I said, indicating a mother with sagging breasts and two toddlers, walking past us.

"What about them?" Anne said, indicating a group of French girls in their late teens or early twenties on beach towels right near us, topless and in tiny string bikini bottoms, who were attracting attention from young men playing paddle ball. The young men kept offering the girls drinks, rides in speedboats, and anything else they could to get their attention.

"They don't seem embarrassed," I said.

"If I had a body like theirs, I wouldn't be embarrassed either," Margot said.

"That's right! We've had babies. We earned our sags and stretch marks. We should be honored. Instead, all we do is suffer from body envy of women who are dying to accomplish what we've already done. The world makes no sense," Anne said.

"No guts, no glory," I grinned.

"I will if Anne will," Margot said, taking off her tee shirt, but leaving on her swimsuit top.

"I will if Margot will," Anne said, taking a swig of wine.

"That's cute, each of you using the other as an excuse," I said. "There's no getting away from it. Americans are prudes."

"You really want me to take my top off and have every man here see my boobs?" Anne demanded, starting to pull down the strap of her bathing suit. For a second I panicked, wondering if she was really going to do it, in which case, did I really know who I was married to? At such times, I told myself, one follows the Golden Rule For Husbands: Never let them see you sweat; give nothing away.

"If you want to. It's your choice," I said.

"Why should we?" Anne demanded.

"When in Rome..."

"All right, you asked for it. I'll do it," Anne said, pulling down the other strap, but still keeping her breasts covered.

"Me too," Margot declared, not making a move, as a pretty French girl began to play racquetball with one of the men, her breasts bobbing with her every move. "God, that girl knows she's sexy as hell and enjoys it. It's inhuman," Margot said, indicating the French girl.

"Neither of you are going to do it, are you?" I said.

"Not a chance," Anne said, pouring us all another glass of wine from the bottle. "You?" she asked Margot.

"I don't have the guts either," Margot said, putting her tee shirt back on.

"You didn't really think we were going to do it, did you?" Anne said.

"Not for a second," I said. "So when is Margot meeting this millionaire?"

"Tonight. We're all going to that new Brazilian nightclub. He should be there. Sally's arranged everything," Anne said.

"Is that the one mentioned by that awful blonde with Prince Maximillian?" I asked.

"You guys go to parties with people named 'Prince Maximillian' and you think your life is boring?" Margot said. She looked around the beach. "I feel like Dorothy coming to Oz where I've only ever seen black and white and now, all of a sudden the world is in color! I love this!"

"Yeah, but you didn't take your top off," I said.

"Well, give me time. This is only my third day. I'm still a prudish American," she said.

That night, we met Max, Sally, Bobby G. and Gaby at the Brazilian club, *Samba Samba*, off the Boulevard Princesse Charlotte. The place was bright with yellow and green lights, fake rubber trees, and crowded with jet setters and tourists. On the bandstand, a samba band was pounding the drums and people were dancing. We ordered *feijoada* stew, the Brazilian national dish, and to drink, *caipirinhas* for everyone except Justin.

"This is delicious. What's in it?" Anne asked the waiter.

"*Cachaça, lime, et le sucre, Madame.*"

"What's *cachaça*?"

"*Je ne sais pas, Madame. C'est Brésilien,*" the waiter said.

"It's Brazilian liquor, distilled from sugar cane," Max said, raising his voice to be heard over the samba drums.

"So how is it different from rum?" Margot asked.

"Beats me," Max shrugged.

"Ask him," Anne said, indicating me. "He knows everything."

"Next to Bernard," Sally said. "Look, there's Thierry," she said, waving at a tanned man in a pink St. Laurent sports shirt across the room.

"So how is it different?" Gaby said.

"Rum is made by making molasses out of sugar cane and then distilling the molasses. *Cachaça* is distilled directly from the sugar cane juice," I said. I had spent time in South America, having set my first book, *Hour of the Assassins*, in the Amazon jungle and had drunk cocktails across the continent from Peru's *Pisco sours* to *Fernet Branca y Cokes* in Argentina.

"See. He's a smart-ass," Anne said.

"No, a writer," I said.

"Same thing."

"That's all right. At least he does something," Sally said. "My husband's just a smart-ass, period."

"Sally just loves me for my body," Max said, grabbing Margot and dancing her over towards Thierry's table. The samba band was loud and the beat was very strong.

"My husband's not even a smart-ass," Gaby said.

"But I'm cute," Bobby G. said.

"*Très mignon*," Gaby said and they got up to samba. Justin wandered over to the bandstand. At first the band ignored him, but he stood there, moving to the rhythm and imitating them. A girl singer in a Brazilian costume pulled him up onto the bandstand.

The bandleader handed Justin a pair of maracas and showed him how to shake them in time to the music. In a minute, Justin had become part of the band to loud applause from everyone in the club. I wanted to dance with Anne, but I could see she wasn't up to it, so we watched Justin. Max introduced Margot to Thierry and Sally was right, they made *un couple formidable*. They looked good dancing a Bossa Nova, though next to them a party of Italian tourists were dancing like spastic lobsters.

The waiters handed out sparklers and people waved them about and danced with them and we drank *caipirinhas* till after one in the morning, finally making our way back to the apartment past Monagasque policemen on empty street corners, who saluted as we toddled by, Margot waving a bottle of *Cachaça* our waiter had given her and Justin shaking his maracas. We hummed Bossa Nova music, Anne singing *The Girl From Ipanema* off-key as we went up the stairs to the apartment.

"So when are you meeting Thierry?" Anne asked.

"We have a date on his yacht tomorrow night. He seems nice," Margot said, yawning.

"Daddy, I'm a musician," Justin said, taking the maracas to bed with him.

"I know, kiddo. You put on a good show," I said, helping him into his pajamas and pulling the covers up.

"That was fun, wasn't it Dad? I like Brazil," Justin said.

"Yeah, it was great. Never miss a chance to have fun, Justin," I said.

"We're good at it, aren't we Daddy?"

"You know, I think we are," I said.

The next morning, while Margot waited outside with Justin, I checked Anne into the *Clinique St. Georges* in Nice for her surgery.

Chapter 31

The Most Amazing Day

The day of Anne's surgery, I dropped Margot and Justin off at the *Parc du Château* in Nice. The park was on a hill between the old town and the port. There were trees and grass and a waterfall near the top and a fenced-in children's playground with a rope-web jungle gym and hand-turned *carrousels*, where Justin could play for hours and Margot could watch him until I picked them up after the surgery. I only saw Anne for a few minutes before they took her into the operating room.

"Can you believe it?" Anne said. "They didn't give me a nightgown or anything. They took away all my clothes and I had to sit here stark naked. Doctors, orderlies, men walking in off the street, trust me, they all got a good look. In France, no one cares if you're naked. One of them winked at me! I'm naked under this sheet right now!"

"I'm sorry, Babe. These things don't seem to bother them."

"It didn't bother the men who were ogling me yesterday. I'm beginning to think the only reason I'm having this surgery is so Dr. De Villiers can have a good look. How do you say 'nightgown' in French?"

"*Chemise de nuit.*"

"Yeah, tell them I want a *chemise de nuit*, okay?"

"I will."

"Justin okay?"

"Margot's with him at the park. I'll get them as soon as this is over."

"I'll be all right. I just hate this," she said. "What if my tubes are bad? I'll never be able to have another child."

"You've got two tubes. Even if this one is bad, and we don't know that, you've got another."

"Don't go anywhere," she said, grabbing my arm.

"I'll be right here," I said and kissed her as the nurse and an orderly came to get her.

"*Ma femme a besoin d'une chemise de nuit*," I told the nurse.

"*Pourquoi?*" she asked.

"*Elle est modeste et aussi parce que je l'ai dit!*" I snapped, acting on the theory that sometimes a display of arrogance is the only thing that enables the average French person to distinguish a human being from a doormat.

"*Ils sont incompréhensibles, les américains*," I heard her mutter to the orderly as they wheeled Anne away.

I sat in the waiting room trying not to imagine all the things that could go wrong. There were magazines on the coffee table, *Paris-Match*, *Le Figaro*, that morning's *Nice-Matin*. I tried to read, but I couldn't. I thought about Justin and was glad he was outside playing, not knowing what was happening. It was lucky Margot just happened to be here at this time and could watch him, I thought. We're lucky, like Auguste the bartender said. Hold on to that, I told myself. We're lucky people. After a while, Dr. De Villiers came out.

"It's over, Monsieur. Your wife is doing well. She is in the Recovery Room and should be waking up within forty-five minutes."

"How did it go?"

"Happily, there were no complications."

"Were you able to save her tubes?" I asked.

"There were no problems with the tubes," he hesitated. "It was not a tubal pregnancy. All the signs indicated that, one could not take chances, but still..."

"Then what was it?"

"It was *une fausse couche partielle*, you understand?"

"What's a partial miscarriage?"

"It is when there is a spontaneous abortion, an abortion of nature, *normalement* either because there is a defect in the fetus or a problem with the uterus. The miscarriage becomes incomplete if the woman does not pass all the tissue from the fetus and the placenta. In your wife's case, nothing passed; that was the cause of the confusion. Without bleeding or tissue passing, there was no sign of a miscarriage; meanwhile the fetal tissue was still sending the hormonal signal that she was pregnant."

"So her tubes and everything are fine."

"Her tubes are good and we did what is done in such cases, suction *dilatation et curettage* to remove the remaining tissue. That solves the problem of the miscarriage."

I took a deep breath. "Can she still have children?" I asked.

He hesitated again. "Your wife's endometriosis has returned. I suspect that, and not necessarily a defect in the fetus, may have caused the miscarriage. She will require additional surgery."

"You couldn't just take care of it right then, while you were in there?"

"We were not set up for that Monsieur," he said. "It was not possible. We need to reschedule another surgery for the endometriosis."

"Is there any reason why we cannot take her on a plane now? We could have it done in the States?"

"None whatever, Monsieur. But sooner or later, it will have to be done."

"But there is no urgency?"

"No Monsieur, *pas d'urgence*. Go to your wife," he said, patting my shoulder. "She will need you."

Anne was still groggy from the anesthesia when she woke.

"How'd it go?" she asked.

"It went fine. You're fine," I said.

I picked up Justin and Margot at the park. We had lunch in the old town and went back to Monte Carlo.

The next day, I brought Margot and Justin with me to see Anne. Colette was there and we cheek-kissed and introduced her to Margot.

"I'm using my French more these past two days than in all the time I've been in France. That's Monique. Breast cancer. She's having a mastectomy," Anne whispered, indicating a dark-haired woman in the next bed.

"We miss you. How's Michelle?" I said to Collete. "Michelle's her older daughter," I explained to Margot.

"Things are better now. Her husband has a new mistress. This one is not married and has her own apartment in the sixteenth *arrondissement*, which is so hard to come by she would be a fool to give it up. And Michelle has a lover also. So everyone is happy," Colette said. "*Et alors*, Georges and Annette ask about you all the time. They said you should spend time with them in Troyes this summer. He says you both can have champagne every day."

"Champagne every day. Are you kidding?" Margot said.

"And Jean-Claude and Freddie feel terrible they missed you in Paris. They want you to come to Picardy for the summer. Freddie loves the little one," she said, indicating Justin.

"We'd love to," I said, looking at Anne. "We have to see about the medical situation."

"We'll see," Anne said. "How'd your date with Thierry go?" she asked Margot, who didn't say anything. "Well?"

"No comment," Margot said.

"Really?! Did you go on his yacht?"

"Yes," Margot said, reddening.

"Who is Thierry?" Colette asked.

"*Elle a un petit ami français*," Anne said. "See, I'm speaking French now! Aren't you proud of me? So when do you see him again?"

"He had to go back to Paris for a few days. After that, we'll see."

The next few days, we shuttled between Monte Carlo and Nice. After bringing Justin to visit with Anne, Margot would take him to the *Parc du Château* so Anne and I could talk. I asked her what she wanted to do about the surgery and the summer.

"We have to go back. It's the only thing that makes any sense. Our insurance will cover the surgery in California and besides you need to go to New York about the book. We can stay with Luke and Julia," Anne said. Anne's sister, Julia, lived in Scarsdale. Her husband, Luke, was a physician who was anxious to see Anne's surgery incisions so he could judge for himself what the French doctors had done and how.

"That's it, then," I said. "We just need to pull things together."

"Where will we stay when we get back to California?"

"With my mother till we find a place. She'll love it, having Justin there."

"She won't enjoy having us?"

"Compared to her only grandchild? Don't be silly," I said.

"Listen, I feel bad that Margot's not really getting a flavor of what it's like here. Why don't you take her out? Take her to the Casino. It's world-famous, we live within walking distance, and she's never even been. Show her the *Salons Privés* or maybe take her out to *Le Sporting Club* or Stuart's pub."

"I'm not comfortable with that. Everyone will think we're having an affair," I said.

"Well are you?"

"Noooo!"

"So what do you care what people think? Besides, you have my permission," she said.

"That only makes it laughable."

"They probably already think you're having an affair. Besides, I trust Margot."

"Ah, you trust Margot and not me?"

"Of course not, you're a man," she laughed, then winced. "God that hurts. You're not sorry about going back to the States, are you, Babe?"

"A little. I'd rather go to Champagne and Picardy for the summer and then back to Eze. We have no choice. The endometriosis is back. You need the surgery."

"Don't forget the book. We have to go to New York. Strike while the iron is hot," she said.

That night, with Sally babysitting Justin, I took Margot out to dinner at Rampoldi's, then the Casino, where she lost a few francs at roulette, then to Stuart's pub.

Max was there, wanting to talk to me about some idea he had about a golf club on the Côte d'Azur, only since the amount of buildable land for a golf course was impossible to find on the Côte, he wanted to create a course about the size of a Par 3 course using a special ball someone had invented that would only go about ¼ the distance of a normal golf ball. He was thinking of calling it 'McGolf.' "It can't miss. It'll be the only golf course on the Côte. I've heard a million golfers complain there's no place here to play. What do you think?" Max said.

"Sounds good to me, but you're asking the wrong guy. I was product manager of the first spreadsheet application ever for minicomputers and didn't have enough brains to port it to a PC. Would've been a multi-millionaire," I said.

We picked up Justin and after putting him to bed, Margot and I had nightcaps and watched the fireworks over Monte Carlo harbor from the balcony. As the summer approached, there were fireworks nearly every night that we could watch from our balcony.

"Thank you for tonight. This is incredible. You must love it here," she said as a burst of white and red light umbrella'd over the water.

"I loved it in Eze," I said. "That was special."

"Then you'll go back," she said.

"I hope so," I said, but in the back of my mind I could feel things changing. Everything was pushing us back to America.

In the morning, I got up early, picked up fresh croissants and the

International Herald Tribune and had my coffee on the balcony as before. Apparently, it had been an amazing finish at the U.S. Open, with nine players tied for the lead with only nine holes left to play. Raymond Floyd had taken it with a 66, nailing it with a birdie on the 16th hole and a par putt on the 18th. I looked down on Sam Cummings' empty rooftop *terrasse* and realized that I was missing people. I missed nodding at Sam as we had breakfast. Ron and Roxanna were touring around Europe, Adrian was away on business, Anthony Burgess was in Switzerland, Nigel and Monika were in England, Bobby G. and Gaby were leaving to see her family in Finland. We weren't leaving the Côte d'Azur, I thought, it was leaving us.

We brought Anne home from the *Clinique St. Georges* the next day and went back to Nice a few days after that to take Margot to the airport.

"I'm sorry you wound up doing so much babysitting. That wasn't what we wanted for your vacation," Anne said as we left her at the boarding gate.

"Are you kidding? It's the most amazing time I've ever had. You guys are living a fairy tale. I'll give your regards to L.A. Unified," she said.

"Don't," Anne said. "We have no idea what happens next."

The next day, Chuck called and asked me to drop by his office. I sat on the couch and he handed me a portfolio.

"When do you leave?" he asked.

"In a week or two. We have to wrap things up here, sell the car. Max's going to help. What's up?"

"Global Systems is in trouble. Not us, the American company. They're about to go Chapter 11. I want to buy them," he said.

"OK. Where do I fit in?"

"I'd like you to check them out. You're going to be in California anyway and I need someone I can trust. See what they've got. Assets, liabilities, business model, how they're marketing, what's working with their distribution, what isn't. What's selling? What isn't? And why aren't they going gangbusters in the U.S., the way we are in Europe? I want to come up with the right price and I want another opinion before I put my money on the table," he said. "You didn't expect this, did you?"

"No I didn't."

"All right," he grinned. "Go ahead, ask."

"OK. What's in it for me?"

"Five percent. Cash plus stock. It's all here," he said, handing me an envelope. I opened it and skimmed the agreement quickly. "Your share could be worth a million dollars," he added.

"Tell you what," I said. "I'll sniff around free of charge. If it looks like something, I'll sign this thing and send it to you."

"Fair enough," he said and we shook hands. Walking out, I thought that I wouldn't have to do that much sniffing around to know what was the U.S. Global Systems' problem. Global was a pioneer in computers for businesses. The history of the technology business was littered with the corpses of pioneer companies. For every Microsoft that got in early and succeeded, there were hundreds that got in early and paid the price of proselytizing for someone else's success. If Chuck had the cash and they didn't, he could pick up all the marbles.

Anne had taken Justin to the beach. The day was hot and before heading back to the apartment to change for the beach and meet them, I decided to stop in at Stuart's pub for a cold drink. Stuart was sitting with a Frenchman at a corner table. When I came in, he waved me over and called the waiter. I sat down and ordered a gin and tonic.

"This is my attorney, David. I'm thinking of buying the Victoria Hotel in Roquebrune. What do you think?" Stuart said.

"Sounds good. If you do, do I get a special rate?" I said.

"Actually, I wanted to propose something else," he said and motioned to David, who did the *"plaisir de faire votre connaissance"* thing with me and left. "I can't get Glenda or the girls to stay at the *mas.*"

"You call that extravaganza you're building a '*mas*?'" (farmhouse) I said.

"Well, that's what it was."

"Calling that a *mas* is like the Vanderbilts calling their place in Newport 'the beach house,'" I said.

"Well, whatever it's called, all they do is complain about it. It's too remote, it's too big, it's too isolated, it's too this, it's too that. Thing is, I like it and I'm damned if I'm going to give it up," he said.

"Good for you. Stand up to 'em. You might be lonely, but you'll have room," I said.

"Don't be sarcastic, it's a dilemma. I still want to be able to go out there every once in a while, but once it's built, I don't want to leave the property empty. I need someone to help keep away those truffle bastards and their damn pigs away from my oak trees. I don't want to rent it out or anything. It's personal for me, a place I've always imagined," he said.

"So what are you going to do?"

"I was planning on offering it to you."

"What do you mean? I can't afford anything like that?"

"No, it's free for you and Anne and Justin as long as you like. Just don't take over the whole place. There are three wings. Leave one for us in case I can ever get them to come out for a weekend or something. We'll have fun. Go skeet-shooting or something."

"I've always wanted to kill a skeet."

"That's why I wanted you guys," he laughed and slapped me on the back. "You'd appreciate it and you know how to laugh at things."

"You've heard we're leaving, haven't you?" I said.

"Oh, you'll be back as soon as you fix Anne up and whatnot. What do you think?"

"You're not thinking I'm going to be the caretaker or anything. I'm not very handy. According to Anne, I shouldn't be allowed within twenty feet of any useful tool."

"No, we've got Hivert there in a separate cottage on the property.

He'll take care of everything. I just want you to live there. What do you say?"

"I'll have to talk to the boss. We have to see what happens in the States. But whatever happens, that's incredibly generous of you. I mean that," I said, shaking his hand.

When I met Anne at the beach, she was all excited.

"What an amazing day! Justin was almost swimming!" she said.

"I've had a pretty amazing day myself," I said. All these offers.

That night, I was reading Justin his favorite French illustrated storybook, *Les Mondes Engloutis*, based on the French TV animated show about a group of wayfarers on a journey under the surface of the Earth, before his bedtime when the phone rang.

"It's June," Anne said, handing me the phone. We spoke for a few minutes and when I hung up, I was literally in a state of shock. Anne and I just stared at each other.

"What is it? What's happened?" she said. I took a deep breath, barely able to speak.

"Either I'm completely totally insane or I'm smart as a fox," I said.

"What do you mean?"

"I just turned down $200,000 for *Dragonfire*."

Chapter 32

Au Revoir Is Not Adieu

"YOU DID WHAT?!!!!"

Warner Books, who'd published *Scorpion* in paperback, had just made a pre-emptive bid on *Dragonfire*. $200,000. I'd told my agent June to turn it down.

"Are you crazy or are you crazy?! Call her back," Anne said.

"I can't."

"Call her back. Tell her you suffered a momentary lapse of sanity but you're OK now and you changed your mind. You want the money."

"I don't want to."

"Why not?"

"Because I want to go to New York and talk to other publishers. And because I think we can get more."

"What makes you think so?"

"Why do you think they made a pre-emptive bid so quickly?"

"I haven't a clue, but I'm sure you're going to tell me."

"Because *Scorpion* is selling and they don't want to have to bid against anyone else for *Dragonfire*."

"What makes you so sure anyone else is going to want it?" she asked.

"Because there's buzz. Because I talked to God. Because it's a Main Selection of the Book of the Month Club. Because it's good," I said. "If we can get some bidding on it, we can make some real money. And maybe Warner isn't the right house for me. How do I know?! I don't know these people or that business. I don't know anything about it. June says my old editor from Macmillan, Laurie, the one who first bought *Scorpion*, is at Simon and Schuster now. She wants to meet with me in New York. June's going to set it up."

"$200,000. My God," she said. "We'd be rich."

"Well, not rich like Stuart or Mark or Chuck or Sam. But definitely OK."

"Wow!" she said, throwing her arms around me and kissing me. "You're beginning to impress me."

"I love it when you talk dirty like that," I said.

We spent the next week making arrangements, making calls and saying goodbyes. We went back to Cap d'Antibes for one last walk on Gatsby's Beach and a drink at the Hôtel du Cap. On the way back, we stopped off in St. Laurent du Var to say goodbye to Colette.

"You can leave the little one here," Colette said. "He can grow up to be a Frenchman."

"I want him to be an American," I said. "I don't want him to think of baseball or Rock n' Roll as something alien. Besides, it's hard enough to grow up. It's really hard when you're an outsider."

"*Eh bien*, when you come back, remember you have a French family too," Colette said.

We went back to Edmund's in Cap d'Ail, where the Italian waiter used to order *spaghetti Bolognese* for Justin as soon as he saw our car drive up. Only he wasn't there. Another waiter told us he had had to go back to Italy to deal with a family emergency with one of his children. We ate there, but it wasn't the same and Justin said the *spaghetti Bolognese* tasted different this time. I wondered if it was the

Côte d'Azur that was changing or whether we were seeing it differently now that we were leaving.

We left a message for Nigel and Monika in England and they called us from Wimbledon. They told us to leave the apartment keys with our neighbor, Madame D'Alessio. We promised to get together again either in the States or in Monaco as soon as possible.

"How was Ascot?" Anne asked Monika.

"The women's hats were unbelievable," Monika said. "The plainest dressed one there was the Queen. I swear she looks like she buys her clothes from a thrift shop. She carries it off though."

"How's the tournament?" I asked Nigel.

"Usual loudmouths about. I may wager a few quid," he said.

"Bet on Becker," I said.

"Becker's German. You know me, Andy."

"Yeah, but you met Becker too. You like him. You told me you did."

He was silent for a moment, then said, "Well, I do like him. He's a good lad. Maybe this once."

Max helped me sell the Renault for only $500 less than I had paid for it. With that and the money left over from June, we would be fine till we got settled. Bobby G. and Gaby were leaving for Finland the next day and we all got together one last time in the garden at Max and Sally's villa. The day was hot and sunny, like the day we had first arrived on the Côte d'Azur. Max broke out a bottle of *Grand Cru Chambertin Clos de Bèze*.

"This is the best wine I know. I've been saving it for a really special occasion," Max said, pouring our glasses. We all toasted.

"Santé!"

"Skoal!"

"L'chaim!"

"Merde!" Max said and we all laughed and drank. The wine was delicious and smooth as silk.

"It won't be the same without you guys," Gaby said.

Anne told them how we'd been saying our goodbyes and about the Italian waiter at Edmund's.

"That's too bad," Sally said.

"Everybody's got problems," Max said and I sensed something was bothering him.

"Do you think people like Mark or Stuart and Glenda with all that money have the same kinds of problems as people like us?" Anne said.

"Absolutely. We know lots of millionaires. I never knew one that didn't have problems," Sally said.

"My great-grandmother Gittel, whom I never met, but who my mother used to tell me about, used to say that if everybody in the world had a basket and everyone put all their troubles in their basket and then they all put all their baskets into a big circle and you could choose any basket you wanted, but you had to pick one, everyone would end up choosing their own basket," I said.

"I'm not sure that's true," Bobby G. said.

"Well, I like it," Sally said.

"I like it too," Max said. "To Great-grandmother Gittel!" he toasted.

"To Great-grandmother Gittel!" we said and drank.

The next day, Max and Sally drove us to Nice airport. We somehow managed to cram all the luggage in, tying a pyramid of suitcases to the top of Max's car, so that driving down the *Corniche*, we looked like the French version of *The Grapes of Wrath*. More than one car filled with French tourists down from Paris on holiday, *les estivants* Madame Finot would have called them, honked at us.

At the airport, we hugged and did our *bisou* cheek-kisses. Max looked at me, his head tilted.

"You know your problem?" he said.

"Which one? I've got plenty wrong with me, just ask Anne," I said.

"You don't like to argue, do you?"

"I didn't know it was a character flaw."

"It is. I was looking forward to having lots of arguments with you about writing, politics, religion, life, sports. You just avoid it. How come?" he said.

"Because people only come in a single piece," I said. "You can't take just the parts you like. Take politics. I often find that people I disagree with politically, I often like as people better than some I may agree with. A lot of people let their emotions get tangled up with their opinions. I didn't want to lose you as a friend."

"Well, I like a good argument," he said.

"OK, I promise. The next time we get together, we'll have a kick-ass argument," I said, shaking his hand.

"It's a deal," he said. "Oh, and see if you can find any investors in America for my McGolf thing. Prince Albert is going in with me."

"Is he kicking in any money?"

"He says he will," Max said.

Sally was hugging Anne and Justin again.

"*Au revoir* is not *adieu*, you know," Sally said. "*Au revoir* literally means 'till I see you again.' This is just *au revoir*."

We did another round of cheek-kissing. This time six each. A new record!

"*Au revoir*, Max, Sally. *À bientôt*," Justin called and waved to the two of them standing in the terminal as we headed for the passenger gate.

In the airport shop, where we went to find a toy to give Justin something to do on the plane, the headline in the *International Herald Tribune* said that Becker had swept Lendl in straight sets to win Wimbledon. I should've put some money down at a bookie when I was in London, I hope Nigel did, I thought. We paid for the toy and headed for the gate.

"I've been thinking about that $200,000. We're going to make it, aren't we?" Anne said, taking my hand and Justin's as we boarded the plane to New York.

"Sure we are," I said. I mentally started to hear my grandmother's warnings and thought, Shut up, grandma. We settled in and put on our seatbelts.

"Well, my mother will be happy," I said.

"Oh God, something to look forward to. Living in that tiny apartment with your mother till we find a new place," Anne said.

I glanced out the window at the terminal, the tarmac white in the sun, the signs all in French and thought we were visitors all this time. France didn't belong to us; we just borrowed her for a while.

"We're going home, kid," I said to Anne.

She put her hand to my cheek.

"No," she said. "As long as the three of us are together, we are home. We've been home all along."

Notes

16. Visitors, Part One: The Budapest Express

1. This was not improbable. In December 1978, three years after the U.S. pulled out of Vietnam, Communist Vietnam invaded Cambodia and fought a vicious war against the Khmer Rouge for the next 13 years. Although both the Vietnamese and the Khmer Rouge were Communists, as is often the case, nationalism trumped ideology. Sawyer's mission was set during this period of extreme instability in Southeast Asia. The border war between the Thais and Vietnamese began to escalate and a large Vietnamese military buildup in Cambodia signaled a full-scale invasion of Thailand. Both the U.S. and Thailand were members of SEATO. An invasion of Thailand by the Vietnamese Communists would have pulled America into a second Vietnam War. Sawyer's mission was to prevent this from happening.

18. The Twelve-Hour Lunch

1. "Why was I not made to litter a brood of vipers, rather than conceive this human mockery?"
2. Years later, we saw the house twice: once in a spread in *Town and Country* magazine; the second time in the James Bond movie, *License To Kill*, where it was used as the villain's lavish hideaway.

20. A Cold Spring In Paris

1. The way one had to deal with tax and other such issues in the time before tax software and the Internet.

About the Author

Andrew Kaplan is the author of two bestselling spy thriller book series: *Scorpion* and *Homeland*, the original prequel novels to the award-winning *Homeland* television series.

His novel *Homeland: Saul's Game* won the *Scribe* 'Best Novel of the Year' award. His standalone novels include the *NY Times* bestseller *Dragonfire*; *Hour of the Assassins*, about the hunt for the Nazi war criminal, Joseph Mengele; and *War of the Raven*, selected by the *American Library Association* as 'one of the 100 Best Books ever written about World War Two.' His most recent novel, *Blue Madagascar*, a #1 *Amazon Release*, won the *Global eBook* and *Chanticleer Best Thriller* awards.

His books have sold several million copies and have been translated into 22 languages. His screenwriting career includes the James Bond film, *Goldeneye*.

- facebook.com/andrewgkaplan
- amazon.com/stores/Andrew-Kaplan/author/B006GQZJM6
- bookbub.com/authors/andrew-kaplan

Also by Andrew Kaplan

Blue Madagascar

Homeland: Saul's Game

Homeland: Carrie's Run

Scorpion Deception

Scorpion Winter

Scorpion Betrayal

War of the Raven

Dragonfire

Scorpion

Hour of the Assassins

Made in the USA
Middletown, DE
03 June 2024

55242952R00215